TALES BY JAPANESE SOLDIERS

TALES BY JAPANESE SOLDIERS

OF THE BURMA CAMPAIGN
1942–1945

KAZUO TAMAYAMA

AND

JOHN NUNNELEY

CASSELL

*This book of personal experiences of the Burma
Campaign is dedicated to reconciliation and
lasting friendship between two great nations*

Cassell Military Paperbacks

Cassell
Wellington House, 125 Strand
London WC2R 0BB

First published by Cassell 2000
This Cassell Military Paperbacks edition 2001
Reprinted 2002, 2003, 2004

The authors' moral rights have been asserted

British Library Cataloguing-in-Publication Data
A catalogue record for this book is available from the British Library

ISBN 0-304-35978-5

Printed and bound in Great Britain by
Cox & Wyman Ltd, Reading, Berks.

Contents

3 OCCUPATION *July to December 1942*

4 ARAKAN OPERATIONS *January 1943 to March 1944*

Acknowledgements

This is a book about the war as seen through the eyes of average Japanese soldiers. It is intended to describe how the common men drafted into military service lived through the Second World War in Burma. The soldiers' frank experiences are written in chronological order, so this can be read as a brief history of the war in Burma from a new perspective, but not as a traditional war history which covers broad policies, strategy and troop movements.

Much of the material in the book is based on soldiers' recollections recorded in regimental Memoirs so as to preserve the memory of the hard and unforgettable war, and was supplemented by interviews. Some stories were abstracted from interviews or lectures given by ex-soldiers at meetings of the Group Remembering the War to audiences, many of whom were from postwar generations. We are grateful to those individuals who kindly agreed to the use of a part of their articles in the Memoirs.

Japanese veterans' associations, such as the All-Burma Veterans Association of Japan, are very well organised and we are grateful to those of their members, survivors of the Burma Campaign, who helped us to locate authentic witnesses and supplied us with a mass of accurate information.

Our warm thanks are extended also to all who kindly read through our drafts and pointed out errors or provided us with additional facts. Among these were: Major General I.H. Lyall Grant, MC; Mr Stanley Charles, CBE; Major Paul Payne;

Mr Richard Spickernell; Mr Kazuo Imai; Mr Satoru Inazawa; Mr Tadahiro Ogawa; Mr Yoshiki Saito; Mr Eiichi Sugimoto; and Mr Shuichiro Yoshino.

We are indebted to Mr Hugh Wilkinson and Mr Satoru Inazawa for guidance in English writing, to Mrs Keiko Ito for her help in typing, to Mrs Hiromo Mori for transcribing taped records, and to Sazanami Tamayama for her untiring support and encouragement.

Preface

by Kazuo Tamayama MBE (Hon)

This book tells us how the ordinary soldier of the Imperial Japanese Army lived – and died – in Burma during the Second World War. Japanese citizens from every walk of life were conscripted into the service of their country. Most of the young graduates of higher education were commissioned as reserve officers but were similar in their attitude and thinking to the rank and file; in these respects they were quite different from the professional officer corps.

In January 1942 some 100,000 troops were despatched from Japan to invade, conquer and occupy the province of the British Empire called Burma (now Myanmar). It was a country, far from their own, of which they – and, indeed, most British people – knew very little. In the latter stages of the long war these soldiers of Japan's Burma Area Army came to feel themselves isolated, almost forgotten, as communication and supply links between Burma and their homeland were battered by the combination of Allied air superiority and submarine attack.

In 1944 yet more troops were sent to Burma to defend the occupied area from the counter-attacking British forces. Due to the acute and worsening shortage of materiel, and poor planning by stubborn generals, 61 per cent of the 305,501 Japanese soldiers who fought in Burma were killed or died of wounds, disease, malnutrition and starvation, so that only 118,352 returned home by 1947.

The book describes the activities and emotions of the ordinary soldier in combat and in peaceful occupation, and also those of fighter pilots, navy men and nurses. It is, in a sense, a history of the war seen through these many pairs of eyes. Wherever possible, stories were cross-checked against other references and witnesses to the events narrated. Readers interested in Sections 1 and 2 may refer to *Burma 1942: The Invasion of Burma*, co-authored by Major General Ian Lyall Grant and myself.

Much of the material contained in the book has been selected from recollections recorded in regimental histories, veterans associations' publications, private papers and personal memoirs. A number of the stories were drawn from interviews; and much valuable material was obtained from a series of lectures given by Burma survivors at meetings of 'The Group Remembering War', of which I was chairman, whose audiences included many from postwar generations.

I have been fortunate in enjoying the enthusiastic support and help of my collaborator and friend, John Nunneley, chairman of the Burma Campaign Fellowship Group, the aim of which is reconciliation and renewed friendship between our two countries. Although I myself had carried out all the interviews and research in Japan, and wrote all manuscript drafts, there was much to be done if the book were to be introduced to Western readers. John Nunneley revised my English writing in such a way as to preserve its essentially Japanese character and style, and advised on the differences between the British and Japanese military systems. Our close association has been both happy and rewarding.

Readers of *Tales by Japanese Soldiers of the Burma Campaign 1942–1945* are asked to address comments or queries to me, not to those whose stories are told in the book.

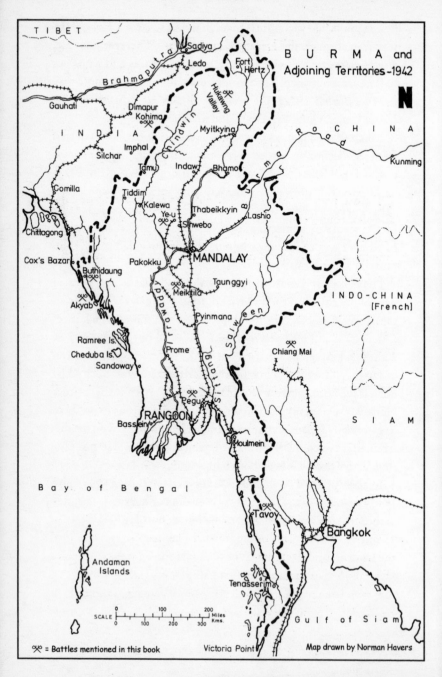

TIBET

Brahmaputra

Gauhati

I N D I A

BURMA and
Adjoining Territories -1942

N

Sadiya
Ledo

Fort
Hertz

Hukawng
Valley

Myitkyina

C H I N A

Burma Road

Kunming

Dimapur
Kohima

Imphal

Silchar

Tamu

Chindwin

Indaw

Bhamo

Comilla

Tiddim

Kalewa
Ye-u

Thabeikkyin

Lashio

Chittagong

Cox's Bazar

Buthidaung

Sihwebo

Pakokku

MANDALAY

Akyab

Irrawaddy

Meiktila

Taunggyi

INDO-CHINA
(French)

Ramree Is.

Cheduba Is.

Sandoway

Prome

Pyinmana

Salween

Chiang Mai

RANGOON

Bassein

Pegu

Sittang

Moulmein

S I A M

Bay   of   Bengal

Tavoy

Bangkok

Andaman
Islands

Tenasserim

Gulf   of   Siam

SCALE   0   100   200 Miles
         0 100 200 300 Kms.

☒ = Battles mentioned in this book

Victoria Point

Map drawn by Norman Havers

Introduction

BURMA – ITS GEOGRAPHY, ITS PEOPLE AND ITS WAR

Major Alan A. T. Hiscock RE 70 Field Company,
King George V's Own Bengal Sappers and Miners
17 Indian Division IV and XXXIII Corps

Rangoon, Prome, Magwe, Meiktila, Shwegyin, Kalewa

Burma, renamed Myanmar in 1989, is a larger and more complex country than the malarial jungle made familiar to the outside world during the 1941–5 war against Japan. It is also a country with a history of civilisation reaching back some 2,500 years.

Its total area is approximately 416,000 sq. miles. Thus Burma is 1.8 times larger than Japan and 2.3 times larger than Great Britain. The Irrawaddy, its longest river, at 1,350 miles, flows from the Tibetan border into the Andaman Sea.

Burma has a coastline of 1,200 miles on the Bay of Bengal and the Andaman Sea. It is surrounded on its land frontiers by three of the world's most important civilisations: China, with a border of 1,357 miles; Thailand (Siam) 1,120 miles; and India 900 miles. Over the centuries Burma has been much influenced by all three and to a lesser degree by Laos (formerly part of French Indo-China) with a border of 145 miles, and Bangladesh (formerly East Bengal) at 120 miles.

A glance at the map on page 12 will show Burma primarily as an elongated central plain through which the main river systems of the Irrawaddy and Chindwin flow from north to south. The commercially less important river systems of the Sittang and Salween also flow from north to south, the Salween flowing through eastern Burma to Moulmein on the Gulf of Martaban from its source in the Himalayas. It is as long as the Irrawaddy but has less commercial and agricultural significance owing to dangerous currents and wide fluctuations in water level as it flows through the deep gorges of the Shan Plateau. It is only navigable for about 100 miles.

There are mountain ranges to the west, towards the Arakan and India, rising to over 10,000 feet in the Chin Hills; ranges to the north and north-east towards China, including Hkakabo Rasi at 19,290 feet; ranges to the east towards China, Laos and Thailand. These mountain ranges are sometimes likened to a horseshoe, the 'open' end forming the Irrawaddy Delta and the Gulf of Martaban, leading in turn to the Indian Ocean and the Andaman Sea. The Arakan forms a separate river system, outside the 'horseshoe', and on the Bay of Bengal with a multiplicity of small creeks and rivers including the Kaladan. The Irrawaddy, lying at the very heart of Burma, is navigable by steamer from the delta for 900 miles to Bhamo. North of Bhamo it continues past Myitkyina and Putao (Fort Hertz), navigable by country boats and rafts until it reaches its birthplace at the confluence of the rivers Meikha and Malihka in the region of Hkakabo Razi.

Burma is typical of countries in South and South-East Asia in that its rainfall is dictated by the Indian Ocean's monsoon winds. Thus the rainy season normally starts with the south-west monsoon winds in May and continues until October when the winds change to north-east.

Rainfall is at its heaviest throughout Burma from June to August. The 'horseshoe' of mountains does, however, protect the plains from the damaging floods experienced in other parts of South-East Asia. Rainfall varies over the whole country, from the coastal regions of Akyab and Tennasserim (120–200 inches per year), the Irrawaddy delta with 60–100 inches per year, and on the leeward side of the mountain ranges and with monsoon rainfall, the melting snows in the far north feed the great rivers in the summer months and thus permit irrigation for a variety of crops.

Burma is notable for its forests and its production of rice. Up to 1941 the exploitation of the forests was carefully controlled by the Burma Forest Service and much of this controlled exploitation was in the hands of large firms such as the Bombay Burma Trading Corporation and Steel Brothers. Forest and woodland cover about 50 per cent of the land area and the controlled extraction of timber, especially teak, ironwood and padauk remains, as prewar, an important resource. Timber is mainly harvested in the Shan plateau up to about 2,000 feet and exported through Rangoon and Moulmein.

It is the production of high-quality rice which has contributed most to Burma's economy over the years. Before 1941 exports amounted to 3 million tons annually and Burma was the world's largest exporter. Exports subsequently fell to 600,000 tons but have now recovered to over one million. Population increase has been a   factor in the decrease of exports but political unrest and insurrection have also been a major problem. Despite this, rice is grown on 9 million acres of irrigated farms in the Irrawaddy delta and also on over 1,500 acres in the central Dry Zone of Upper Burma. This area also produces cotton, tobacco, peanuts, sorghum, sesame, beans, maize, sugar cane, rubber, tea and jute on 3.7 million acres.

Burma has other potential and actual sources of wealth. Of these, oil and gas are the most immediate, and the prewar oilfields at Yenangyaung and refineries at Syriam play an increasing part in Burma's revenues together with iron ore, tungsten, lead, silver, tin, mercury, copper, plutonium, zinc, cobalt, antimony and gold. Not only this, but Burma has rubies, sapphires and jade to add to its wealth.

It is clear that the movement of people and the products described above has depended and continues to depend heavily on the river systems. Nevertheless, railways had been built before 1939 from south of Moulmein as far north as Myitkyina and including Rangoon and Mandalay, Lashio, Toungoo and Prome.

Over the centuries, from the original settlement by the Mons, part of the Mon-Khmer language family, about 2,500 years ago, there has been constant movement and development of the ethnic make-up of Burma. In the very simplest terms the Mons established the Buddhist tradition in Burma and this was transmitted to successive waves of peoples, especially including Burmese at the time of King Anawrahta, about AD 1000. The language of the successive major ethnic groups was generally of the Tibeto-Burman family and this remains so.

Following many wars between these groups the population in 1941 was approximately 17 million, ethnic division not being precisely known but estimated as follows on 1931 figures:

Burmese	65.75%	Shan	6.8%
Karen	9.6%	Chin	3.4%
Indian	6.8%	Kachin	3.4%
Chinese	Not known	Arakanese	Not known

By 1994 the total population of Burma had grown to 46,527,000 according to the UN. The ethnic division is similar to 1941, with 68 per cent Burmese but additions for Arakanese at 4 per cent, Chinese 3 per cent and Mon 2 per cent. Not surprisingly, in view of the 1942 exodus, the Indian proportion has declined to 2 per cent.

Thus, despite the upheaval caused by the 1941–5 war and the subsequent internal dissension, Burma has kept a surprising balance between its ethnic groups, and has continued its overall population growth.

It is sufficient in this brief Introduction to say that by November 1941 war between Japan and the USA and Great Britain (plus the Netherlands) was imminent. On 8 December came the attack on Pearl Harbor and the invasion of Thailand. Victoria Point at the southern extremity of Burma was occupied on 15 December by the Japanese 143 Regiment which had crossed the Thai border at Kra Buri nearby after a seaborne landing.

At this stage, with virtually the whole of the Thai border available to them, it is clear that the Japanese commanders had a rich choice of invasion routes. Despite many difficulties the Kra Isthmus was initially the main focus for seaborne assault. This route was also supported by the Singapore–Bangkok–Chiang Mai railway, enabling men and equipment to be moved rapidly north to Chiang Mai and Chiang Rai. Unfortunately, the British plan to cut this railway at Prachuap failed on 16 December. Tavoy was occupied by the Japanese on 19 January, Mergui on 20/22 January and Moulmein on 31 January. The movements covering these operations were complex and difficult and both British and Japanese found problems in the dense hilly jungle with few roads, often with tracks suitable only for pack animals. These operations were the first in the Burma Campaign and also the first in which dense jungle was encountered.

For the British, the loss of the Kra Isthmus, Tavoy and Moulmein was shortly to be followed by the disaster of the Sittang Bridge in which it is estimated that half of the infantry of 17 Indian Division were lost due to premature demolition of the bridge. This led inevitably to the abandonment of Rangoon on 7 March and the 650-mile-long fighting retreat to Imphal. The retreat, mainly through the centre of Burma, mostly in the dry season, took the British through Prome, Magwe, Yenangyaung, Kyaukse, and finally Shwegyin, Kalewa and Tamu. Much of the route was in open country, paddy fields in the south and plantations of peanuts, maize, tobacco, cotton and sugar in the drier and more open areas of central Burma. It was possible to deploy tanks of 7 Armoured Brigade until the Chindwin was reached. Thick jungle came together with the Chin Hills and along the Chindwin and this new terrain marked a change in tactics for both Japanese and British.

The rains in the Chin Hills and Manipur started on 18 May 1942, just at the time when the exhausted units of 17 Indian Division, 1 Burma Division and many other units were arriving to a cold and wet welcome, with little food and shelter. Re-organisation, re-equipment and retraining went ahead, accommodation constructed, roads cut through the hillsides and units redeployed. New units, notably 23 Indian Division, arrived and began to take a full part in IV Corps activity. Among the many vital projects started in this initial period were a motor road south to Tiddim, about 150 miles, improvement of the road to the railhead at Dimapur, upgrading tracks in the Naga Hills, and improvement of the mountain road between Tamu and Palel. All this, and the building of four airfields in Manipur of course required an immense effort, the intention being to attack the Japanese Army at the earliest opportunity.

The Japanese Army was preparing to do the same. The 600-mile railway from Rangoon to Lashio was repaired with some discontinuities by the end of May and played an important part in subsequent operations. A motor road from Ye-u to Kalewa was built in 1942 by the Japanese. In the meantime the Japanese had pushed on and occupied Akyab in the Arakan early in the same month. Orders were issued by the British commanders in September to reoccupy Akyab and northern Arakan. This proved a difficult and costly struggle and by the end of May 1943 the British were back where they started, a lack of training and morale having proved decisive.

The idea of long-range penetration was now being developed and the first Wingate expedition, 3,000-strong crossed, the Chindwin in February 1943, returning less some 1,000 killed and missing in May. This operation undoubtedly puzzled the Japanese in the first stage. At the same time they realised that it was possible to move and to fight effectively in the mountains and jungles of the Chindwin and its region. The material results of the Wingate expedition for the British were relatively poor but the effects on morale were altogether positive.

The remainder of 1943 and early 1944 was a busy and active time for the British in the Tiddim/Fort White area. Not only was there continued effort to improve communications but there was a good deal of aggressive patrolling and skirmishing, especially by 48 and 63 Brigade of 17 Division.

It had become known that the Japanese intended to strike in the Arakan and across the Chindwin in early 1944, coinciding with a British offensive also planned for the same time. The

Japanese attacked in the Arakan on 4 February but after heavy fighting over three weeks withdrew. A major Japanese offensive aimed at Imphal now became evident: IV Corps decided to concentrate and fight on the Imphal plain, a decision which was, for some, difficult to accept but which proved to be correct; 17 Division at Tiddim (163 miles from Imphal) was particularly isolated but by careful and methodical withdrawal accompanied by resolute fighting spirit Major General Cowan succeeded in moving his division first to Tonzang and then over the Manipur river bridge, later destroyed, by 26 March. Subsequently 17 Division, overcoming various Japanese units, arrived at Imphal on 5 April.

The new-found ability of the British to withstand and overcome Japanese roadblocks played a significant part in the subsequent battles along the Tiddim road and elsewhere. Effective training with new tactics and support from the air had changed the whole balance between the two armies. The second Wingate expedition flew into northern Burma on 6 March, adding to the better profile of the British. The decision to concentrate IV Corps on the Imphal plain was now about to prove its worth. The battles of Bishenpur in April, May and June, together with Torbung in May had shown a decisive advantage for the British. This added to the hard-fought battles in the Kohima area from 5–18 April and 18 April–22 June which were finally disastrous for the Japanese who withdrew in some disorder via Ukhrul to the Chindwin.

In following the detailed progress of the two armies from Imphal to Rangoon, it is not possible here to make an appreciation of Wingate and his second 'Operation Thursday' in which he was killed in an air crash on 24 March 1944.

In the autumn of 1944 both Japanese and Allied Forces reorganised their command structure. Both Japan and the Allies had changed their perspective and now looked for an initial confrontation in central Burma. The Japanese ideas of an invasion of Bengal assisted by the Indian National Army and a pro-Japanese Burmese Government under Aung San had been much modified. Allied ideas too had changed, and XIV Army was specifically to take Mandalay with Rangoon taken by a seaborne and airborne operation.

Leaving aside descriptions of this long trek from Imphal to Tamu which many, including this author, had completed in the opposite direction in May 1942, the next task for XIV Army was the crossing of the Chindwin. This was, of course, dependent on the Palel–Tamu–Kalewa route being passable without a major battle. In fact, crossings were made by 11 Division, 19 Division, 20 Division and 2 Division between 30 November and 19 December. These crossings were followed by the remainder of XXXIII and IV Corps. The open country of the Shwebo plain now allowed rapid movement for both infantry and tanks; 19 Division had advanced 400 miles from the Chindwin to Shwebo in about five weeks. After the occupation of Shwebo 19 Division turned its attention to Mandalay and finally crossed the Irrawaddy together with the tanks of 254 Tank Brigade and 7th Cavalry. Mandalay was entered on 8 March but the task of clearing the Fort had not begun; 2 Division made its Irrawaddy crossing on 24 February and 20 Division, after three weeks of heavy fighting, finally crossed near Myinmu, west of Mandalay.

The taking of Mandalay by 19 Division with the support of 2 Division and 20 Division was an important boost for morale both in the X1V Army and in the wider aspect of the war. It is at this time that the heavy losses inflicted on the Japanese began to affect their ability to continue with the same high morale as previously. The capture of Mandalay, although important, was not the final, decisive, battle. This, as intended by General Slim, was Meiktila. The capture of Meiktila destroyed any chance the Japanese had of recovering either Central or Lower Burma. Following General Slim's orders, 17 Division crossed the Irrawaddy at Nyaungu on 18 February 1945 with 255 Armoured Brigade leading the assault. The distance to Meiktila is 80 miles and the first defensive battles took place at the village of Oyin where 200 Japanese were killed. Sporadic fighting took place as 17 Division advanced and by 28 February 17 Division was poised to make a definitive attack. The capture of Meiktila took four days and by 3 March all organised resistance was at an end. Some 2,000 Japanese bodies were counted in the town area.

The quick capture of Meiktila surprised the Japanese and steps were speedily taken to build up an adequate force to recapture the town. As this proceeded 17 Division pursued an policy of active and aggressive defence. The next phase, the siege, lasted until the Japanese order to withdraw on 28 March. It should be realised that the British were, after an initial period, entirely dependent on air supply and that control of the airfields was a vital necessity if the division was not to rely on air-drop. Although there had been fierce fighting in the capture of Meiktila, the next phase, the siege, in which reinforcements of battle-experienced units were brought in by the Japanese, was very tough indeed, with heavy casualties.

Rangoon is about 340 miles from Meiktila via Pyinmana or 440 miles via Yenangyaung and Prome. Mountbatten, the Supreme Commander SE Asia, was looking beyond Burma to Malaya and Singapore. It was clearly necessary to retake Rangoon before the monsoon and the first of June was the latest date before the rains made movement virtually impossible. The British decided to go forward down both of the routes with XXXIII Corps taking the longer route via Prome and IV Corps the shorter route via Pyawbwe. The Japanese 33 Army under Lieutenant General Honda Masaki had planned to intercept IV Corps at Pyawbwe 26 miles south of Meiktila. This proved to be a disaster for 33 Army and one which sealed the fate of the Japanese occupation of Rangoon. There were two problems for 33 Army. First, its units were, in almost every case, in a poor condition to withstand an enemy whose equipment was superior and whose confidence had improved immensely since 1942/3. Secondly, much valuable equipment, including guns and tanks, had been lost and the highly competent handling of armour and artillery by the British proved too much for units which were weak in numbers and near exhaustion. This did not mean that Japanese officers and men had ceased to fight hard. There was much bitter fighting in Pyawbwe before it was taken on about 14 April.

Next after Pyawbwe came Pyinmana, captured on 19 April with Toungoo and its airfields reached on 22 April, still 167 miles north of Rangoon; 17 Division was on the edge of Pegu on the night of 29 April, 50 miles from Rangoon. Pegu was completely cleared by 1 May despite vigorous Japanese opposition. Hlegu, 27 miles from Rangoon, was reached on 6 May by 17 Division and the seaborne 26 Division. By this time the rains had arrived in earnest, two weeks earlier than anticipated. By this time also 'Operation Dracula' had started its sea and airborne landings; 50 Indian Parachute Brigade was dropped on Elephant Point on 1 May, thus allowing seaborne units of 26 Division, as already noted, to deploy north of Rangoon.

After the British regained air superiority over Burma in 1943 supply to Burma had become a critical problem for the Japanese. Ships could no longer come to Rangoon from Singapore, and many ships were sunk between Japan and Singapore by American submarines. These heavy shipping losses forced the Japanese in Burma to fight with insufficient military supplies.

What of the Japanese forces? This brief Introduction is not the place to describe the problems and dissensions faced by the Japanese commanders. The decision was made to evacuate Rangoon and concentrate on Moulmein while 28 Army was more or less isolated in the Pegu Yomas. However, the battle for Rangoon and for Burma had already been lost.

Alan Hiscock

As a Royal Engineers subaltern in 1941, Alan Hiscock was posted to King George V's Own Bengal Sappers and Miners in India. He joined 70 Field Company and arrived in Rangoon on 3 March 1942 to join 17 Indian Division which had suffered the disaster at the Sittang Bridge on 22/23 February. Incidents in the long retreat to Manipur by 17 Division are described in this and other publications. Alan Hiscock himself remained with 70 Field Company until September 1943. During that time he had been building tracks, roads and water supply in the Naga Hills to Ukhrul (50 miles from Imphal), and in the Tiddim/Fort White area (126 miles from Imphal). He was attached for many months to 48 Brigade. Later, both Ukhrul and Tiddim were to see heavy fighting but at this stage – mid-1943 – there was mainly patrol activity and casualties were light.

His move in September 1943 was to IV Corps Troops Engineers in the Imphal plain from which he joined Chief Engineer XXXIII Corps, thus providing continuity as units changed. He finally achieved his ambition as Officer Commanding 76 Field Company for the final advance on Rangoon, and thus became one of the few to start and finish there.

This was not to be his final task in Burma, however, because he found himself involved in re-raising an engineer unit for the Burma government under an agreement with Aung San. There had been a prewar sapper and miner unit and the first problem was to find and train as many Burmese and Karen officers as possible. This plan was thrown into confusion by the assassination of Aung San in July 1947.

After Burma, also in 1947, Alan Hiscock completed his professional engineering training. This took place at graduate and postgraduate levels at the Royal Military College of Science and led to Instructor appointments with postings to Japan with the British Commonwealth Forces, Korea, and also to Singapore.

1

TO RANGOON

January to March 1942

1 · From China to Burma

Lance Corporal Koji Kawamata 3rd Company, 1st Battalion,
214 Infantry Regiment, 33 Division

Bilin, Rangoon

In the morning of 8 December 1941, I went to Suhksien railway station. As I was expecting to be discharged soon, after serving 3 years in the army, I applied for a transfer to China where I hoped to get a job in the North China Railway Company. I explained this to a man at the station, who stared at me in amazement and said to me, 'Your discharge is most unlikely. Look at this.' He handed me a newspaper with a headline saying that Japan had declared war against the USA and Britain. What a terrible situation! I ran back to my Company and I told my fellow soldiers, 'Discharge is out of the question. It's war with the white people!' Their reaction was, 'What did you say, Kawamata? Don't play the fool with us.' When I showed them the newspaper, everybody just said 'Oh!' The company commander returned from the regimental headquarters and ordered us to pack the weapons, ammunition and clothing needed urgently for operations. Packing was finished by the evening of 9 December and the soldiers moved everything to the railway station. Then we boarded trains for Nanking.

We embarked on a freighter and sailed down the River Yangtze. While we waited off Formosa, a big convoy of more than 60 boats was formed. We were not allowed to go ashore, but some soldiers who went ashore on official duty brought us fresh bananas which tasted very good. On 31 December the convoy moved south escorted by the cruiser *Natori* and 16 navy vessels. We celebrated the New Year with Japanese sake. One day a destroyer headed back at high speed leaving a big wake, and the submarine alarm was sounded. We could see flashes of an explosion far away. Later we found out that a boat carrying a parachute regiment had been sunk by spontaneous combustion of powder in its cargo but everybody on the boat had been saved. As we sailed south, our low wooden bunks became as hot as a steam bath. We did some gymnastics and played quoits on deck, trying to keep up our morale and strength. Several shepherd dogs that some soldiers had brought in astutely went down the ladder to the holds to enjoy cool air. There was a lot of ice stored there for the care of the horses which were not used to such hot conditions. On 9 January the boats were going up the River Menam, and we understood that we were to land in Thailand. We enjoyed looking at the green scenery on both sides of the river, after having spent about a month only staring at the vast sea. Next day we disembarked at Bangkok and marched along a tree-lined road. Thai people waved Rising Sun flags, shouting 'Nippon! Nippon!' We stayed in houses with bright electric lamps and ate fresh vegetables and shiny-looking rice. We wandered around the city for a week and relaxed, and I wrote a lot of letters to my parents, relatives and friends in Japan and also to many soldiers from my home area who were now in various places. I felt this might be the last chance to send messages to them, as we were going to fight against the British Indian troops who had modern weapons, whereas we were poorly equipped with old-type rifles and guns. No improvements or additions had been made when we moved out of China.

We spent several days in Bangkok. I received 40 per cent of my pay in Thai money and went out to the town as soon as permission was given, enjoying my freedom, and gazing at the houses of southern design. Young Thai people on the streets were walking briskly along and seemed to be enjoying their lives, something we had not seen in China. I drank beer at the Nippon restaurant operated by the Japanese Army, then strolled around the town until late in the evening. We left Bangkok in a small train pulled by a wood-burning locomotive. Then we had to walk over rough terrain carrying one week's rations and everything we needed on our shoulders. In addition we had to help build the road along which were walking. We had to leave behind many items including our steel helmets. We marched along this rough road for 20 days and arrived at Pa-an on the River Salween. We marched during the night when it was not too hot. The sunshine in Burma was very bright and it was very hot during the daytime.

When we crossed the Thailand–Burma border, the commander detailed the strict and concise orders of the 15th Army. We had to be very careful not to repeat the foolish mistakes made in China which had alienated almost all the local residents. So we were not allowed to go into a Burmese house alone, and provision of food or materials from residents could only be made on the command of a staff sergeant or above. Looting and arson were strictly forbidden.

I GREW UP IN a village called Inukai-mura which is about 100 kilometres north of Tokyo. At the age of twenty, I took the military physical examination held at my village, and was rated as First Grade. I and about 40 men from my village went to the barracks of the 29th Regiment Home Unit at Aizu-Wakamatsu on 10 January 1939. When our basic training was finished, on 25 March 1939, the 214 Infantry Regiment was formed, to which we were transferred. The regimental commander went to the Imperial Palace and received the regimental flag from the Emperor. We were issued with brand-new rifles in place of the ones used for training. My bayonet was ground to give it a sharp edge, which impressed strongly on me the reality that I was going off to a bloody war. We put on 'White Tiger' badges above the star mark on our caps. The badge was the idea of Lt Col Junnosuke Hamada who later became the second commander of the 214 Regiment. The 'White Tigers' was a group of young men (samurai warriors) of Wakamatsu who fought in the civil war of 1867 and are highly respected by Japanese people. We left the port of Niigata on 4 April 1939 and went to central China where we fought with the Chinese Army until 1941.

2 · Advance to Tavoy

Corporal Buhachiro Nakai, 55 Mountain Gun Regiment, 55 Division

Tavoy, Pegu

Tavoy is a small town in south-east Burma, not far from the Malayan peninsula. When the war began on 8 December 1941, the Japanese army landed in northern Malaya and marched south to capture Singapore, the most important British fortress in Asia. In order to protect the Japanese army advancing on the Malayan peninsula, it was important to avoid attacks by the British air force from airfields in Tavoy and Victoria Point, which were relatively close by. The Japanese army therefore decided to occupy these airfields. Though Tavoy is only 280 kilometres from Bangkok, the capital of Thailand, as a plane flies, the steep Bilauk Taung mountain range lies between the two places.

I left Sakaide port on the beautiful Inland Sea of Japan in a freighter crammed with many soldiers and horses, and landed in northern French Indo-China on 26 November 1941. At the outbreak of war we were loaded in trains and arrived in south-west Thailand. Then the mountain gun platoon that I belonged to was assigned to the Oki detachment which was bound for Tavoy. The detachment consisted of one infantry battalion (three rifle companies, six medium machine guns and two 70mm guns), one mountain gun platoon (two guns), one sapper platoon and supporting groups; a total of 1,500 men.

We took small boats going up the River Keonoi and arrived at a small village near the Burma–Thailand border on 7 January 1942. Here we were told to send back to the rear all spare materials and unnecessary personal belongings, although we had carried them with great effort. As we had no experience of fighting with the British Army, it was thought important to carry as much ammunition as possible, so the amount of food we could bring with us was limited: one week's rations on a reduced basis and two packets of biscuits as an emergency reserve. The horse feed was reduced to one-third of the standard, in the hopes of supplementing it with local grasses. We hired about thirty Thai people and had them carry four shells each. Though we managed to persuade them to get close to the border, they eventually ran away saying, 'We are not fighting the war.' So each of us had to carry one shell on our already heavy knapsacks.

The forced march through the jungle was very, very hard. I tried my best to keep up with the group. Meanwhile we crossed the border but still there was not any road, just a narrow animal track. We went through grass fields and came to a forest; almost dark even in daytime. Then the forest turned into tall, thick bamboo. On the second day the animal track petered out and we advanced across a steep cliff where the sappers worked hard to make a passage. We had to be very careful not to let the horses and oxen tumble down into the valley. We had oxen for carrying some of the shells. As we advanced to the west, a plane flew overhead to show us our forward route. We could make only 2 or 3 kilometres per day, and ran out of rice on the eighth day. We did not know how many more days we had to walk, as we soldiers did not have maps and did not know where we were. Still our advance through thick forest continued. When could not stand the hunger, we peeled off the skin of the paddy carried for horse feed and ate the rice as porridge. The poor horses had to eat bamboo grass. Finally it was decided to eat one of the oxen carrying ammunition. The oxen in Thailand are quite different from those in Japan. Its meat was too tough and after two meals my gums were swollen and ached, so I could take only beef soup. Then, as we could not carry the ammunition which had been carried by the ox, we left some shells to be picked up later.

On 14 January we were told by the plane that the march through the mountains would be over in a day or so; we were encouraged and made preparations for fighting. The next day we finally came to a plain covered by tall grasses. We saw the blue sky after ten days of torment. Every one looked so pleased and some even shed tears. Emerging from the dense forest to an open plain, we felt the strong sun beating down on us, while at the same time a comfortable breeze swept around our bodies. We were filled with deep emotion to think that we had come to Burma, so far away from our homes. On the 16th we were told to keep up with the infantry as we might meet the enemy at any time, so we walked as fast as we could. After a while we heard the sound of rifles. We grew tense at the sound of shooting for the first time since we had left our home country. It seemed that our advance column had encountered the enemy. The platoon leader shouted 'Quicken your pace!' After ten minutes the shooting stopped. As we advanced we saw a village with about twenty houses on a hill. It was Myitta, where a soldier was waving a big Sun flag. It was a sign that the village had been occupied. We rested in the village until sunset, attended to our weapons, and started towards Tavoy. As the road was wide the mountain guns were now assembled and drawn by horses, ready for combat. Up to then they had been carried in several pieces on horseback. As we advanced along the winding road for two hours and arrived at Kyauk-medaung village, we heard heavy firing. A messenger came from the infantry and asked us to move forward. We advanced, braced for action. About 600 of the enemy were drawn up in line, and three of the detachment's advance party were killed by them. Guided by the infantry, we went up a hill and placed our guns. Our first shell landed close to the target, then all of the enemy began to retreat. After five shots, the 'Cease fire!' was called. Our section leader seemed disappointed, and I also felt we had not contributed very much.

After sunrise we covered ourselves and our horses with tree leaves and branches, so that it looked as if trees were walking. Enemy aircraft flew over us twice, but as we hid on both sides of the road we were not discovered. When the evening sun set in the west beyond Tavoy, we came to a three-forked road. It was at a town called Pagaya. We stayed here overnight while the enemy positions were scouted by our patrols. As soon as we laid down our weary bodies, the sound of snoring was heard here and there.

Next morning we were woken before sunrise. As the road was becoming worse, the guns were disassembled and carried on horseback. The infantry advanced so quickly we had a hard struggle to follow in their footsteps. We went through dry paddy fields and saw simple country houses occasionally. The strong sun rose and burnt us. Shortly before 9 o'clock we heard enemy gunfire; we assembled the guns and hurried to the front line. We could see a wide plain, then beautiful rows of houses and streets. This was Tavoy. We placed our guns behind the infantry's extended line. I heard the order: 'Load in succession.' As 1st gunner, I opened the breech mechanism, then 3rd gunner Private Akashi loaded a shell. While 2nd gunner Private Kitaoka was adjusting the aim accurately, I kept a tight hold on the trigger rope. 'Fire!' the section leader ordered, and I pulled the trigger. After I had let off ten shells, the 'Cease fire!' came, and we waited for fresh orders. At this point we heard the whirr of propellers and saw enemy planes coming up one by one and circling. It seemed that there was an airfield to the east of Tavoy. The planes flew away northward as Japanese Zero fighters appeared. After that our mountain guns advanced their positions twice, but did not open fire. In the afternoon, when the sun was still shining, we saw black smoke rising high from the streets of Tavoy. The town had been occupied completely. Though twenty men were killed in the infantry, no one in our mountain gun platoon was killed or injured. We rejoiced at our well-being, and celebrated the victory in our first combat. The platoon leader also seemed happy.

3 · Night Attack with Bayonet

Captain Tadashi Suzuki, Gun Company, 215 Infantry Regiment,
33 Division

Sittang, Monywa

On the night of 10 February 1942, we crossed the River Salween, and on the next night the Second Battalion of our regiment attacked British troops around a small village on the river called Kuzeik.

The battalion attacked according to a traditional Japanese system in which soldiers were not allowed to load bullets in their rifles; and their bayonets were dulled by spreading mud on them, to prevent them from reflecting enemy gunfire, and conceal the moves of the Japanese under cover of a moonless dark night. They charged into the enemy positions using only bayonets as their weapon.

My company was located with the regimental headquarters. We got no message, but British gunfire was heard continually for a long time. We were worried at not knowing the progress of the night attack; if it did not succeed we would be at a disadvantage as the British had superior gun power and air power. So I proposed that the major portion of my company attack the rear of the British position and this was approved. The two 75mm infantry guns were left just a few gunners, and loaded with shrapnel shells with instantaneous fuses, in case they were attacked.

The rest of the company, armed with rifles and bayonets, advanced in high spirits, bypassed the west of the hill where the enemy might be positioned, and kept moving south along the River Salween in the early morning light.

Unexpectedly we found several tents. We advanced and stabbed a few men who were outside. When we entered a tent which looked like a combat headquarters I saw a wounded commander (a British Lieutenant Colonel) sitting upright with several of his men. He signed to us to shoot him and died in a serene frame of mind. His attitude really was in keeping with the honour of a military man. I sincerely respected him and wished I might do the same.

Thanks to the determined attack of the Second Battalion the enemy in Kuzeik were almost completely destroyed. This was our first victory in Burma. Then we marched westward with heightened morale.

4 · The Battle of Bilin

Lance Corporal Koji Kawamata (continued), 3rd Company,
1st Battalion, 214 Infantry Regiment, 33 Division

Bilin

I crossed the River Salween on 10 February 1942 in a small wooden boat belonging to the local people and then walked westward during the night, sleeping during the daytime in the forest.

Late in the evening of 14 February, we came to the River Bilin and were looking out for a suitable place to cross. We heard someone approach, panting. We challenged him: 'Who goes there?' The answer was 'Ochiai.' He was with an advance party which had left several hours before us and was carrying a wounded soldier. He told us the advance party had been attacked by the enemy and had suffered great losses.

The river was about 80 metres wide and one metre deep and was not too difficult to ford. However, we had to be careful as the enemy might be waiting on the opposite bank. We spread ourselves out along the bank as the second platoon quietly started to cross the river. We gazed at the opposite bank with our fingers on the triggers of our rifles.

After five minutes or so a signal came from the advance platoon that there were no enemy. We felt relieved and entered the water with our rifles and ammunition on our heads. In the middle of the river I was almost up to my neck but fortunately no higher. After fording the river we immediately started to march in our wet uniforms.

We followed the signs that the advance party had left on the paths in the jungle, sheets of paper torn from a magazine marked with a letter indicating our unit. Soon we lost track of the signs and walked blindly towards the west.

Then we were allowed a long rest period and I fell asleep by the roadside. A small frog came jumping on to my face and woke me up. The sun was shining already. So I woke everybody up, as it could be very dangerous to stay there. Then a soldier appeared with his rifle on his shoulder; he was Private Tobe who had gone with the advance party. I asked him, 'Tobe, what happened?' He answered, 'I don't know what to do! My platoon leader and many of us were killed, and we lost touch with each other. I myself am trying to rejoin my company and have walked here.'

The commanding officer shouted, 'OK, anyway climb up that hill with a red flag on top.' As we climbed up through the jungle close to the summit, we saw a building which looked like a Buddhist temple. Two priests came out. I asked them in broken Burmese, 'English?' They answered that there were no British soldiers there. Trusting what the priest said, we spread out on the hill in fighting positions. Most of our canteens were empty. At our request the priests willingly brought two water pots on their heads. Burma is a Buddhist country and priests have high authority and influence, so we had to be very careful not to offend them.

I could see the River Bilin from the hill. After a while British planes appeared firing their machine guns at Japanese troops crossing the river. I hoped that nobody would be shot. Then British armoured cars were seen, moving towards the Japanese units.

The British encountered the leading Japanese. I saw our soldiers attacking the armoured cars with hand grenades. A medium machine gun located on our hill started shooting at the armoured cars with armour-piercing bullets but this was not effective; they all bounced off. Meanwhile the leading armoured car was immobilised by the bold attack of Japanese soldiers from close quarters, and came to a stop. Other cars turned around and went back, but most of the soldiers who attacked the armoured cars were killed. I felt deeply that an unprepared surprise engagement like this was really a miserable business.

After dark I and nine others were ordered to go on watch at an advance post. When the long night had almost passed and the eastern sky was becoming lighter, I heard somebody talking at the foot of the temple's stone staircase. I crawled close to the voice and saw three soldiers with flat helmets just climbing the steps. I fired, and the three men fell. Then as more started coming I threw a grenade. The sound of the shooting alerted the whole company, who then attacked the enemy; they retreated leaving behind twenty dead.

As we continued to watch, three men came up the steps. I signalled to my comrades not to shoot and beckoned them forward. They seemed shocked for the moment but soon raised their hands and came towards us. We surrounded them as they stared at us in puzzlement and fear. They seemed to be an officer and two non-commissioned officers. They too were evidently thirsty and repeated, 'Water, water.' Some of our men said, 'They have a nerve as prisoners to ask for water.' But we had water brought to them by a priest. To our surprise one of the prisoners fell down dead face upwards as soon as he had drunk three cups of water. It was a strange and unusual experience. Was it heart failure? The remaining two men were disarmed and sent to the regimental headquarters.

The next night we moved to a new position in the jungle. We dug a deep trench and remained there during the daytime, and during the next night advanced to another trench 50 metres outside the jungle. That night enemy guns shelled the trenches where we had been during the day, and this was followed by an advance of their infantry to within 50 metres ahead of us. Because they did not venture any further, our night position was relatively safe. In the morning, after several days of eagerly awaiting, Japanese planes flew over us and bombarded the enemy gun position on the hill, which was covered completely by the smoke of the bombs. We waited there all night, fearful that the enemy would be sure to take massive revenge. But the night passed without any shelling. We told each other that it was uncomfortably unnerving and odd that the enemy was not attacking us. Then the company commander, Lieutenant Matsumura, ordered me to scout the enemy's main position with five men. I felt considerable fear at being ordered to approach an enemy who strangely was not attacking us.

We went forward, hiding in the jungle as much as possible and then moving ahead very carefully, trembling with fright. As we met no enemy on the way we finally reached what seemed to be the gun position, but there was no indication of any enemy presence. As a precaution I threw a stone and we hid ourselves and watched. But there was no sign of anyone moving. I imagined that the enemy might be keeping silence in an attempt to capture us, and kept staring at the enemy position, but there was no such sign. So I made up my mind to go in. I left one man where we were and went ahead. I found a bundle of about twenty telephone wires and cut them with my bayonet, expecting the enemy to come out. But there was no reaction. We circled the hill, which was burnt, but still no enemy. There should have been many casualties as a result of yesterday's bombardment, but there was no sign of dead bodies. While we looked around here and there, I somehow became calmer and imagined that the enemy had retreated carrying all their dead and injured. While we were eagerly looking all around, we came to a point ahead of the man I had left. Hearing the action of his bolt I cried, 'It's me.' He said 'Oh, you gave me a shock!' and we looked at each other saying, 'Good, we have escaped the danger. Now let's look for the gift rations from Mr Churchill.' (That is how we referred to the food or clothing captured from the enemy supplies.) Many bread rolls and cans filled with water were scattered by the roadside. I thought of eating the bread but stopped, as it is foolish to be tricked by the enemy. So we opened some completely packed boxes, and found corned beef, cheese, butter, coffee and tea. Sandbags, which were piled up for protection, were filled with sugar. As we had no bags, we put some of the food from one box in our trousers, hung them around our necks, and returned to our position. We lined up in front of the commander and reported that there was no enemy. My comrades came running, grabbed the food and filled their stomachs. This was a big blessing for us as we had been eating only boiled rice and a thin soup with local wild grasses since we had entered Burma. The soup was made by putting dried soybean paste in hot water. Rice was available locally but vegetables were scarce. Refreshed by the present from Mr Churchill, the company moved towards Sittang that night.

5 · The Sittang Bridge

Private Yoshizo Abe, 1st Company, 33 Engineer Regiment, 33 Division

Sittang, Prome

We were to have a long rest period at a temple. After a hurried march during the night through a mountain path in the jungle, many from the engineer company had dropped out of line or lagged behind. So we were waiting for them. It was the early morning of 22 February 1942. My platoon leader and section leader were at the end of the column, as a team to handle the drop-outs, so they had not arrived at the temple. After an hour or so the roar of gunfire was heard from the front line, and Japanese battalion guns opened up. We assembled under orders from Warrant Officer Hasegawa and were ordered to hurry to the front line under the direct command of Lt Tamogami, our company commander.

We started to run, carrying our full complement of knapsack

and rifle. They were so heavy that many had to drop out of the race. The leading group included the commander, Warrant Officer Hasegawa, Corporal Yanagi, myself and several more. I was the only private among them. Behind us I saw five or so others following us within 100 metres. After running 7 or 8 kilometres, we reached the headquarters of the first battalion. The commander told us, 'It seems that there are several enemy armoured cars in the town. Let everybody leave knapsacks and rifles here and carry anti-tank mines and hand grenades.'

The houses in the town were all burning and British armoured cars came bursting through the flames. We threw grenades and mines into the cars passing through the town. I did not take note of how long it lasted. I was euphoric and did not remember what I had done. Four or five armoured cars were left stalled, on which some senior soldiers wrote 'Occupied by the Engineers' in chalk. I noticed that I had slight burns on my face and arms. It seemed there were no enemy in the town. Lt Tamogami and WO Hasegawa started running up the sloping road leading to the bridge. Yanagi and I followed them. When we climbed up the slope we saw Indian soldiers spread out ahead and advancing towards us. Hasegawa and Yanagi hid behind palm trees and I lay down under cover of a lorry. Hasegawa called to me to see if I was all right, and I answered him, 'I'm OK.' As I peeped from behind the lorry the enemy came closer, firing their automatic rifles from the waist. I had then only one anti-tank mine and a bayonet at my waist, so I started gradually to move backwards. Being only concerned with the enemy in front I fell down a steep embankment, fortunately feet first. Being a private I did not know which way to go. As I was walking down to the river, I met my commander. Then he went to the infantry commander who had been his classmate in the Military Academy and requested his company to make a dash for the bridge. The infantry tried to advance several times with little progress. I rested in a house, still worried about what had happened to the two men, Hasegawa and Yanagi. The fighting lasted a full day and night. At about 6 o'clock, before dawn on 23 February, we suddenly heard a big explosion. The British themselves had demolished the bridge. The enemy facing us stayed and retreated by evening. As soon as they had gone, I went to the spot with the commander and recovered the dead bodies of the warrant officer and the lieutenant. I felt extremely hungry as I had not eaten since the previous day. I found some biscuits and milk in the enemy position   and ate them and felt better. Then I joined the company and Yamamoto and I cremated the remains of the two men; it took ten hours to do so.

6 · Securing the Hill Overlooking the Sittang

Private Shiro Tokita, 3rd Company, 1st Battalion, 215 Infantry Regiment, 33 Division

Sittang, Kokkogwa

While the engineers were fighting in the town, we ran up a steep hill by the river. Shells from anti-aircraft guns located on the opposite side of the river were exploding over our heads. I was a medical corpsman in an infantry platoon led by Second Lieutenant Kiuchi. On the hill were a Burmese-style pagoda and a square wooden building, the floor of which was used as a temporary field hospital. The enemy there surrendered without any resistance, and we captured 27 men, vehicles and machine guns. There were three doctors among those who surrendered, a lieutenant colonel, a captain and a second lieutenant. I heard later the lieutenant colonel had been a friend of Lt Hiroshi Wakasa, the doctor of our battalion, while they were studying in Germany. The doctors who surrendered took good care of the wounded Japanese soldiers.

We could look down on the long bridge of the River Sittang from the hill. At about 11 a.m. shells were bursting continuously on the hill. I went into the trenches dug around the top, together with some wounded Indian soldiers. The hill was uneven in contour and we could see little of our fellow soldiers; 2nd Lieutenant Kiuchi suspected that our own guns might be shelling us and held a Japanese flag high trying to communicate with the battery. A piece of shrapnel hit his head and he died. It was unfortunate that we had not carried steel helmets, in order to reduce our load in crossing the difficult terrain. When the shelling was over we took up defensive positions. Enemy soldiers approached in groups. We shot at them through the bushes at close range. After sunset the enemy seemed to have retreated, but we could not relax. We felt very hungry as we had not eaten since the previous night. I and Kurimoto, who was at my side, encouraged each other saying, 'We have stuck it out staunchly. We are alive!'

Before dawn we heard a big explosion. The enemy had left, and the sun came up. I saw from the hill that the bridge had collapsed in the middle. There were many fish floating on the water, killed by the explosion. On the river bank I saw a lot of shoes and clothing scattered here and there. The Indian soldiers must have swum across the river. Because of the hard walking in the mountains and jungles for a month my shoes had developed holes in the soles. I replaced my torn shoes with a suitable new pair.

7 · First into Rangoon

Lance Corporal Koji Kawamata (continued), 3rd Company,
1st Battalion, 214 Infantry Regiment, 33 Division

We spent four days at the River Sittang clearing the battle-field and then rested to recover for just a while. Those who had dropped out during the rapid advance arrived, and the supplies we had left on the way were brought up to us. Although two spans of the Sittang Bridge were demolished, our engineers made a temporary narrow wooden plank bridge across. We walked over the spans carefully holding on to the guide rope, as we were carrying heavy equipment on our shoulders and at our waists. We marched throughout the night, trying to reach the forest west of Pegu so that we would not be located by the enemy planes, crossing the railway from Rangoon to the north before sunrise. Our officers proudly told us that we had cut the notorious Burma Road, which had been used to carry military supplies from the Allies to China. Every day we walked from sunset until dawn. During the daytime we slept in the dense forest, which was still dark and also humid, as little air circulated and mosquitoes assailed us. We could not sleep well at all, but we were told to make a dash for Rangoon whatever the difficulties.

At sunset on 7 March we were ordered to go on an even worse forced march. We saw the huge glow of oil tanks burning in the southern sky, and encouraged each other saying. 'The place where it is burning is Rangoon, our goal,' and continued our march as fast as we could, carrying rifles, ammunition and other necessities. Even though we infantry men were accustomed to walking, the soles of our feet were covered in blisters and calluses. Almost everybody in the platoon had developed blisters. We asked our medical corpsman to treat our feet during our short rest period, but finally he had to give up. The forced march was the hardest I had ever experienced.

Late in the night we heard the sound of heavy firing close on our left, but our company continued the forced march without a halt. At last we entered the city of Rangoon. It was 8.50 in the morning of 8 March 1942. We could not see a single enemy soldier, though we had expected to fight in the streets. We advanced, writing 'Occupied by the Third Company, 214th Infantry Regiment, 33rd Division' on the walls of buildings. As we came to a pier and were writing on the wall of a big building, the Japanese navy landing force arrived from downstream carrying a naval ensign. The naval officer told us to move to another building as the navy had occupied this one; he explained that the formal first ride into a city should be made by a troop with a military flag, marching in formation. We and our platoon leader, disappointed at not officially being the first to enter Rangoon, found a shady place under trees and fell asleep.

8 · Pushing on to Rangoon

Lance Corporal Tokutaro Mizushima, 7th Company,
2nd Battalion, 215 Infantry Regiment, 33 Division

Sittang

We crossed the River Sittang 30 kilometres north of the Sittang Bridge on 2 March, marched through jungle, marsh and dry plain and arrived at a village 60 kilometres north of Rangoon during the morning of 6 March. We heard the sound of guns far to the north-east. Someone said that this was the 55 Division fighting at Pegu. A strong sun shone down on us, and British planes flew overhead several times, so we had to be careful not to be detected. We rested until the evening of 7 March. We finished eating supper, and had prepared two meals of boiled rice to keep in our mess kit. We lined up ready for departure. Captain Sunagawa, the company commander, calmly told us, 'Now we have received new orders. We are going to make a dash for Rangoon, the capital city. Distance 60 kilometres. We are the advance unit.' Upon hearing this, we let out shouts of joy and 'Banzai! as enthusiastically as if we had already occupied Rangoon.

We walked through the jungle again. The battalion commander was at the head of the column with Captain Sunagawa. The officers had white headbands and the non-commissioned officers wore white armbands. When we came to a paved road, we saw several tanks advancing in the moonlight. We lay down flat on the ground and waited. We ran across the road when the sound of the tanks was no longer heard, and ran through the thin forest south of the road. From then on we marched, half running, not keeping in formation; those who could kept up with the rapid pace of the commanders. By sunrise we were walking on a paved road in the suburbs of Rangoon. My feet ached, treading a hard pavement after marching all night. Some Indian people with small moustaches offered us coffee and milk. Although I hesitated to take them, their offers were repeated, until finally, as I was so thirsty, I grabbed a cup of milk and drank it at one gulp. It tasted so good. The battalion commander cried, 'Don't drink what is offered by the inhabitants!' He was worried in case it was poisoned. Our soldiers were moving hurriedly, not in formation, and the local people mingled with us offering their services. Everybody took the drinks, while keeping their eyes on the commander. The officers pretended not to see us. Since the inhabitants are our friendly allies, unlike in China, we were not able to reprimand the people for hanging around us. Soon we saw the Governor's Building on a hill. We reached the building without meeting any resistance, and a soldier went up to the rooftop and hoisted a Japanese flag, which was small and tattered, with many names written on it. The soldier held high a rifle in one hand and a container of the ashes of dead comrades in the other hand. We lined up in the forecourt and shouted 'Banzai!'. It was 9.55 on the morning of 8 March 1942.

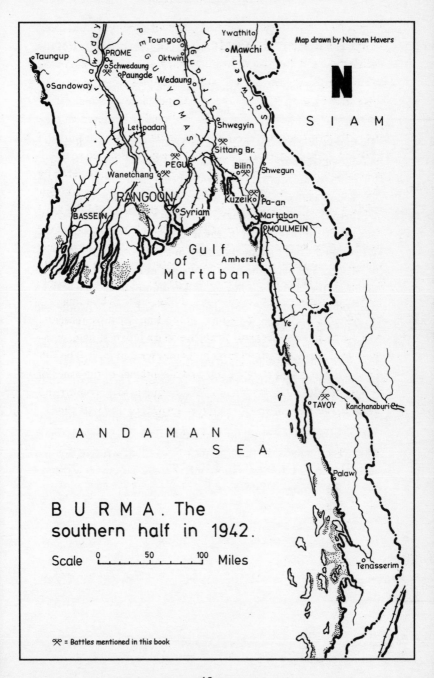

Map drawn by Norman Havers

N

Taungup
Sandoway
PROME
Schwedaung
Paungde
Wedaung
Toungoo
Oktwin
Ywathito
Mawchi
SIAM
Letpadan
Shwegyin
Sittang Br.
PEGU
Bilin
Shwegun
Wanetchang
Kuzeik
Pa-an
RANGOON
Syriam
Martaban
BASSEIN
MOULMEIN
Gulf
of
Martaban
Amherst
Ye
ANDAMAN
SEA
TAVOY
Kanchanaburi
Palaw
BURMA. The
southern half in 1942.
Scale 0 50 100 Miles
Tenasserim

✂ = Battles mentioned in this book

9 · The First Message from Rangoon

Corporal Toshio Miura, Radio Unit, 33 Division

Rangoon

In the evening of 7 March 1942 I was walking towards Rangoon following the right-hand column, 215th Regiment. It was a forced march. Mountain guns were being towed, making a rattling sound as the horses were whipped and whipped. On the way we met vehicles heading out of Rangoon several times. So someone proposed that we get on the next one. Soon a big bus came. We stopped it by blocking the road, took away the weapons of the passengers and made them walk. We put our radio on it in order to reduce the load on the horses. When about 20 kilometres from Rangoon, we took milk porridge offered by Burmese people and were greatly refreshed. As we continued the forced march, Major Yamanoguchi, staff officer of the 33 Division, came to take the radio with him to Rangoon, so my section leader and I went in his big saloon car. An Indian was driving the car. There were four of us including the major's messenger. We entered Rangoon, and the staff officer said that nobody before us had entered the city. Japanese planes were still bombing the oil tanks. At half past ten, I keyed out a message that the staff officer had written: the first official report of the occupation of Rangoon. This news was soon broadcast throughout the world.

10 · Attacking the Last Train

Lance Corporal Seiichi Aoyama, 1st Company,
33 Engineer Regiment, 33 Division

Wanetchaung, Imphal

On 7 March 1942, we were walking along a path thickly covered with the fallen leaves of teak trees. We were a small independent group of engineers with a platoon of infantry, accompanied by several horses carrying explosive materials. Our mission was to blow up the railway in order to prevent reinforcements coming from the north and to stop the enemy leaving Rangoon. We had ferried infantry across the River Sittang in folding boats, and followed the Harada Regiment in a forced march when the crossing was done. Then we advanced on our own to the railway. Suddenly we heard the roar of planes flying at a very low altitude. A British aircraft was being chased by Japanese planes; we had good protection from our airforce. Encouraged by this we marched on, carrying heavy supplies.

After we passed through damp forest and came to a path in a teak forest, we were told to have a quick lunch. I sprinkled powdered soya bean paste on the boiled rice in my mess canteen, which smelled slightly odd, and ate this plain lunch. I threw away the remaining rice. I put on my equipment and lay on the ground. Then I put in my mouth a small piece of raw sugar made from the flower bud of palm which I had bought in a village the previous night. It tasted good with a pleasant flavour, a luxury for us. At my side Corporal Yamazaki was already sleeping with his knapsack on his back. Soldiers could and did sleep even in a short rest period, but those who handled the horses had to do a lot of work; they unloaded the horses, gave them water, attended to the scratches under the saddles and let the animals rest. They had no time to rest themselves. A slight relief was that they could have their food carried on the horses while they were on the march.

Any rest period was always too short for the tired soldiers. We were ordered to start moving, and after we had walked for some time, I don't remember how long, we came out of the forest and into a plain covered with low bushes. On the far left we saw a green field and a railway line glittering. Our commander told us that our target was close. Then we saw an armoured car racing from the direction of Rangoon. The enemy were already retreating ahead of us, and this made us tense and strained. After a while another motor car passed at high speed, seeming to indicate confusion in the capital city. We crossed the railway carefully and arrived at a village surrounded by banana fields. The people of the village seemed disoriented for a moment by the sudden arrival of a group of Japanese soldiers, but they soon turned friendly towards us. It seemed that the information that the Japanese army had captured key cities like Moulmein and Sittang and were approaching Rangoon had spread even to a small country village like this.

In order to keep our intentions secret, our company commander had sentries stationed around the village to prevent people from coming in or going out, and we started to prepare explosive materials and to cook meals. We were warned not to make any smoke. I helped Doctor Serisawa treat the slight shoe sores of the soldiers and then joined in the cooking. A section leader hurriedly came to call me: a soldier was badly wounded. I went with a first aid kit, and found that he was gravely injured, having been gored by a buffalo. The buffalo, which was in an enclosure, had become excited by seeing unfamiliar soldiers with rifles in their hands, and the soldier had touched the nervous animal, which in a reflex action had attacked him. He had a gash from his upper thigh into the abdominal organs, with severe bleeding, and died within several hours, despite intensive care by the doctor. When the sun was about to set, we heard the continuous sound of firing and the roar of tanks and other vehicles moving, and saw white smoke or dust, we could not distinguish which, in the direction of Rangoon. As we were told on the following day, there must have been fierce fighting between the advance unit of the 214 Regiment blocking the Rangoon road and the British Indian troops and armoured corps who tried to break through it.

At about 8 o'clock we left our horses and unnecessary supplies and equipment in the village and set out towards the railway. That night the moon was almost full and was reflected on the barrels of our rifles. We walked towards Wanetchaung station in an ominously tense silence. The company halted and spread out beside a small river 3 metres wide. On our left we saw the railway bridge which we were going to blow up. Lt Tamogami went ahead with demolition teams and attached explosives to the bridge. No enemy patrols appeared. Then, as a train approached from the south, the commander gave the order 'Detonate!' A flash was seen with a heavy explosion. The train, which had stopped at the station, soon started to move. It was a long one pulled by two steam locomotives. The first locomotive passed over the bridge as normal while we were eagerly watching, but the second gradually slowed down on the bridge, and we heard the screaming sound of steel and the crushing sound of colliding coaches. The train then stopped.

On the order 'Charge!' we dashed towards the train. As the first few men were climbing over a fence by the side of the railway, a flash with a deafening sound of gunfire came first from above the tender of the locomotive and then from all the windows of the coaches; the enemy must have been expecting such an attack and their counteraction was fierce. We were in a dreadful situation. We retreated a little, reorganised, and began shooting and throwing hand grenades, but the enemy's fire was so severe that we were forced to cease firing. As our grenades emitted fiery smoke when they were ignited before throwing, the positions of the soldiers were clearly seen in the night and soon attracted concentrated enemy shooting, so it was quite suicidal to use the grenades at night.

As the headlight of the first locomotive illuminated part of our force, Corporal Makita went round to the front and destroyed the light with a rifle shot. Our situation became more and more unfavourable. I heard our wounded groaning in pain, then we heard another train coming from the direction of Rangoon. The front light of the second train illuminated the rear of the first train. Then the light was turned off but the train seemed to have hit the halted one and the coaches in front of us were shaken back and forth. Owing to the shock, the enemy firing stopped for a few minutes. But since more soldiers were on the second train we were even worse outnumbered. Our soldiers kept as low as possible, as anybody who made a sound or showed any movement was fired on immediately. This worst possible situation continued for a while until a black cloud covered the moon and it became dark. The soldiers made use of this opportunity and crawled away. I untied my puttees, tied them to the ankles of a wounded man who was close to me, and pulled him away from the trains. When I came to a hollow, I tried to put on a temporary bandage. His thigh muscle was cut by bullets and he was not breathing any more.

'Assemble at the village.' Staff Sergeant Wakasa relayed the order in a low voice and we went back to the village in twos and threes, dragging our tired feet. The company assembled there and checked the names of those missing, before we were allowed to sleep for a few hours.

Next morning, just before sunrise, we went out and attacked the trains from a distance with light machine guns and mortars. There was no enemy reaction. Sergeant Kamiya approached the train in Burmese clothing and reported that there were no enemy there; they must have left on foot. We reached the train and recovered the dead bodies, and prepared for the cremation of the eight soldiers killed. The trains must have carried the equivalent of a regiment of soldiers, against whom we could never compete. We should not have attacked them.

Our soldiers were delighted to find a lot of canned food, brandy, beer and cigarettes, and ate as much as they could and filled their bags with them. Around noon on 8 March we had to start moving. We now carried wounded men, captured weapons and some food on ox-carts, and marched in daylight, which we had not been able to do before in Burma. On the road to Rangoon we saw destroyed tanks and armoured cars; some of them were still smoking. There were many dead bodies of British and Indian soldiers left by the roadsides. It was a miserable sight. Our soldiers did not know where to walk to avoid the dead.

It was almost sunset when we entered the streets of Rangoon and took shelter in an allocated house. It was the basement of a building on a narrow side street.

11 · A Disaster at Pegu

Private Toshiaki Tadokoro, 8th Company, 3rd Battalion,
112 Infantry Regiment, 55 Division

Tavoy, Pegu

I had been walking almost every day for two months since my battalion came to Burma in early January 1942. We had rested for only a few days at Tavoy and Moulmein. We crossed the River Sittang during the daytime, fortunately without being attacked by British planes, which flew over us from time to time, for which reason our commander ordered us to hurry.

One night, while we were passing through a town called Waw, I saw the moon ahead of us. It gradually waned and almost disappeared. Nobody talked about this eclipse. I thought it unlucky, as a lunar eclipse might be a prophecy of declining fortune for us soldiers.

Platoon Leader Second Lt Shioze told us that we were going to capture Pegu and then proceed to Rangoon, the capital of Burma. We started to move as soon as it got dark. We had to cross four or five shallow rivers. Whenever we did so, water got into my shoes which made an unpleasant squelching noise as I walked. The shoes stopped making this noise after I had walked for a while, then the next river was waiting for us. Because of this repeated soaking of my shoes, I had painful soles. We heard the sound of engines being started, so we were ordered to go into the forest and dig trenches. I was ordered to be a member of a three-man scout patrol. I thought of mentioning my aching soles, but refrained and went with the patrol.

After we had advanced about 2 kilometres, the situation became somewhat clearer. Tanks! As we went closer we saw many tanks, and there seemed to be some infantry. Soldiers were talking in loud voices. As our time limit was nearing we hurried back and reported the situation. The platoon left immediately, making a detour to the left, trying to avoid the tanks that the patrol had found. We crossed a paved road which we were told was the Rangoon–Mandalay road, or the Burma Road, leading to China.

In the dry season in Burma, there is usually some mist around sunrise, and this morning was no exception. We advanced platoon by platoon towards the British tanks under cover of the mist. We could see the tanks through gaps between the village houses. Our leader was delighted at this opportunity. Everybody must have imagined capturing a tank, as we had done so often in drills before we left Japan. When we came to the houses, our leader lifted his sword and we rushed forward. Then we were fired on very heavily. We could not tell where the bullets were coming from. Anyhow, we were forced by the shooting to lie down flat. I thought that our attack had failed and we were in danger. Soon the houses in front of us caught fire. Burmese village houses, made of bamboo poles, tree-leaf roofs and mat-rush walls, burn easily.

Unfortunately, the straw which was piled up behind us also started burning. It was about 8 o'clock in the morning, and the sun was shining brightly, heating us up as well as the fire. We felt pain rather than heat. My steel helmet got so hot that my head ached. I felt as if I would soon become a baked and dried human being. The houses in front were burnt down, so now we were clearly visible to the enemy tanks. There were scores of them lined up. All the top hatches of the tanks were open and soldiers with automatic rifles were watching us. They must have thought that all of us Japanese were dead. When an injured man moved even a little because of the unbearable pain, he was immediately shot at. I made up my mind to keep pretending to be dead, but to do so was intolerable torture. The dry paddy field was soaked by my sweat, my nose was choked with mud, and I had to breathe through my mouth.

I do not know how long the torture lasted. To me it was a very very long time, as if it were years. I heard a British order shouted, and all the tanks started their engines. I held tightly to a hand grenade, as I expected that the tanks would come to trample us down. If they did come, I would throw the grenade straight and true into a top hatch. But the tanks stood still with their engines running. I was very nervous wondering what they would do next. At that moment a Japanese scout plane flew very low over the tanks. Immediately the tanks changed direction and made off. It was just noon. My body had lost so much water, heated by the sun and the fire, that I could hardly stand up. It was a pity that we did not have any anti-tank weapons. Fifteen men had been killed and as many were injured. The boiled rice that we had prepared the previous evening before our departure had gone bad due to the heat, so we boiled fresh rice, taking care not make any smoke.

On 6 March two portable mines were issued to our company for the first time, and tank attack teams were organised. We laid the mines and waited under the bridge, but not a single tank came. After dark all the men of the company marched silently in a single file through paddy fields. We were now less than half our original number. Later that night it became too dark to walk, so the company commander allowed us to have a long rest. The soldiers went to sleep on the spot with their knapsacks on their backs.

When I was woken up, it was nearing sunrise. I looked around, but most of the company were not there; only a part of our first platoon was left behind with me. Maybe one man in the single file had not awoken, or if he had he might have forgotten to wake up the next man. Second Lt Shioze had been sent to hospital from Payagi, and now there were no officers with us. We could not find any footprints of those who had left. Meanwhile, the mist cleared up and we saw a forest ahead. We proceeded towards a pagoda among the trees. When we arrived there and looked down from a hill, we saw many enemy tents. Though we were few in number, about fifteen, we had three machine guns, so we started firing around the tents at close range. We continued shooting as fast as the cartridge cases were loaded. I saw several enemy soldiers rear up and fall flat, dead. When we had used up all our ammunition, we heard heavy firing close to us. Possibly the main body of the company had attacked the enemy positions. We were few in number so we did not charge the enemy, who were a thousand or so strong. A mortar shell exploded by a tree near the temple. As I had had some experience of mortars, I went into the pagoda with Private Sako, who loaded the cases. As soon as we entered, more than ten shells exploded near the pagoda. When the shelling had finished, five men came in to take shelter. Seven men were injured and were being taken care of by a medical corpsman. Two men had been killed. While I was looking for a place to cremate the dead, a Burmese man came to me calling out, 'Japan master'. He closed his eyes and inclined his head. I went with him and found that all the men of the company lay dead, company commander Kitaoka and 53 men. Looking at such a tragedy I felt sweat running down my back. They had been killed only 300 metres away from the pagoda where we were.

The seven of us who had survived, or rather who had failed to die, collected the dead bodies, helped by Burmese people, and laid them on wooden railway sleepers in a dry river bed. We started cremating the bodies after sunset to avoid enemy bombing. It was still too hot to recover the ashes the next morning, 8 March. When the heat lessened in the afternoon we wrapped the ashes individually in lawn cloths with the names on, and put them on a temporary altar. We sat in front of it and mourned, crying. I thought of what would have happened to me if my comrade had not been half asleep. Men's fortunes are changed by a slight incident. Had the lunar eclipse affected my destiny?

The seven of us remaining from the 8th Company went to the regimental headquarters. We were treated as an independent unit. Later in March we seven were ordered to escort Colonel Oharazawa, commander of 112 Regiment, to a military hospital in Rangoon. As the 55 Division did not advance to Rangoon but went north from Pegu, we were among the few who were able to visit the capital city.

12 · A Japanese Lady in Syriam

Private Sojiro Maeda, 2nd Company, 1st Battalion,
112 Infantry Regiment, 55 Division

Moulmein, Arakan

We crossed the River Sittang on 3 March 1942 and walked day and night towards the south. Our battalion was ordered to make a dash to Syriam to secure oil tanks and facilities. It was really a torture to continue the forced march with little rest, under the tropical heat. We were guided by young soldiers of the Burma Independence Army who rode Burmese ponies and waved the Peacock Flag. When we came to a big village about twenty Burmese ladies welcomed us with smiles, holding water bottles and bamboo baskets piled with tomatoes. This was repeated at every big village and was a consolation and help for our painful, hard march. We felt that Burmese people were eagerly looking for independence and sincerely thanked us for our help. It had been our understanding that we would see no women and children near the battlefield.

After six days we approached Syriam, our Horiuchi platoon leading the advance. At the entrance to the town we saw an elderly Japanese lady waving a small Japanese flag. We talked with her, and she was so happy to know that our unit was from Kagawa-ken in Shikoku Island where she came from. She invited us to her house and offered us a nice meal. The lady, Nobu, was married to a Briton for thirty years, and when the war started was put in a jail in Rangoon but she managed to escape by bribing the gaolers. Her husband was Mr John Henry Edward Smith, an engineer of the Burma Oil Company. Even after all the British had left for India he remained in Syriam expecting that he would be safe as his wife was Japanese.

Although Syriam is just across the river from Rangoon, we did not feel the war as stores in the town were open as usual and people were nice to us. Our only regret was that the oil tanks were burning with masses of black smoke. We stayed in the town for two days then headed back north to Toungoo trying to catch up our 112 Regiment. The town people offered us enough rice and many ox-carts and saw us off cheerfully. We started the march refreshed.

MR SADAHIKO ISHII, a nephew of Nobu, who served in my regiment told me what then happened to them. Mr Smith was arrested and was accommodated in a hospital in Rangoon, and Nobu visited him every day with food and took care of him. Fortunately, Nobu was able to meet Gendarmerie Major Hideo Akiyama who came from the same area as she, and with his help Mr Smith was released and confined informally in their home in Syriam.

In April 1945, when British planes came to attack Syriam, Mr Smith ran up to the rooftop of the town hall and signalled to the scout plane using a white flag that indicated 'Japanese troops are not here. They have already retreated.' Thanks to this message the town was not bombed and avoided disastrous destruction. The town people appreciated his action very much and presented him with a silver statue of a horse as a token of their thanks. Moreover, the town decided to call the day 'Smith Day' and an event remembering their gratitude has been held every year.

After the war ended the couple lived in Singapore for a year and then went back to Folkestone, John's native town. They stayed in Japan for three years from 1960 and then returned to England.

2

ADVANCE

March to June 1942

13 · Advance to the North

Lance Corporal Masakichi Kanbayashi, 7th Company,
2nd Battalion, 215 Infantry Regiment, 33 Division

Kuzeik, Sittang

We marched a long way from Thailand and on 8 March 1942 raced into Rangoon, which had just been deserted by the British army. We stayed in a school building near Lake Victoria in the suburbs of Rangoon. We had a completely free time for about ten days; no duty, no sentry and no service work. A paradise for soldiers, the first I enjoyed in my military life. We had a lot of food and were given plenty of luxuries such as whisky, canned food, coffee, cocoa, milk, butter, cheese, corned beef, jam, cigarettes and others which I did not know. They were brought from British warehouses and were called the gift ration from Mr Churchill, then British Prime Minister. We had parties every night and sang cheerfully, danced, ate and drank enough. We really enjoyed ourselves. We lacked fresh vegetables so when fried leech was served it tasted good. A comrade made tasty doughnuts.

After a very relaxing ten days we were told to advance north to chase the retreating British. Our Machine Gun (7.7mm) Company and units with horses departed the evening of 18 March, and we left Rangoon on 19 March in lorries that the British had left. The drivers were short on training, one lorry hit a roadside tree and another an ox crossing the road, but we arrived at Letpadan safely where the lorries went back for a shuttle service.

We crossed the great Irrawaddy River by small boats, and arrived at Henzada where we stayed for a few days. On 24 March we started marching north along the west bank of the river. We walked at night to avoid strong sunshine but it was still very hot. Burmese people who lived along the road welcomed us enthusiastically day and night as we passed. They cried 'Dopahma! (Hurrah for the independence of Burma)' and offered us fruits and water continually; their hearty reception impressed us greatly.

On the march we usually walk 4 kilometres in 45 minutes and rest for 15 minutes. We made use of the valuable 15 minutes to sleep and recover from fatigue by lying flat on the ground with knapsacks on. We lay down with our feet in the line of advance, so that we could move in the right direction when we woke up. Otherwise we might have gone off sideways and dropped into a roadside ditch when we started half asleep. The Burmese people were so keen to be nice to us, and sometimes woke us up and offered us water. Though we were keen to get some sleep we had to thank them for their kindness.

After walking about 100 kilometres we crossed the river during the day of 27 March, where many ox-carts were assembled for us. All of us in the Second Battalion went on the ox-carts; light wooden carts with big wheels pulled by two oxen. Three of us shared a cart with a Burmese driver, and travelled towards the north through a wild plain. As it got dark and quite cool the drivers disappeared one by one; probably the enemy were close. We could not force them to continue driving, as we had done in China. Meanwhile our driver also fled, afraid of being involved in fighting. So we had to drive by ourselves. I had never handled oxen, but when I tried it was not a problem; the oxen obediently followed the cart in front. So each of us drove the cart in turn and the other two slept on it.

The night had almost passed and I was still half asleep on the cart, when I heard the shouted order, 'All men get off, prepare for fighting and come forward on the run.' We left the cart as it was and started running with full equipment. This was the beginning of the battle of Schwedaung!

14 · The Battle Begins

Second Lieutenant Yasushi Sakamaki, 2nd Machine Gun Company,
2nd Battalion, 215 Infantry Regiment, 33 Division

Schwedaung, Tiddim Road

In the morning of 29 March 1942, our Second Battalion occupied Schwedaung village after light fighting by our leading platoon. The battalion was far from the rest of the regiment as we came in on ox-carts moving throughout the night and the commander decided to secure the village which lies at a natural bottleneck on the Prome–Rangoon Road. From inhabitants and our scouts we knew that a large group of British troops and tanks had passed the village southbound only five hours before our arrival.

One infantry platoon and our two 7.7mm machine guns were despatched to 2 kilometres south of the village as an advance guard, expecting that the enemy might return. Several anti-tank men were hidden under a small bridge on the main road and the rest hid on the west side of the road. Soon three lorries loaded with soldiers came from the south without noticing us. We shot at them crossing the bridge with full firepower, and lorries tumbled down. The enemy were thrown into confusion and ran away, leaving behind some dead bodies. Around noon about twenty soldiers were seen approaching. Taking the chance when they moved in front of our position from right to left, we opened concentrated fire, killing most of them. About 2 p.m. a large number of soldiers were seen in the forest one kilometre ahead of us and the sound of caterpillars was heard. The enemy must have found us and full-scale attack seemed under way. Soon a passenger car drove out of the forest and a man who looked like a commander came out and gave orders. Moreover, men with red cross armbands came nearer and started carrying dead bodies on stretchers.

Almost at the same time a whistle was heard, and the village we were in was covered with exploding smoke and sand dust. When

62

we thought that shelling was dying down, smoke shells fell on the village and to our front, and about 300 soldiers came forward trying to encircle us. We kept shooting them through gaps of smoke. When we saw the smoke had gone, the soldiers had also disappeared from our sight.

Once again we heard the noise of tanks getting louder. It seemed that the enemy was planning to attack us again. It was almost sunset. Already we had received a radio message to retreat, so we gradually broke off from the enemy and went back to the main position of the battalion. Our battalion commander was happy when we stopped the attack and left time to defend Schwedaung. After that night intensive attacks by the enemy began.

15 · A Brave Enemy Soldier

Major Misao Sato, 2nd Battalion, 215 Infantry Regiment,
33 Division

Kuzeik, Schwedaung

Our battalion captured Schwedaung village in the early morning of 29 March 1942 after a light fight. Everybody was busy as there were about ten casualties, and positions were being set up on the south and on the north of the village where a strong enemy attack was expected. As I was standing at the three-way crossing at the south end of the village, I noticed occasional sniping fire from a certain direction. The shooting was so persistent that I sent out a section to look for the sniper, who brought back a young British soldier with his lower body stained with blood. This wounded soldier alone had bravely continued sniping from a bush.

I went to see him lying in the shade of a tree. He was young-looking, about 18 years old, a handsome British soldier. He was treated by our doctor Kikuchi. A bullet had gone through his abdomen, and the doctor told me there was no hope of survival. I asked him in my broken English, 'Where are your father and mother?' He said just a word, but clearly, 'England', and as I asked, 'Painful?' he again said a word, 'No.' I knew that he must be suffering great pain. It is torture to be shot through the abdomen, and more painful as his intestines were ruptured.

As I looked at him closely I saw a thin stream of tears coming from his eyes. I understood that he was enduring his pain with all his might, his young, pale face contorted. Ah! his attitude was really dignified. He was doing his best to maintain the pride of the Great British Empire while his life was ending. Unconsciously I cried and held his hands. I would never forget the last minutes of that young British soldier! At that time I really discovered the origin of the strength of the British Empire.

16 · Tank Attack

Lance Corporal Kesazou Higuchi, 8th Company,
2nd Battalion, 215 Infantry Regiment, 33 Division

Schwedaung

As soon as we arrived at Schwedaung village we received orders for its defence. I collected glass bottles from the villagers and filled them with petrol plugged with cloth, and made instant petrol bombs (or flame bottles in Japanese).

As the main road which went through the village was one to two metres higher than the ground, we lay flat, close to the edge of the road which was in a dead angle of the tank guns, and covered our flanks with bags of rice. At about 9 p.m. shells and bullets came at us. During an interval of shelling enemy tanks came advancing at high speed in the centre of the road. As I was lying flat on the ground, the tanks had already passed in front of us when I raised my head to look. I thought that this was no good, as we could not throw the petrol bombs. I, with my comrades, moved a lorry which was left on the roadside and blocked the far side of the road by turning it sideways, so that the tanks would come close to us. We waited.

The next tank which came speeding slowed down and followed the route as we planned. I waited patiently until the tank was level with my eyes, and threw the petrol bomb when it was changing direction. The bottle exactly hit the front of the tank, and the tank crew bailed out, seeing the vast flame in front of them. The company commander, who happened to be near us, asked, 'Who threw the petrol bombs?' So Corporal Hirasawa and I reported our names. He commended us, saying, 'Well done'. Another bomb thrown by one of us landed inside the third tank from its opened hatch. The tank kept going for a while and the crew escaped. We missed them because of the dark night. No more tanks showed up for the time being.

At about 9 p.m. many big shells exploded around our position and the fighting continued. I suffered three shrapnel wounds in my right leg and was sent to a field hospital, to my regret. Later in the evening Corporal Hirasawa was killed at his second close-range attack.

17·Enemy Tanks Advance and Retreat

Second Lieutenant Tatsuya Maruyama, 5th Company,
2nd Battalion, 215 Infantry Regiment, 33 Division

Schwedaung, Thododan, Tiddim Road

After the attack by three tanks, probably a reconnaissance in force, the village came under fierce shelling. We crouched in a roadside ditch to avoid being hit. After sunrise on 30 March the enemy attack became stronger and we suffered heavy casualties. By noon we had to retreat from the south and moved to the west of the main road; we fired spontaneously at the approaching vehicles, causing several lorries to tumble down the embankment or to catch fire. My platoon was ordered to secure the bridge at the north end of the village. There was a river 50 metres wide and 5 metres deep but with no water flowing due to the dry season. The bridge was of concrete span, about 4 metres wide.

The first tank to arrive struck a portable mine on the bridge and its caterpillar track exploded with a big bang. The tank tried noisily to go back and forth, then came to a stop. A crewman opened the hatch to look around, so I moved close and tried to snipe at him with a rifle. Then the enemy found me and a long tank gun rotated as I hid behind a lavatory. Bang! it went, and I was covered by earth from the lavatory wall and did not dare move for a while. Close-range attack crews threw petrol bombs at the tank from the other side of the road. As its interior got too hot three men climbed out and tried to escape. Our light machine gun killed two of them.

The tank had stalled on the bridge, blocking the only retreat route of the motorised enemy. The second tank half-climbed on to the stalled tank and tumbled down into the river on its side. The third and fourth tanks on the bridge could not move as many lorries which followed were desperate to move on and were hitting the rear of vehicles in front. The road was closely packed with vehicles, which our troops hit with the full force of machine guns, rifles and a 70mm gun. Japanese planes attacked the enemy in the south. Finally, the enemy left their vehicles, guns and heavy weapons, and fled through jungles towards the north, disorganised. The rest of the tanks managed to cross the dry river, climbing up the steep river bank, and retreated. As we were clearing the dead bodies on the lorries, enemy guns from the direction of Prome fired incendiary shells on the village and vehicles, which were soon in flames. We tried to move the lorries, which were so valuable to us, but this did not go well. Many lorries were burnt out. By sunset the fight, which lasted for a full day and night, came to an end. As we were so tired we soon fell asleep, after a quick supper.

18 · Heavy Fighting at Thadodan

Lance Corporal Umeo Tokita, 7th Company,
2nd Battalion, 215 Infantry Regiment

Sittang, Shwedaung

'Unload bullets from your rifles,' the section leader ordered in a loud voice in the late evening of 11 April 1942. This was the order we often heard in China and in Burma before night attacks. By repeated bayonet drills and past experiences we had come to realise that the bayonet is the only and best weapon that protects ourselves and strikes the enemy in night fighting.

Soon after sunset we started moving. I was recalling the order that our section leader gave us before departure. In contrast to the hard fighting at Shwedaung of about ten days ago, we were going to attack positions of a famous armoured corps.

That night we were walking, quite relaxed, as we were not the advance section. 'Rest fifteen minutes!' came the relayed message from up front. I sat down on the ground and slept holding my rifle. As I looked up at the sky the Southern Cross was shining brightly and beautifully. For a moment I thought of my home country which lay beyond the far end of the sky. After midnight I heard sounds of shooting far on our left. A lot of flares brightened the sky, and more sounds of shooting. After an hour or so it became silent and dark, as it had been before. It might have been our 1st Battalion attacking Kokkogwa, involving my good friend Yamaguchi.

Our company came to the main road, our first target, without any resistance, and continued to advance along the lower edge of the road in single file. We heard voices on the other side of the road. A soldier crossed quickly and we awaited his report, keeping absolute silence. It was the enemy. About 100 metres beyond the road was an enemy position. Although they might not have noticed our approach, we were already deep in their ground;

fighting would start within a few minutes and several of us could be killed. I might be one of them; I felt more forlorn. It already became dim. The situation was not in our favour. The enemy had more men and better weapons, so we preferred a night attack. But time passed and the sun came up. Heaven did not help us. An enemy sentry must have noticed us. Firing began at once. Under the circumstances I would only fight with the 'do-or-die' spirit.

The enemy position was spread widely ahead of us, and at our back was a vast, wild plain scattered with clumps of palm trees. I dropped into a roadside ditch and placed my gun on the road surface. In front was a village, and at its entrance a tank with its gun pointed towards us. Enemy soldiers were seen from time to time behind the tank. I went on shooting towards the soldiers. I could not afford to check the effect of my shots and just continued firing. Our platoon leader was on my right and was shouting but I could not hear what he said due to the noise. Enemy mortars started shelling: they seemed to be overshooting us as we were so close. However, the occasional explosion of shells deafened my ears for a moment. The terrain was not to our advantage. On the far right, hand-grenade fighting began. I heard the platoon leader shout: 'Retreat one by one to the men in the back! Retreat!' He ordered the retreat by calling our names in turn. This time our infantry gun shelled the enemy to cover our retreat. I gripped my light machine gun firmly and waited for a chance to jump out of the ditch. I took the drastic step of getting out and ran for my life. I was saved! I tripped on a root of a palm tree, and checked my body. No injury! Our company seemed to have assembled in a group. Several comrades were wounded.

It was then, much against our will, that we had to retreat, and we had to fall back once more to a river where no water was flowing during this dry season. The river was a natural anti-tank trench as its depth and width were both about two to three metres and its flat bottom was covered by pebbles. Most of us went into it. 'Tank coming!' someone shouted. As I stood on tiptoe to look, I saw a tank in front, swerving about, and then it stopped at 300 metres from us. It seemed to be watching us. By and by more tanks came and were moving freely ahead of us. We were like mice in a trap! Nothing we could do; we had only rifles, machine guns and grenade launchers.

After a while the tanks started up and came straight towards us, firing their machine guns. At the same time skirmishers behind us on the hill began shooting at us. Bullets flew overhead, and we kept as low as possible. The tanks got close to us, but they could not aim low enough. We were not that afraid of them, but we could not raise our heads due to firing from the other side. The tanks turned around when they got near, probably afraid of our close-range attacks; more tanks approached and then turned back. One tank came close and threatened us by showing a part of its caterpillar track above our heads which made us uncomfortable! We were really lucky as tanks could not cross over the dry river nor move along the river bed.

To protect myself I tried to dig a hole on the river bank and hid my body as much as I could. My clothes and face were covered by mud. Mid-April in Burma is very hot and strong sunshine heated up the pebbles on the river bed, which made it even hotter. This would mean more torture for patients on stretchers left on the river bed but there was nothing we could do for them. We could hardly repulse the approaching infantry with our fire and some of us were wounded.

Meanwhile, we ran out of drinking water. Some men climbed out of the river to get water but several of them were shot and injured. I dug a deep hole in the river bed, scooped up muddy water and kept it in my mess canteen until it settled, then drank. The crew of a 37mm anti-tank gun pushed up the gun and its first shot pierced a tank's track but that was all. No more shells penetrated the armour. Most of our gunners were killed by the concentrated fire from tanks and the gun itself was run over by a tank and smashed. In order to use a petrol bomb or 'Chibi bomb' (glass container filled with an acid) in close-range attack we had to leave the river bed, which itself was suicidal. A soldier went out to attack a tank and did not come back, but this brave and self-sacrificing act seemed to have some effect and tanks no more tanks approached.

Then tanks repeated their attacks from our front and also from our rear. The dry river bed was chaotic with men moving around. Whenever a tank came near we would stick to that side of the river bank, looking for a dead angle to avoid enemy fire. When another tank came from a different angle we had to move to the other side. More men were wounded but we could not attend to them. Injured men who could not move had to endure pain and fear, leaving their fate to heaven.

Under these unfavourable conditions it passed noon. I prayed that the sunset would come quickly. I would never again experience such a long day in my life. Then information circulated from an unknown source that Japanese tanks were coming to rescue us. Having seen a group of tanks moving far away, all of us were encouraged and shouted 'Banzai!' (Hurrah). This had an unexpected effect on the enemy, who might have thought that the reckless Japanese were going to start a massive close-range attack. The tanks turned around one by one. Encouraged by this, we cried 'Banzai!' again and again. But in fact it was not the Japanese which we saw; more British tanks were arriving. But then we were saved from the critical situation. Soon afterwards Japanese heavy shells (150mm and 105mm) started to explode around the tanks which then retreated and did not come back to attack us.

When the sun went down, the enemy infantry went away and the shooting ceased. We moved back, with the dead and wounded on stretchers in the dark plain, which then was strangely quiet. We hurried, feeling we were being pursued. We cremated the dead at a village about two kilometres from the battlefield, and then moved westward towards the River Irrawaddy.

19 · Attack on Kokkogwa

Sergeant Yoshiro Tsukagoshi, Signal Company, 215 Infantry
Regiment, 33 Division

We left Allanmyo on 9 April and arrived at Iwaza village about sunset on 11 April. There my radio section was assigned to 1st Battalion who were to attack Kokkogwa. We left the village soon after sunset. There was no moon but the stars were beautiful. Under the dim starlight we walked quietly; I did not know at all where our objective, Kokkogwa, was situated.

After walking for about five hours, we came to a sandy plain, and saw palm trees silhouetted in the sky. There was a small village, where we left the horses, and carried radio equipment on our shoulders. We started once again after a short rest, and in an hour or so came on to soft, uneven sand, which seemed to be a wide river with no water. As I looked at my watch, using a firefly lamp, it was about 1 a.m. We kept moving, then a whistle was heard, to my surprise; then silence prevailed as before. Staff Sergeant Fukuhara told us in a low voice, 'Rest for a while here.' So everyone sat down, but some noise was inevitable, being relaxed after a tiring march. Someone warned, 'Be quiet!' but suddenly we were shot at from a short distance with the sound of machine guns and lines of tracer bullets.

We lay down immediately but, being surprised, could not afford to fight back. I was unable to move, but tried to dig in the sand so as to keep my head low; being hit in the head is fatal. As I turned my head I felt bullets and saw tracers flying only 20 centimetres above me. Rifle companies in the front started to fight back. But as the enemy knew our movements, our confident night attack could not proceed as we wanted.

Our attack by rifle companies did not go well, and the charge by 1st Company did not succeed, resulting in high casualties, including its commander killed. The battle situation was miserable.

I prepared to destroy our radio equipment in case of the worst. As I heard the groans of soldiers wounded by the shelling still continuing, I called out the names of five men in my section one by one; 'Ebinuma, are you all right?' 'Yes, I am all right.' By repeating the call I found all my men were safe. But who could know when a bullet might hit me? Probably the very next bullet! As I reflected that I might not mind being killed, strangely I felt very sleepy. I neither heard the fierce sound of shots nor did I see the tracers and I felt as if I was drifting into unconsciousness. I do not know how long it lasted. When I recovered my senses, I heard the battalion adjutant crying, 'Retreat, retreat!' I felt an inexpressibly strong fear. How could we escape from this critical situation? Bullets were still raining fiercely. I told my men, 'Listen, we are retreating now. Follow me!' I ordered the receiver, transmitter and generator to be carried on their backs and we crawled, moving slowly, though I was impatient to be quick. After we crawled 300 metres or so, we got out of the enemy's range. We sheltered in a good hollow in the ground and I checked that all in my section were uninjured. We rejoiced in our well-being.

After a few minutes I heard men talking. It was battalion headquarters. I asked the adjutant if there was any message to send out. He asked, 'Can you radio now?' I replied, 'Yes, I will contact regimental headquarters.' I started transmitting, hoping that the noise of the generator would not attract enemy attention. Headquarters answered immediately. I was impressed that they were awaiting our call. But the coding team was not there and it would take time to locate them, so I asked permission to send a message without ciphering. The battalion commander thought for a while and said, 'It's inevitable. Send as follows: Kokkogwa has not been occupied. Request shelling on Kokkogwa.' So I keyed the message in reverse sequence. Having heard the answer, 'Understood', my tension relaxed and I felt very weary.

At that moment a beam of light swept before me. It was the headlight of an enemy tank. I lay down flat and kept quiet. The tank went away. Now it was dangerous to stay, so we started to move and arrived at the village where we left horses and other equipment at around 4 a.m. We went into an allocated hut, installed the radio and contacted regimental headquarters.

The sun came out and I enjoyed the fresh morning air and had a quick breakfast. Then we heard a tank gun close by. Tanks moved in and shelled our positions. We received a telegram from headquarters. We deciphered it: 'From Harada to Mugita. Daytime is dangerous. Do not overexert yourself.' Though brisk, it was a considerate message from our Regimental Commander, Colonel Harada, to 1st Battalion. Major Mugita carefully read the telegram and bowed his head in assent.

20 · Defeat at Kokkogwa

Lance Corporal Shiro Tokita, 3rd Company, 1st Battalion,
215 Infantry Regiment, 33 Division

Sittang

We retreated from Kokkogwa and reached Songon village in the morning of 12 April. An advance guard of six men was sent out from 3rd Company, and I was its youngest member. While I was on watch I heard the sound of planes, and I looked around but could not locate them. I was searching in the sky when three enemy tanks appeared in front of me on the road. As the road sloped downhill towards us, the tanks advanced with their engines off, so their noise was mixed up with that of the planes. The tanks stopped at the barrier we had laid, and as I watched from a shelter, the hatch of the top tank was opened and a man stood up. He seemed an officer of about 50 years of age, and scanned around with his binoculars. Soon he gave an order and the tank guns started shelling our anti-tank gun position about 300 metres behind us.

We had no petrol bombs or mines at our position, so I tried to shoot him with my rifle but I lost a chance to fire as I was in hot haste. The second tank found me and fired its machine gun at me. Instantly I lay down in a gully and retreated through it as instructed. The tanks climbed up a hill on the left, which our guns started shelling, and then went away.

At about 3 p.m. 3rd Company was resting under the floor of a temple. Suddenly two tanks came as close as 50 metres, shot at the temple for five minutes, then left. As we kept quiet, the tanks must have tried to check whether Japanese were there or not. Fortunately no one was injured. We were surprised to find that a shell had gone through a big wooden pillar, leaving a big hole. By evening the enemy had left the battlefield and it became quiet. Major Mugita assembled his battalion and praised our brave fight. He was standing on an enemy tank which a sapper had captured by throwing a flame bottle on to its back and killing three crew escaping from it.

At midnight we started marching towards Nyanbegin which was 30 kilometres west of Songon, and arrived there next morning. That evening most of the battalion went back again to Kokkogwa to recover the dead bodies we had left there. It is a disgrace for our unit to leave behind the bodies of our comrades, which should be cremated and sent to their families.

We arrived at Kokkogwa next morning without meeting any enemy, and found that the bodies of the commander of 1st Company and other men had been buried. We appreciated the enemy's humanitarian behaviour.

21·Entering Yenangyaung

Private Yoshizo Abe, 1st Company, 33 Engineer Regiment,
33 Division

Sittang

Our group left Allanmyo in the evening of 9 April. After being carried on lorries for 40 kilometres, we started advancing on foot towards the north through the hot, desert-like area where the temperature was above 30 degrees centigrade even at night. I was posted with the headquarters of 214 Infantry Regiment as an order-receiver (messenger) of 2nd Engineer Platoon.

Late on 11 April we were told to keep as quiet as possible as we were to advance along a dry river to get beneath a bridge that was guarded by an enemy sentry. All of us, and our supplies carried on horses, were covered with tree leaves, and riding on horses was prohibited as tall figures are distinguishable against the night sky.

Soon after midnight, emerging from a big bend of the dry river, we saw the bridge, about 15 metres long. I saw a sentry standing on the right of the bridge. I was worried that my shoes were making some sound as I walked along the sand of the river bed. A British tank came from the left, making a lot of noise, and stopped at the bridge. The sentry ran to the tank and said something. Then the tank rumbled off to the left. I walked as though in a dream. After about an hour we heard a relayed message: 'Passage completed. Everything OK at the tail end.'

When the sun rose we looked at one another and laughed as our faces were all dirty like mud dolls, but everyone was so happy that we had passed through the critical line safely, undetected by the enemy. We walked across the arid plain, avoiding villages, towards the sky lit by red flames. The temperature was unbearably high and there were no flowing rivers, nor springs; really a hard march. Fortunately a sergeant from headquarters was an expert in well-drilling. He pointed out places on the river bed where water might be available; we dug about one metre and found water. We gave it to the horses first and then filled our canteens.

At 3 a.m. we arrived at a hill north-west of Yenangyaung. Big British lorries were running towards the north, lighting the road below us brightly with headlamps. As the enemy seemed not to have noticed us, we slept, waiting for further orders. At sunrise of 17 April we went into Yenangyaung, following 3rd Battalion via the River Pin Chaung.

22 · Hot Breakfast

Lance Corporal Keiichi Yokoshima, 7th Company,
2nd Battalion, 214 Infantry Regiment, 33 Division

Bilin, Sittang

We advanced to the north-east of Yenangyaung before sunrise of 17 April. We heard the sound of our light machine guns ahead. As we ran forward there was a wide, paved road, on which stood three big lorries still stained with human blood. Indian soldiers were lying on the lorries. Our doctor had pulled down two lightly wounded men from a lorry and was treating them. They were young soldiers of about twenty years old and seemed uneasy while being treated. Enemy lorries which followed stopped with a screech of brakes and the soldiers in them jumped out and ran off.

After sunrise about fifty soldiers came out and surrendered to us. They were men from supply units, not the infantry. Our company went up a hill with a pagoda on top. There we found breakfast ready to eat with steaming milk and tea. We enjoyed the present from Mr Churchill.

23 · A Sharp Action

Lance Corporal Jin-ichi Abe, 12th Company, 3rd Battalion,
214 Infantry Regiment, 33 Division

Bilin, Sittang, Yenangyaung

In the early morning of 17 April, our 3rd Battalion was separated from the main force and went to the north of Yenangyaung. We saw many vehicles and several tanks speeding towards the north on a wide road. We approached the road and our platoon leader ordered me and five men to blast the road. We laid five anti-tank mines on the road and watched them from twenty metres behind.

A group of vehicles came. A jeep at the front hit the mine which did not explode because of the vehicle's light weight, but the next big lorry exploded with a huge noise and was in flames. The road being blocked, a tank which followed put on its bright light and was on full alert. At that time the 2nd Platoon on our left started shooting with three light machine guns, so we were able to block the road but were in trouble, having nothing with which to fight the tanks. The battalion commander, seeing the hopeless situation, ordered 12th Company to retreat, but we could not do so immediately as our 3rd Platoon was fighting on the other side of the road. We could not let them die before our eyes, so we fought on until 3rd Platoon moved back. In the fight Sergeant Nakayama was killed.

We planned to resume the attack when night fell, but then we were told that all the regiment should assemble at Yenangyaung (Twingon) in order to block the enemy's retreat route.

Next morning our company was left of regimental headquarters and I was at the left end of our line. When the sun rose our medium machine guns fired at enemy soldiers who came to draw water, and this sparked off a severe fight. The enemy increased more and more, and when a tank on to our left approached to within ten metres, I threw a magnet mine with my full force. The tank did not reappear but we came under heavy shelling as our position was known. I covered my foxhole with a steel plate and hid deep in it. When I peeped outside after a while our mountain guns and tanks were fighting. Soon our regimental headquarters were attacked by troops and tanks. Our commander decided to hold the position and made preparations to burn the regimental colour in case of the worst. Our platoon rushed forwards and fought. Men of the Signal Company attacked tanks at close range and hit two of them with flame bombs, which started burning but retreated while quenching it with fire extinguishers.

24 · A Flag of Truce

Sergeant Mitsuru Ishida, Headquarters, 214 Infantry Regiment, 33 Division

In the afternoon of 18 April 1942, while we were busy issuing orders, digging trenches and receiving surrendered men from the front, three enemy tanks with about fifty men approached headquarters. We took up defensive positions but, despite our best efforts, they crossed over the ridge of a small hill and came straight at us.

At 500 metres from us, the tanks stopped, opened hatches, stuck out a white flag and waved it. We stopped shooting and stood up and swung our arms in answer to them. Then a British soldier jumped out of the leading tank and ran to us with a white flag in his hand. When he reached our trench he asked for an English-speaking man. He was a nice youth with blond hair; he wore the 'Black Cat' badge and three angular stripes. He was armed with a pistol at his waist, and moved smartly. He was a sergeant. He spoke calmly, not showing any fear, while many of us surrounded and watched him.

Interpreter Ishibashi, Lt Uchida and 2nd Lt Yuzawa came out

to meet him. What he said meant, 'Let us stop this foolish fight right now and be friends.' Our answer was, 'As we have one whole division in Yenangyaung, your unit has no way of escaping. Please tell your chief to surrender to us.' The Briton answered, 'I understand', smiled and left after shaking hands. We admired his dignified attitude and saw him off until he got into the tank. We felt encouraged that human beings could talk in such a life and death situation. It was an indescribably heart-warming moment on the bloody battlefield.

As soon as the British sergeant went inside, the tanks started firing with full power until their infantry retreated beyond the ridge, in the evening light.

25 · On the Road from Yenangyaung

Lance Corporal Ryozo Watanabe, 2nd Company,
1st Battalion, 214 Infantry Regiment, 33 Division

Bilin, Sittang

Huge black smoke high up in the sky! We had been walking towards the enormous smoke cloud for three days. The fleeing British Indian troops had set fire in confusion to an oilfield in Yenangyaung, even though many of them were still located south of the city.

On our way we were ordered to go to Yenangyaung by boat up the River Irrawaddy, passing through enemy lines to help our regiment. We boarded the boat at night. We were thankful for the boats as we were really tired by our hard marching. We heard the faint sound of explosions far away.

In the evening of 18 April 1942 we approached our planned landing site and saw an enemy tank-car drawing water from the river. We landed without any resistance. A good surprise operation. We marched after dark through many oil towers, which

79

impressed us. To my great surprise I saw tall figures walking by. At first I thought they were Japanese, but was shocked to hear them speak English. As it was so unexpected neither side could believe it and passed each other without any disturbance.

Next morning we advanced on an asphalt road which was soft due to the terrible heat. As our company came to a ridge we saw many lorries moving on the road 400 metres in front of us. Our company commander ordered 3rd Platoon to attack them and I, as machine gunner of 1st Section, started firing. As I shot about 100 rounds we received concentrated shelling of mortars and everybody moved away looking for shelters.

I continued shooting, losing heart without knowing it. Then I noticed that the second lieutenent who had been giving orders on my right was not there. He might have taken cover to avoid the shelling. I felt lonely having been left behind alone while mortar shells exploded around me.

I must have had good fortune, for the shelling stopped after a while. I realised I was still alive in the quiet battlefield, and felt relieved. At that time Sergeant Morohoshi called my name several times so I answered, 'Here!' I was so pleased when he patted my shoulder saying, 'It is good that you were safe.'

Several hours later we descended to the road. As we were so thirsty, five of us went into a valley to look for water. We heard men speaking so we went towards them and found six Indian soldiers scooping water eagerly from a small puddle. Though they were armed they showed no intention of firing at us. Feeling a little strange, we took away their weapons, but they still acted as if we were their friends. We drew water, feeling a little worried. Even though none spoke the others' language, it was possible to communicate with them by signs. We captured the Indians without any trouble and sent them to headquarters. The friendship communicated with enemy soldiers on the bloody battlefield remained a pleasant memory.

The fighting ended in three days and then we were able to rest in a splendid house for a week. Even though it was a short period we forgot war, ate a lot of presents from Mr Churchill and drove leisurely around in automobiles. What a difference between the pleasure and the torture!

26 · Reinforce Yenangyaung!

Staff Sergeant Shuukou Namba, Headquarters, 215 Infantry Regiment, 33 Division

Sittang, Tiddim

After the hard battles of Thadodan and Kokkogwa our regiment moved and dug in by the River Irrawaddy for a few days. In the late evening of 18 April I was woken by a messenger. I was an assistant to Captain Tadashi Suzuki, chief operations officer of the regiment. Regimental Commander Colonel Harada, who was looking at a map with Captain Suzuki under candle-light, told me, 'Prepare for departure immediately. Tell all units to assemble on the road by 3 a.m.' After I had gone around to relay the order, I was shown a telegram which said, 'Our units which occupied Yenangyaung are fighting against counter-attacking enemy about 5,000 strong, with twenty tanks and many guns.' We had to hurry to rescue them.

We boarded boats operated by engineers and on 20 April landed on the east bank two kilometres south-west of Yenangyaung. Not far from us great flames were billowing high in the sky. We moved towards the city but shelling sounds came from the far north. We entered the city and rested for a while.

That evening we marched to a hill in the northern outskirts of the city. About midnight we heard the sound of machine guns which had been so familiar in China. On 22 April we crossed the river again to the west bank and arrived at a small town called Nyanguan. People there welcomed us warmly and offered houses to sleep in, prepared meals and brought water to wash our bodies.

After resting comfortably for three days we left the town on the evening of 25 April, sorry to part from the townspeople who stuck out lamps from their doors while many followed us to the town boundary to see us off. We were picked up by lorries, and after driving through roads so bad we had to push the lorries many times, arrived in a forest on the other side of Monywa at 6 p.m. on 30 April. 2nd Lt Katayama, with men of the Burma Independence Army, crossed the River Chindwin in a small boat and scouted around Monywa. The enemy there seemed unaware of our arrival, so boats and troops were secretly moved to our crossing points.

27 · Prelude to the Battle of Monywa

Private Kenji Ohara, 1st Machine Gun Company,
1st Battalion, 215 Infantry Regiment, 33 Division

Monywa, Tiddim

'We go to the crossing point by lorries. Leave your heavy and unnecessary stuff here.' This was the order I received in the early morning of 1 May. I put food and rifle bullets in my shoulder bag, and thought we might have to expect hard fighting this time. I was a member of the medium machine gun section and only I had a Type 38 rifle, not because I was good at rifle-shooting but because I was the most junior member.

A short ride by lorry brought us to the river where motor boats were already waiting. We climbed aboard the boats, which started immediately. I hoped the engine noise would not wake up the enemy. Soon the boat hit the bank, and the section leader gave a low but sharp order, 'Good, jump off!' The enemy did not shoot at us; the crossing in front of the enemy went successfully. The eastern sky was dawning.

We set up the gun by a trench in front of a pagoda. The trench might have been dug by the enemy. Fighting began here and there. We saw about 50 men with their bayonets shining in the morning light spreading out and advancing towards us. Orders were issued one by one: 'Keep grenades in your hands!' 'Fix your bayonets!' I prepared my mind for the close-range fight as I had done in training. But as our machine guns started firing, the enemy began to retreat. We advanced. A Gurkha soldier came out from a grass shrub holding his hands high and I saw an enemy's face for the first time. I checked that he did not have any weapon, according to the procedure, and tied his waist with a band. He looked young and his eyes seemed to be pleading with me to help him. As the enemy retreated after a little resistance, we moved north and took up position at the south end of Monywa.

28 · Gun Versus Tank

Lance Corporal Yoshiyuki Kobayashi, Infantry Gun Company, 215 Infantry Regiment, 33 Division

Sittang, Monywa

We left the horses in a village, so we had to carry or pull our Type 41 mountain gun. Just after dawn on 1 May we crossed the river and landed at Monywa by steel boat and advanced to the main road east of Monywa, where enemy tanks and lorries were now coming from the south. Rifle troops of 1st Battalion who were in front of us ran back in disorder, crying 'Tanks! Tanks!' Captain Suzuki cried out, 'Attack tanks! Why run away?'

At that time the guns of the tanks started firing and their shells made a tremendously loud noise hitting the pavement. We lay down behind the roadside trees. Only I and Lance-Corporal Baba stayed with the gun. I could not see our platoon leader nor our section leader. Around us was a vast field dotted by trees and cactus; nothing to shelter us. I cried, 'Bring forward ammunition!' several times. The section leader had not yet come back: nothing we could do if the tanks attacked us; we had only the gun but no shells. After a while the section leader appeared from behind a cactus, looking tense. Private Shimura came, dragging two boxes with three shells each in them, so I felt relieved. I opened the breech mechanism and quietly loaded a shell. More shells were then delivered to the gun. Two Mk III tanks came to attack us, but for some unknown reason the second tank turned around and went off. So it became better: one gun versus one tank! The sun shone strongly on me lying flat on the ground, but I could not move despite the heat. As the tank gun was aiming at us, we would die if we moved. Many minutes had passed; I felt every minute as if it was an hour. I thought of attacking but was prudent. Baba also seemed calm. While we were suffering, the enemy must also be in torment. The inside of tank must have been hotter than we were and one man, probably a gunner, opened the hatch and jumped out and ran away. The next moment the tank started and its caterpillar track climbed on the pavement. That was the chance! Baba aimed at the track directly at a distance of 400 metres, and I pulled the trigger rope several times on signals from him. No shooting came from the tank: white smoke and then flame billowed out of it. The smoke went heavenwards as if to mourn the death of the brave soldiers.

We chased the enemy for a while and then we returned to Monywa, set up barricades on the road and surrounded our gun with bags of salt and sugar carried from a warehouse. In the night Indian refugees in lines passed in front of us and went through the town. As our infantry was good at night attack we did not worry much about an enemy offensive. From sunrise of 2 May the enemy counter-attack became stronger and ten or more tanks and twenty guns shelled us. As we had supremacy in the air, we were only afraid of the tanks, but we had confidence in beating them from our experience of the previous fight. By evening the enemy had retreated towards the east. During the day a light-machine gunner of our self-defence section was killed and several men were wounded. Our horses were brought forward from the river crossing.

Next day we advanced towards Budalin, which we captured on the evening of 4 May. We saw two crippled MkIII tanks on the way. We were told that we Japanese had captured six British tanks at Schwedaung which were then used by us to fight British tanks. One of them was destroyed by shells shot by a British Mk III tank gun. We were impressed that British tanks had powerful guns able to pierce through their own armour plate.

29 · The Advance on Shwegyin

Corporal Hiroshi Ishikawa, 8th Company, 2nd Battalion,
213 Infantry Regiment, 33 Division

Shwegyin, Arakan

We left China on 24 February 1942 and arrived at Bangkok on 11 March in the last group of 33 Division who had moved to Burma. We joined our regiment at Monywa. There our battalion embarked in forty of engineers boats, on 4 May and went up the River Chindwin. We covered our boats with leaves of banana and palm as enemy planes flew over us several times, and advanced through jungle where many monkeys were seen.

In the late evening of 9 May we landed on shore undisturbed by the enemy. Two reconnaissance groups went out and reported that the enemy seemed to be waiting to cross the river, so we advanced in the pitch dark. It was a really hard march through the jungle. Around midnight we were made leading company and advanced until we heard the engine noise of enemy vehicles. We ate breakfast and as we were just getting ready to attack enemy, we were suddenly fired on by enemy machine guns.

Our mountain gun, machine guns and mortars started to shoot

and 1st and 2nd Platoons attacked the hills in front of us. The enemy fired on us more fiercely and Company Commander Ootomo was shot through his right arm bones and was sent to the dressing station. He told 3rd Platoon Leader to command the company. In a short while two platoon leaders were killed and another leader was wounded, but 1st and 2nd Platoons fought bravely, climbing up the rocky cliffs and capturing the target hills.

A support unit led by Warrant Officer Jiro Inomata advanced along a narrow path between the hills. The unit had about thirty men who usually did clerical, supply or maintenance jobs. We advanced under heavy shelling and the officer was killed. Then Sergeant Sasaki led the remaining men and charged into the enemy and was able to secure a hill close to the river despite persistent counter-attacks.

After the severe fight, lasting the whole day, our company was almost wiped out; only twelve men headed by Sergeant Sasaki survived.

30 · A Hard Fight

Lance Corporal Masaichi Nagai, 6th Company,
2nd Battalion, 213 Infantry Regiment, 33 Division

Shwegyin, Arakan

After we disembarked from the boats we advanced, leading our battalion and, after about six hours' march, rested for a while and then 8th Company took over the lead.

Suddenly we heard heavy firing; 8th Company had penetrated the enemy positions and was fighting desperately. Our company commander ordered Koizumi Platoon to attack the heights on our left front and its Nogami section was able to get to the highest point. Then others followed the company and occupied the hill. This took about one and a half hours.

Shells continuously fired by enemy tanks cracked the rocks of the hill and soldiers lay flat in shallow depressions but were shot through their bellies and killed one by one. We had no time to care for the dead; we could only pull at their legs and drop them into a valley to be covered with fallen leaves.

A platoon leader came retreating from the front. The battalion commander boiled with anger and slapped his face, and the platoon leader went back, trying to regain his position. Soon he died bravely. Finally, we ran out of ammunition. A mountain gun was disassembled and carried to the top of the hill and its first shot stalled a tank but six shells burst around the gun and it was put out of action. Soon Indian soldiers in a large group came charging towards us with their black faces strained. As we had just run out of bullets our company commander ordered us to shout loudly. All of us shouted, 'Yah!' Though our voices were not so loud as we hoped, the enemy flinched and slithered down the hill. We thought we were relieved until they came crawling up with much noise. As we shouted, on the order of our commander, they again slid down the cliff. The sound of shooting was heard from behind them and once again they came crawling towards us, but we drove them off with our shouting.

Then we heard the loud noise of engines in a valley on our right. The very hill was vibrating. The tanks were going to encircle us, but were hidden by the enormous sand cloud they stirred up from the vast sandy plain in our rear. Although the engines sounded loud, the tanks seemed to have stopped, possibly as their caterpillar tracks became stuck in the sand. Shelling became heavier than before and more men were killed, including several of my friends who were due to be discharged soon from military service.

The sun was shortly going to set and it seemed that we would have to carry out a night attack, but as time passed the battlefield became strangely quiet. A scout came back and reported that there were no enemy, but our company commander said, 'It cannot be true', his face strained and alert. 'Go and see once more.'

After a while Sergeant Kurihara returned and confirmed that there were no enemy to be found.

The fierce battle was over. The enemy had escaped into the mountains leaving behind many dead bodies, plenty of weapons and vehicles with their engines still running. There was much food piled up here and there. We ate and drank: a really big feast. But I soon had bad loose bowels and my cheeks and eyes hollowed. It had turned into a miserable treat.

31 · On the Road to Mandalay

Lieutenant Toshihiro Matsumura, 5th Company,
2nd Battalion, 112 Infantry Regiment, 55 Division

Kyaukse, Mandalay

On 26 April 1942 we were moving on lorries towards Meiktila on the trunk road connecting Mandalay and Rangoon. We fought at Pegu, then moved northward and fought with the Chinese army at Toungoo before heading for Mandalay, the second largest city in Burma.

At about 3 p.m. my platoon was leading 2nd Battalion and advanced carefully, watching the surroundings. Suddenly several British tanks came from our front right. As we were jumping off the lorries the tank guns started firing and petrol drums carried on our lead lorry went up in huge flames. We hid ourselves lying by the roadside but, as we had no anti-tank weapons, we could do nothing to combat the tanks. Our mountain guns were with the main column and were not in a position to help us in time. I was afraid if the tanks came forward, crossed the road and encircled us, my platoon would be all killed. We were in an immense plain and there was no shelter nearby. I felt great fear and stared tensely at the tanks.

Tanks shelled our vehicles, a few rounds of which burnt or

destroyed most of them, then turned around and went off to our right, probably to attack our main column which must have been 1 or 2 kilometres behind us. Then we heard tank guns and machine guns firing in that direction. After a while our mountain guns shot a few rounds. In the evening the tanks returned north, and we assembled our kit, or whatever was left, and were allo- cated lorries to continue our move.

In the evening of 28 April we were approaching Kyaukse, an important town on our advance to Mandalay. There were British positions before Kyaukse on both sides of the trunk road. We got off the lorries and spread out on the west side of the road. During the night two tanks came charging at us at high speed but soon retired, causing no casualties. At about midnight one regiment of 18 Division arrived group by group and spread out on the east side of the road. After sunrise the enemy concentrated mortar shells on our positions; as the aim was accurate, many of our men were killed or wounded. We had no option but to retreat into a forest in a confused state.

Our heavy guns arrived later in the morning and shelled the enemy positions. When we thought it might be time to resume attacking to our front, we were ordered to leave the battlefield and go to Myingyan to block the retreating British. Although it was undesirable to be pulled away from the engagement, an order is an order and has to be obeyed. We were unhappy as it might be thought we had been defeated. Next day, when we arrived at Myingyan, we saw no enemy and were told that none had passed through. So we only made a big detour to go to Mandalay which had been already occupied by 18 Division on 1 May. Frankly speaking, we were not given a chance to be the honourable first into Mandalay, nor had it been so into Rangoon.

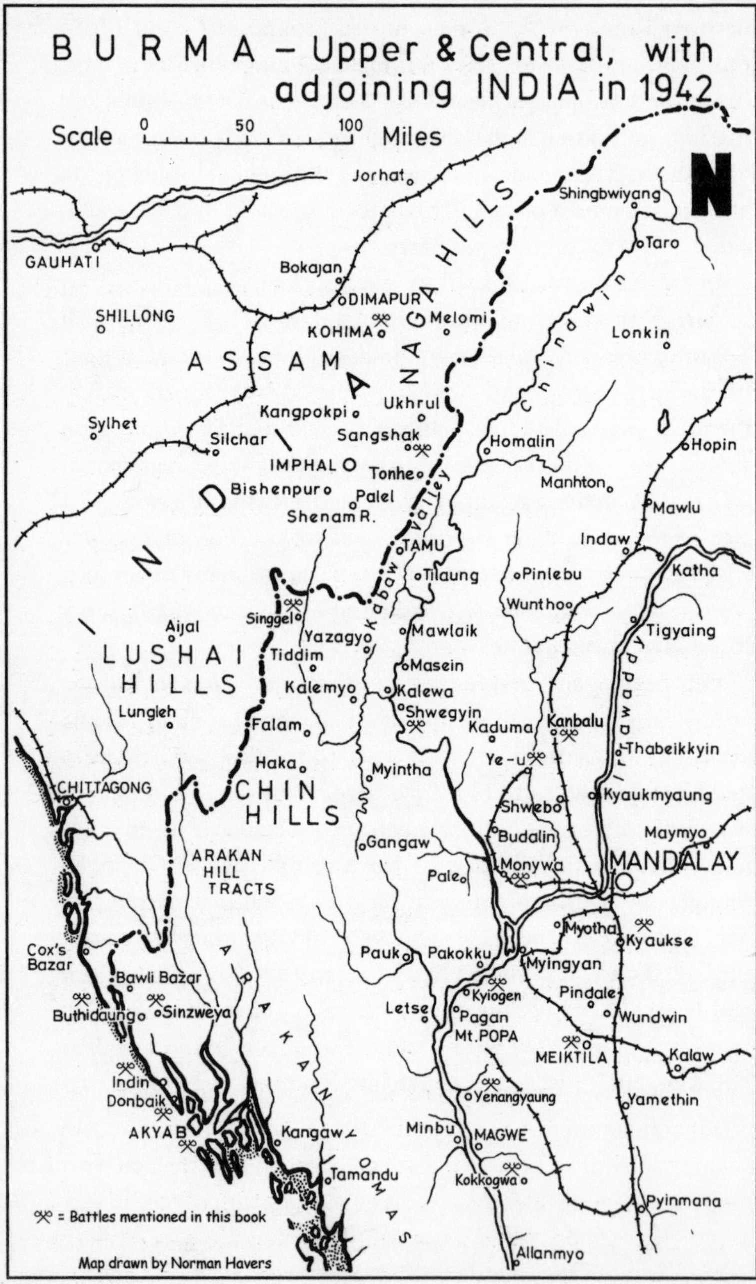
BURMA – Upper & Central, with adjoining INDIA in 1942
Scale 0 50 100 Miles
N
Jorhat
Shingbwiyang
Taro
GAUHATI
Bokajan
DIMAPUR
SHILLONG
KOHIMA
Melomi
Lonkin
NAGA HILLS
ASSAM
Chindwin
Ukhrul
Kangpokpi
Sylhet
Silchar
Sangshak
Homalin
Hopin
IMPHAL
Tonhe
Manhton
Bishenpur
Palel
Shenam R.
Mawlu
INDIA
TAMU
Indaw
Kabaw Valley
Tilaung
Pinlebu
Katha
Wuntho
Singgel
Aijal
Yazagyo
Mawlaik
Tigyaing
LUSHAI HILLS
Tiddim
Masein
Kalemyo
Kalewa
Shwegyin
Lungleh
Falam
Kaduma
Kanbalu
Irrawaddy
Thabeikkyin
Haka
Ye-u
Myintha
CHITTAGONG
CHIN HILLS
Kyaukmyaung
Shwebo
Budalin
Maymyo
Gangaw
MANDALAY
ARAKAN HILL TRACTS
Monywa
Pale
Myotha
Kyaukse
Cox's Bazar
Pauk
Pakokku
Myingyan
ARAKAN YOMAS
Bawli Bazar
Kyiogen
Pindale
Buthidaung
Sinzweya
Letse
Pagan
Wundwin
Mt. POPA
MEIKTILA
Kalaw
Indin
Donbaik
Yenangyaung
Yamethin
AKYAB
Kangaw
Minbu
MAGWE
Tamandu
Kokkogwa
Pyinmana
= Battles mentioned in this book
Allanmyo
Map drawn by Norman Havers

32 · Cholera!

2nd Lieutenant Mibu Hirano 3rd Battalion,
214 Infantry Regiment, 33 Division

Monywa, Tiddim Road

We arrived at Monywa on 2 May 1942 after 215 Regiment had captured the town and then moved towards the north-east. We came close to Ye-u and were resting under trees by the River Ye-u, when a non-commissioned officer started vomiting severely followed by violent purging of white liquid faeces every three or four minutes. His hands and feet became cold and wrinkled, and he was badly dehydrated. This was the dreaded outbreak of cholera. It was essential to supply water to the body by injection as he could not take even a drop of water by his mouth. Meanwhile, similar patients arrived in large numbers, and our senior doctor requested isolation of the whole battalion in order to stop secondary infection. Many preventative measures were ordered. Quicklime was sprayed on faeces, and when we ate meals two men took turns to beat off the swarming flies while one man ate. The injection of Ringer's (saline) solution and heart stimulant was the only treatment, and a very large amount of the intravenous solution was needed. The battalion had only six bottles of Ringer's solution which were not enough even for two men, and the field hospital had only a limited capacity to make up the solution to cope with such an explosive increase of patients. We badly needed sterile water in large quantities!

Sergeant Oikawa came up with the idea of injecting juice of palm fruit as a desperate measure. There was no time to lose. Rather than watch many patients about to die without doing anything, this was tried, and was found surprisingly effective. So all the healthy men went around nearby villages and collected a lot of young palm fruits. Medical staff extracted juice from the buds by hypodermic syringe, and injected it into patients with some salt added. When juice from five to eight fruits was injected into a patient, he showed signs of recovery. Thus we could avoid the disaster. Almost all of our 70 patients were saved.

By our preventative measures, the outbreak of cholera was terminated, and we could start pursuing the enemy five days later. When we arrived at Shwegyin, a river-crossing point to Kalewa, we found a large number of trucks and tanks left on the roadside but all British Indian troops had already retreated towards India. To me, it was strangely impressive to see white mosquito nets left by the enemy swinging in the jungle.

33 · Zero Versus Hurricane

Staff Sergeant Yoshito Yasuda, 64th Fighter Squadron, Southern Army

On 24 March 1942, I took off from Chiang Mai airfield in northern Thailand as the second plane of Captain Anma's formation, and flew over the British base at Akyab. Our squadron was the only unit that had the new Zero fighter (Oscar, Type 1 Fighter or Hayabusa 'Falcon') in South-East Asia.

Two Hawker Hurricanes were circling over the airfield as overhead guard. Captain Yasuma, with his formation, immediately attacked the two planes. The Hurricane was a unique plane with twelve 7.7mm machine guns which caused deadly damage if we were shot from behind. Its diving speed was much faster than the Zero. Therefore, when we fought with Hurricanes we attempted to counter its fire power with the better manoeuvrability of the Zero and tried to hit its radiator, bringing the engine to a stop. Even with the poor fire power (two 13mm guns) of the Zero, Hurricanes could be shot down merely by a hole in the radiator.

Captain Anma positioned himself just behind a Hurricane and fired one burst. The Hurricane became unstable and crashed, probably because the pilot was hit. I chased the other plane, which dived sharply and escaped. I stopped pursuing it, but I could not locate my captain. Then I found a formation of three planes above me and tried to catch up. It was the formation of Captain Otani heading toward Rangoon. As we were still close to the enemy base, I watched carefully behind and upward while sometimes looking below and behind by swinging my tail and wing. This was important as an enemy could be where I could not see him from my seat.

The Otani formation was flying at high speed, being not far from the enemy base. When I reached 2,000 metres, I banked the wing slightly. Then I saw something. I took off my pilot's goggles and opened the windshield to watch. It was a Hurricane, camouflaged in brown and dark green paint, about 3,000 metres behind me at an altitude of 500 metres below me. I pretended not to see it and continued to follow Otani's formation. If I turned around and attacked it from the advantageous higher altitude, it could escape by diving immediately. I waited for it to come closer. It would start firing with its twelve guns when it was 600 to 700 metres away, but I could be behind and above if I looped when it came to 600 metres. I swung my tail gently so that it would not be noticed, and peered at the enemy by putting my eyes close to the wind shield. It still came closer gradually, assuming that I had not noticed it. It approached to 700 metres, while our three planes were 300 metres ahead of me.

The time had come. I fully opened the throttle and lowered the nose. Speed gradually increased. Distance 600 metres. I pulled hard back on the stick. The nose of my plane went up. At the top of the loop I looked down on the enemy plane which was starting a sharp left turn. But it was too late, I was on its tail and above it. Captain Otani's formation started a sharp left turn, noticing my irregular manoeuvre. The Hurricane came exactly into my line of fire against a background of wavy blue sea, the perfect aiming and pursuing position. I pressed firmly on the gun button, and tracer bullets flowed out from both sides of the engine. Distance 100 metres. My shots concentrated on the engine of the enemy plane.

When I was within 30 metres, I pulled the stick, and then turned left. Steam came from the Hurricane's engine. I had shot right through the engine radiator.

Our three Zeros were moving towards the Hurricane. Suddenly it lowered its nose and dropped, swinging like a falling tree leaf. A black mass emerged from its seat, and a white band stretched from it. The pilot had bailed out. The long white band continued to fall. His parachute had not opened fully. He went into the sea with a splash. Then the plane fell close to the splash. Captain Otani and the two others were looking at me, amazed. We landed at Rangoon (Mingaladon) airfield, which had been occupied by the Japanese army two weeks ago. We were the first in the squadron to land there. Captain Otani patted my shoulder saying, 'You saved the life of one of us three. I'll buy you a drink!'

A large number of Japanese bombers and fighters made a surprise attack on the British airbase at Magwe on 21 March 1942 and destroyed many planes on the ground. The attack on Magwe was repeated on 22 March and on Akyab on 23 and 24 March. Our squadron shot down four British planes and destroyed three others during the four days.

Because of the great damage caused by these attacks, the British air force seemed to have retreated to India, but P-40 fighters of the American Volunteer Group in China were still active. They attacked our base at Chiang Mai on 6 April. I and three men were on standby for emergency take-off ('scramble') but were taken by surprise in the dim evening light. I ran towards my plane, but dust spurted up at my heels – I was in the sights of an enemy plane. I lay flat on the ground, fortunately in a small depression. I felt ashamed but there was nothing I could do. If I dared to take off, certainly I would be shot down very easily. One, two, then three, Zeros started burning. Then our anti-air machine guns started firing, and soon the enemy went away. Even though our guns shot down one P-40, three of our Zeros were burnt and four were destroyed, which was heavy damage.

3

OCCUPATION

July to December 1942

34 · Angels in White Uniforms

Lance Corporal Katsumi Ohno, 2nd Company, 1st Battalion,
112 Infantry Regiment, 55 Division

Pegu, Shwebo, Mandalay

After we took Mandalay some of our regiment went north as far as Walawbum in the Hukawng Valley, and returned to Mandalay in early June 1942. Having occupied all Burma, a ceremony was held at our headquarters to mourn the dead of all nationalities in the Burma Campaign. We were told that large memorials, one for Japanese dead soldiers and one for unknown British–Indian dead were erected at Yenangyaung. Our company remained near Shwebo to guard the area.

Because of the rapid advance and continuous battles, which lasted four months, sometimes with poor meals of just rice and salt, we soldiers were tired out and a third of us in the company were suffering malaria, dengue fever and dysentery, and were not able to serve on duty. Lance Corporal Kuramoto and several of my friends died of sickness. Although I had managed to stay on duty despite my poor health, I developed fever and was sent to the field hospital in Mandalay. My comrades came to see me by turns when they came to Mandalay on official duty, and urged me to take it easy to recover, but my situation become worse and I developed a high fever which made me almost unconscious around 2 o'clock every afternoon. Although I pleaded to return to my section, wishing to die by the side of my comrades, I was transferred to the base hospital in Maymyo which was far from my unit. A few days after I arrived at Maymyo, my fever got worse and I was moved to an intensive care room, where I remained unconscious for three days until a hospital orderly who had been attending me shook me and woke me up. Several days later the doctor told me that I had recovered miraculously, but my body did not recover and I suffered fever in the afternoons.

Maymyo's climate was the best in Burma, where cherry and plum trees blossomed and we could enjoy the best environment with plenty of good food, in contrast to the hard war that I had experienced. I felt sorry for my comrades who were on strict duty. As I got better I went to the doctor and asked to leave hospital, but he sternly told me I had not yet recovered.

When I had spent 50 days in the hospital, I heard a rumour that Japanese nurses were coming from the mainland, and I had the faint hope of seeing them, even for a glance, though I was eager to go back to my company. Then the news was confirmed that the nurses would arrive next day and 60 or so patients in my quarters were really excited. I could hardly sleep at night. The short Burmese night passed and we waited and waited. Then, hearing a shout, 'Here they are!' we dashed to the corridor although it was time for rest. As our quarter was far from the medical room, with a binocular borrowed from a friend, I was able to see the figure of three nurses walking. I felt a yearning for people from home; a common experience on the battlefield. Two days later I was allowed to leave the hospital and went back to my company, with some regret that I did not have a chance to meet the nurses. Thanks to the excellent hospital care I did not suffer more sickness and so never met the angels in white uniforms.

In the summer of 1942 we were in Prome. As there was no fighting we soldiers spent an idle daily life. When we were not assigned on duties we could spend the time as we wanted. Some were keen on chess or 'Go' games; some started to learn poetry, singing or Japanese dancing. I was interested in the *Burma Newspaper* published in Rangoon, and sent my articles to the column open for readers. It was my first experience of writing a short article. The first one I sent was in the paper fifteen days later, and then more were accepted one by one. It was a pleasure to see my words printed in the newspaper. When an article was accepted three picture postcards of Burma were sent to me. This was the only pleasure for me who had no other speciality. In the summer of 1943 I went to Captain Abe, my commander, to officially report my return to the mainland. He said to me, 'You seem to have a literary talent, which you may find useful in the homeland'. I was impressed that he knew my personal interest.

It was in the later part of September 1943 that I left Singapore on a big ship of 15,000 tons. Our comrades who were ordered to return to Japan were mostly those drafted in 1938 and had been in the army for almost five years. At that time the voyage to Japan had became dangerous due to American submarines. In our convoy of six ships only ours arrived back in Japan without any trouble. Just a day before the ship arrived at Shimonoseki Port, one of our comrades died of tropical malaria fever in the shabby cabin. It was early in the morning of 4 October, when rice ripened and the autumn village festival would be held in his home area. We felt so sorry for him, having died only a day before landing in the home country; we could well understand how sad he was. He was vigorous when we left Singapore, and was dreaming of happy times after his discharge from service. We had to drop his body into the rough waves of the Japan Sea while my friends played the sorrowful melody of the military funeral march.

35 · Fishing

Sergeant Isawo Aihara, 8th Company, 3rd Battalion,
55 Mountain Gun Regiment, 55 Division

Mandalay, Arakan

We pursued Chinese troops in the Shan Highlands and then came to Minge, 20 kilometres south of Mandalay, on 29 May 1942. Our lodgings and facilities were already arranged by the party led by Warrant Officer Ogata, and our company was allocated ten nice houses which had been the residences of former British railway engineers. Between our houses a river of about five metres wide was flowing with a high level of water and we could fish for catfish and snakeheads (China fish) in our spare time. As there was broad grassland, wooden fences were made for pasturing and our horses ran around in groups; they must have been reminded of Hokkaido or Kyushu where they were raised.

Soon after we settled down in Minge about fifteen new recruits arrived from Japan and brought us letters and comfort bags. To most of us these were the first letters received since we had left our homeland seven months earlier. Everybody opened the letters immediately and read repeatedly word by word. Although there might have been happy news or sad reports, everybody seemed relieved by the messages from home. We were allowed to mail postcards to our parents and friends, but because of military secrecy we were able to write only that we were in 'southern countries', though we really wanted to tell them that we were in Burma, far away from Japan. One day our Divisional Commander, Lt General Takeuchi, came for inspection and our regimental commander designated our company to drill in encounter battles. We were able to commence firing quickly in conjunction with infantry, which seemed to satisfy the general.

Our company commander always paid attention to the health of soldiers, and also he liked catching fish. He said that he would cut a channel from the river to bring water to our camping ground and collect fish, the only locally available protein, and he ordered me to do the work. While wondering whether fish could be caught by this most unexpected idea, I started driving stout wooden piles in the river with several soldiers despatched from other sections. By evening the piling was completed; wooden plates placed on the piles blocked the flow of the river, while the river bank was cut to let water flow into the camp's grassland. After letting the water stand overnight, we drained it into the downstream next morning. Two hours or so later the water level fell and grass was seen; to my surprise we found here and there a big snakehead 30 centimeters long, a kind of carp, a catfish with long barbels and others. We collected a bucketful of fish for the day's meal, and this was repeated every day.

101

One morning I found the water level of the river very low and I ran to the commander to report it. He was excited to see the river and told me to prepare to drain it, and rode to battalion headquarters on his horse. Soon he came back and declared, 'I will command the battalion's fishing operation!' Soon liaison men came from other companies, and he allocated the river to three companies. Of course, we got the best area and collected six drumfuls of fish from the muddy river bed. The commander's pride knew no bounds and he ordered Sergeant Kurokawa in charge of supplies to slit the fish open and salt and dry them. Handling fish was a weak point of the sergeant who was a Buddhist priest and his religion did not allow the killing of any fish. Seeing that he was at a loss, I volunteered to help him. The salted fish was served at our meals, and dried fish proved very useful later on our long march in the first Arakan operation, as our only source of protein. I also made Japanese-style fish sausages, using local materials. Our commander helped me to make them and brought some to the regimental commander who, I was told, was very pleased to eat it in Burma.

36 · A Soldier Servant

Private Yoshiaki Masuda, 7th Company, 2nd Battalion,
112 Infantry Regiment, 55 Division

Arakan, Bassein

In October 1942 we were in Sagaing with regimental headquarters when colours celebration and other functions were held. Solders were talking eagerly about returning to Japan, as the occupation of Burma had been successfully achieved. At the end of November our company moved to Bassein to guard the area and stayed there for about two months. I was despatched from the company as a soldier servant (orderly) of Military Governor

Makino who was in charge of five prefectures in the Irrawaddy Delta. He lived in a big, two-storeyed building by himself, and I spent a relaxed, happy life as there were no officers or senior soldiers. It was a peaceful time; only one or two enemy planes flew over at high altitude almost every day.

As a soldier, I did not know what the Governor was doing. He spoke English, Chinese and Burmese and never wore military uniform. He went to the office at 9 o'clock in Burmese dress and came back to the residence at 4 to 5 o'clock and usually went out to various hotels to meet Burmese high-class people, returning home around 11 o'clock. In addition to the Governor and me, one Indian cook, one Burmese driver and one cleaner lived in the house. I had been a soldier servant (messenger) of a battalion commander back in 1940, but my job here was very different. The Governor drove the car himself and worked day and night. I went shopping in the town in the sedan driven by the Burmese driver, and often I was embarrassed by soldiers saluting the sedan which looked like the one for high-ranking officers.

Ladies of a big Burmese landowner or high official, wearing red, blue or purple silk lungi and sandals, came to the house. All of them played the piano. There were two pianos in the drawing room. Sometimes they played to my military songs. It was my job to give them a carton of cigarettes when they left. (There were plenty of cigarettes in the house.) When the Governor ran a high temperature due to malaria, the wife and a daughter of the landowner attended him day and night for a week. Close by there was the fine house of a judge and I was often entertained to lunch there. A daughter of the house who looked like a dark-skinned Japanese came to me everyday, teasing for cigarettes.

While Burmese men came to the house rarely, Chinese people came to visit the Governor regularly every day. It seemed they came to ask for the right to use former British property such as hotels, factories and many others, and offered various presents. The Governor might have lost a game of patience and gambled away a factory to a Chinese!

On Sundays Sergeant Onozaka and Private Kanaishi visited me to chat, and every time I gave them a lot of presents. One day Sergeant Onozaka drove the Governor's sedan and by mistake damaged it a little, for which I was severely scolded.

One evening a beautiful Burmese lady came to visit but the Governor was not at home, attending a conference at a hotel. She stayed in the drawing room until 9 o'clock. (This lady often came in the evening and spent some time talking with him.) When the Governor came back at 10.30 I told him that the lady had come and stayed for some time. He told me that the key for the safe in the military government office was missing. There was cash to the value of 50,000 yen in the safe – a large amount as the pay of a private was then 13 yen a month and one yen could buy 40 kilograms of rice. We searched around in vain. Then he hid a pistol under his lungi, ordering me to come with my rifle, and drove his car to a big village in the suburbs of Bassein. Burmese youths armed with bamboo spears were guarding the entrance of the village. He said something to them and went into a big house and talked with his friend, the lady. We learned from her that she had hidden the key behind a big mirror in the drawing room and we hurried back to the house and found it, to our relief. I was told that there were many spies among Karens who had been pro-British.

While I was spending such a pleasant life, the British offensive in Arakan became active and my company was ordered to go to Akyab urgently. As I would feel lonely to be apart from my good comrades in the company, I insisted on leaving although the Governor wanted me to stay. Finally a replacement came from other unit and I joined my company. It was really a drastic change, from paradise to hell!

37 · Supplying Water to Soldiers

Second Lieutenant Shuichiro Yoshino, 11th Epidemic Prevention
and Water Supply Unit

Taunggyi, Hukawng, Meiktila

I was born in Matsutou, a provincial town in central Japan, which was in beautiful country with a view of a mountain range to the south. A female poet wrote many well-known Haiku (seventeen syllable poems) on the life and locality of the town. I went to a middle school and then to a pharmaceutical college in Kanawaza, and was employed by a drug company. At that time military service was compulsory for men and I was rated 'Class A1' in the military physical examination and awaited my call. In March 1941 I was enlisted in the 50th Infantry Regiment in Matsumoto. After passing the examination for reserve officers, I was trained at the Military Medical College in Tokyo and then at army hospitals. I was commissioned officer cadet (which in fact is similar to second lieutenant in the British Army), and in July 1942 I was ordered to be attached to 11th Epidemic Prevention and Water Supply Unit, stationed in Taunggyi, Burma. I said goodbye to my parents and went to Tokyo where the men in my group were gathering.

On 15 August 1942, we assembled in full uniform and marched to Shinagawa Railway Station to board a train to Ujina, a port near Hiroshima. I was made adjutant to the commander of transportation because my voice was loud and strong! That night, before we embarked, my group was separated from the commander and most of the other men because of the ship's limited capacity. This put me, a raw officer, in an awkward position where I had no sweets and cigarettes for our men. It was too late to obtain them from the commander. Meals were supplied on the ship but we had to bring our own luxuries. My group of 60 men boarded an old 5,000-ton freighter. Eight ships formed a convoy escorted by a submarine chaser, and moved at a very low speed. We stopped at Talao in Formosa where I was able to buy plenty of bananas, which was a small luxury for our men.

We stayed in Singapore for five days. The sunken boats in the harbour made us realise this was war, but we were able to get some cigarettes and condensed milk. We sailed to Rangoon, and from there took a train to Thazi where we were met by lorries from our unit. We arrived at Taunggyi on 21 September 1942 and reported to Lt Colonel Inoue, commander of the unit. Only half of the group who went with me were able to return to their home country because of the severity of the war, which lasted for three more years.

The Epidemic Prevention and Water Supply Unit is an unique organisation which was formed after a serious outbreak of cholera while the Japanese were fighting in Shanghai in 1937. The unit had seven doctors and one pharmacist, three other officers and 250 men. To supply clean bacteria-free water (even from muddy sources), the unit used porcelain micro filters. We had four sets of automatic regeneration filters on automobiles (remodelled from fire engines) with a capacity of 30 tons per hour, and eight filters carried on horseback (weight 90 kilograms) with a capacity of 720 litres per hour. These filters gave better water more efficiently than our former method of using alum and 'chloride of lime', followed by boiling. The unit had 30 folding canvas tanks with aluminium frames and 70 small water bags carried on the shoulder.

At Taunggyi our commander lived in a separate house where the officers met at lunchtime. All the other officers lived in a pleasant brick building with a garden dotted with marble statues. We were ordered to maintain the property carefully without alteration, as we Japanese were not occupying the building but were renting it temporarily. To our delight, there was a 'Victrola' gramophone and a big collection of classical records in the house. My roommate, Kanīichi Chiba, a doctor, prepared a complete list of the records, and being a music fan really appreciated the quality of the handsome high-class collection. We knew quite a few classical music enthusiasts in Japan who collected records, but we had not seen such a distinguished collection of superb quality. The owner assuredly had excellent taste and loved music deeply. I felt sorry for him having to leave behind his valuable collection. When we moved to Maymyo in January 1943 we transferred the property to the military government, stressing the importance of the collection and hoping that it would be returned to the owner. If it was given back, the owner must have been happy to know that there were Japanese sharing the same tastes.

Abstract from the Memoir of the Unit, 'Kiku no Bokyu'

The 11th Epidemic Prevention and Water Supply Unit was formed in Tokyo in 1938, and went to South China. On 8 December 1941 part of the unit landed at Kota Bharu in northern Malaya while all the boats were damaged by British aircraft attacks. The major part of the unit landed on 22 January 1942 together with the 18 Division, and proceeded towards Singapore. Our old lorries had to drive at high speed on paved roads.

When we arrived at Johore Bahru, just north of Singapore across the strait, we were ordered to go to Burma and turned back. We boarded trains and the unit arrived at Phitsanulok in Thailand on 15 February. We tuned our lorries and filter cars and left for Burma. Small passenger cars and motor cycle side-cars were loaded on the lorries, and our most experienced soldiers drove the four filter cars. The road to Burma, which Japanese and Thai engineers had built hurriedly after the war had started, ran through rugged mountains with many steep hills and bends. The road had been opened to lorries a few days before our journey and construction work was still going on. The crossing of the Thailand–Burma border was really hard work. Along the way, we saw lorries that had fallen deep into the valley and a big forest fire threatened to burn a wooden bridge. As water could only to be obtained from far away in the valley we extinguished the fire with sand.

After we had crossed the border, the road became a gradual downward slope and we saw a person wearing a red skirt, who turned our to be a man when we came closer. We were relieved to have reached the Burmese plateau without losing any vehicles. One section stayed in Moulmein for several days to supply water to the town. As the main pipe to the water tank in the town had been blown away, we used the pump of the filter car to raise water up to the tall tank. As we advanced we saw on the road many dead bodies and damaged tanks and armoured cars, where hard battles had been fought at Sittang and around Pegu. Our advance party, led by Lieutenant Matsutani, arrived at Rangoon on 9 March and occupied the Pasteur Laboratory, the Medical College, the Citizens' Hospital and the Epidemic Hospital for the use of our unit. At Mingaladon airport we obtained four big tank lorries, to which we welded pipes and valves that could feed water directly into men's canteens. Two of these lorries were destroyed later at Pyinmana by British tank guns. At Rangoon we were given various allocations of captured goods such as whisky, chocolate and chewing gum. We were given two packs each of chewing gum, which caused all members of the unit to suffer from diarrhoea. Our pharmacist lieutenant then discovered that it was not a candy at all but a medicinal chewing gum for children containing a laxative!

The unit went north together with the 18 Division. Our problem was, April being the driest season, it was very difficult to find sources of water. Even if we found a well used by villagers it soon dried up, and we had to wait patiently for the water to appear. It was very, very hard to keep up with the demands of the thirsty soldiers. After Mandalay had been occupied, the unit moved to Taunggyi, leaving Sections in several towns. Later on, the material we had left in Thailand was brought on to us. Thirty NCOs and soldiers who had been with the unit since its formation returned to Japan. They were replaced by a group headed by Officer Cadet Yoshino, who arrived in September 1942.

38 · Taunggyi to Kalewa

Private Denkichi Yatsuda, 11th Epidemic Prevention
and Water Supply Unit, 18 Division

Taunggyi, Kalewa, Hukawng, Meiktila

After advancing north with 18 Division until the capture of Mandalay we settled down in Taunggyi in mid-east Burma in July 1942. The disease prevention team of which I was a member went around villages near Taunggyi for vaccination and study of the health situation. We were delighted that beautiful and efficient Burmese and Indian nurses came to help us. When we went to a village, probably by instruction from the local chief to the village headman, a space under a big tree in a temple was cleared for us. When we arrived mothers from the village assembled, carrying or leading their children whom we injected with vaccines for cholera. We brought soothing medicines for toothache and skin diseases, and treated the villagers. Although injection was disliked as being painful, medical treatment was always welcomed by local people.

As we were allocated one or two villages each day, the work was finished by 2 or 3 o'clock in the afternoon, when we were invited to the house of the local chief or village headman and were served Burmese dishes. It was really enjoyable to eat the food talking with the beautiful Burmese ladies and children in the Burmese language which we had just learnt. This gave me a chance to improve my Burmese. It was my best memory in my hard military life that I had such a happy peaceful time. However, it ended in September 1942, when Private Takeuchi and I were assigned to Engineers who were to build a road to Kalewa.

Before we left there was an entertainment show at Taunggyi where artiste soldiers selected from each unit performed songs, dramas and comedy acts. We soldiers were pleased as well as made melancholy by the participation of pupils of a Japanese

Language School. They came on stage and bowed their heads according to an order of a senior boy. 'Salute!' he said in innocent Japanese. 'We will sing and dance though we are not skilled. It is our pleasure if Japanese soldiers enjoy them. Please take good care of yourself and fight with your whole heart.' The well-dressed girls sang Japanese rhymes that we all learned in our primary schools, and some war songs. The children learned songs at the school; I wondered whether they knew the meaning of songs such as 'Father, you were strong' and 'Duty of an infantryman'.

As they sang their songs one by one, we were reminded of our children, brothers and sisters in our homes and tears came to our eyes. Nobody expected to hear Japanese songs by such young children in the mountain area of Burma. I felt so at ease with the children and kept clapping my hands in applause. Then a soldiers' band played a popular song, 'Moon over the Castle Ruin' and a Burmese girl danced to the melody. I still remember her sweet performance. The Japanese Language School was established soon after we arrived in Taunggyi, recruiting children from good families. Through the eager instruction of Corporal Kohiyama the children made good progress in Japanese in four months.

I left Taunggyi in a truck of engineers, and when we came to a T-junction several Burmese nurses who were on their way to work found me, shook hands and saw us off: one of the happy memories of the town.

I was assigned to the 3rd Company of 12 Engineer Regiment and worked with its medical corpsman, Private Yoshikawa, while my comrade Private Tekeuchi went to its 2nd Company. My first task was supplying water using a portable porcelain filter at the construction site of a bridge at Ye-u. I dug a hole near the stream and installed the filter and provided drinking water every day by operating the pump handle. The company commander and engineers gazed at my work with wonder initially but soon started drinking the filtered water without any worry and their increased demand made me busy. I was impressed that the work of the engineers was really very hard. They went into the river naked and drove in piles, carried heavy materials, and assembled bridges. The bridge construction was finished in two weeks and we moved to Shwebo. Road building continued in jungles and swamps, and it was in December that we reached the end point of road construction, Kalewa, after three months of hard work. During that time I looked for a water source and moved the filter whenever the company moved, and supplied drinking water.

The main part of our section had already arrived at Kalewa by boats from Mandalay together with 55 Infantry Regiment. We lived in a temple near the River Myittha, and when we first boiled a meal British planes which must have noticed the smoke came to attack us. We were surprised and took shelter. After that air-raids were repeated almost every day.

39 · General Sakurai

Lieutenant Eiichi Sugimoto, Adjutant to Commander of
33 Division

China, Shwedaung, Sagaing, Tiddim

In July 1942, our 5th company of 215 Infantry Regiment was resting at Ye-u. We were relaxed after the conquest of Burma; our objective was achieved. One day I was called to Major Sato, the Battalion Commander. When I reported to him, the regimental commander was also present and I was told that I should be an adjutant to the Divisional Commander Lieutenant General Seizo Sakurai. I protested quietly that being a reserve officer (EAO) I would not be suitable for such an important post. However, as I was told, 'This is an order!' I had to accept it reluctantly. I was sad to say farewell to men in my platoon with whom I had fought severe battles in China and at Bilin, Sittang, Shwedaung, Thadodan and Monywa. My only consolation was that senior soldiers who had been with the company for more than three and a half years were to be discharged and would return home soon.

General Sakurai was on an inspection tour and I reported to him at Sagaing. The divisional commander was the man 'high above the clouds' whom we low-ranking officers never met. He was in a narrow, dark room at Sagaing and I saluted him standing stiffly just like a steel pole; with a kind smile on his dignified face, he bowed his head and said to me, 'Welcome! Do your job as it has been done.' Although my experience had been limited to front-line battle and I did not know what I should do, I just replied obediently, 'Yes sir, I understand.'

A few days later I was invited by the General to dinner with my predecessor Lieutenant Tanaka, who was to be transferred as a tank commander, at his residence in Yenangyaung. He asked me, 'Do you drink sake?' I answered, 'Yes, I drink some.' He said, 'You must be a pretty good drinker as you said so in front of me!' Later I was told that the General selected me because of my distinguished combat performance; I was one of the two in the regiment to be honoured with a citation while alive.

The General's daily schedule started early in the morning. He left the residence at 8 o'clock and rode his horse for about an hour, escorted by a section of the cavalry platoon, then went straight to the headquarters office. In the mornings he approved operation papers. Next to his room was my adjutant's room, where the chief of staff and heads of departments came and checked whether the commander was in, and then explained papers to him to get approval. Some officers said to me, 'Sugimoto, do get this sanctioned', and left the paper with me. After the morning work was finished he rode his horse back to his residence, this time escorted only by me.

The residence of the divisional commander was a two-storeyed building by the River Irrawaddy. On the right-hand side of the ground floor was a room of about 65 square metres which was used for receiving the official salute of transferred officers, and also for parties for his commanders. On the left was my adjutant's room of 37 square metres, and behind it was another 27 square-metre room. There were two rooms upstairs: a living room of 65 square metres and a bedroom of 46 square metres. The general often lay down on a couch reading books, wearing only short trousers. His staff brought papers even after he came back to the residence. As I took the paper to him, he smiled and said, 'Excuse me for being naked,' and sat straight up and read it. I thought he could have read the paper lying as only his private assistant was present, but he might have thought it rude to read an official paper lying down. He always said, 'Thank you' or 'Well done' to me or to his servant-soldiers in a gentle voice. In his residence three servant-soldiers, a driver-soldier and I, a total of six, lived. When a party of commanders was held in the ground floor room, I had to go around to pour sake to everybody as there was never a girl in the residence and men did not pour sake for each other in the presence of the General. When the party ended, the General held a 'beanfeast' for us in the servants' room, when he talked over a bottle of sake, relaxed and laughing loudly. It was as if he was playing with his own children, and had real affection for the young, naive soldiers. Private Kurosawa had been a professional singer and Private Sato was good at chanting Chinese poems. These two were so happy when they were offered a cup of sake from the General with words of praise for their performance.

The General never allowed women to come into his residence. He told me, 'Our soldiers think of the divisional commander almost as a god. Even when they are struggling in hard battles, they believe that I would help them. And in a battle they may lose their lives because of my order. So it is inexcusable for me to enjoy a party where females are present.' However, there was an exception. Two girls came for a New Year greeting. They were not Japanese, but a mixed race of British and Burmese and wanted to express their thanks as they had been protected by an order of the chief of staff and had grown up chastely. I asked the General to meet them as it is good for reconciliation of the races in the spirit of our war. They were aged about 18 and were very pretty, a characteristic of mixed race. The General met them as a polite gentleman would, probably because of his background as a military attaché in France. Later, when headquarters moved to Kalaw, the girls followed us.

I came from a rifle company and had not ridden horses. As the General rode every day to maintain his physical strength, I asked Lieutenant Kaneko, leader of the cavalry platoon, to teach me to ride; he commented that it would take me three years to be a good rider! The General's horse was big and stout with fine hair. The name of my horse was unluckily 'Sakurai-go', which I hesitated to call it as this was same name as the General. It was rather old, 17 years, but very well trained and did various performances, such as Spanish trotting, on its own initiative.

One day an entertainment troupe came to Yenangyaung. Their military hotel faced the riding ground. Young ladies of the troupe came out and watched us riding. Then a staff officer came to join in for the first time. As he was in his thirties, he might have wanted to show off to the ladies. But then my horse started doing its performances, one after one, so I must have looked like the best rider!

When the General received his salary he gave me 100 yen telling me, 'Pay my personal expenses from this.' At that time 100 yen was big money. As I came into the army with little social experience, I thought it must be normal to pay his personal expenses from the money I received from him monthly, so I paid tips at hotels and restaurants, meals on dining car and various expenses from it. Later I found out that high-ranking officers could use a secret-service fund, just like entertainment expenses in business companies, and most of such expenses could be paid out of the fund. But I did not know that technique; I still think if I did use the fund he would have scolded me, judging from his fine personality.

He was very good in calligraphy with a dignified style. After conquering Burma, we had some peaceful periods in Yenangyaung. He was often asked by bereaved families of soldiers who died in Burma to write inscriptions for their tombstones, which he did willingly and had the writing sent to the families.

At that time there was a plan to erect a monument of victory which would also be a memorial to our dead soldiers. The General thought it premature as the war would become harder, but he agreed, probably as it would help to improve the morale of soldiers. At the same time he ordered a memorial to British unknown soldiers to be erected by its side. (This memorial impressed Lord Mountbatten and I was told that the General had been treated especially well in the POW camp at Mandalay after the war.)

In March 1943, General Sakurai was transferred to be Director of the Armoured Corps and I was ordered to accompany him to Tokyo. We boarded a plane from Rangoon to Singapore with General Iida, Commander of 15 Army, who was succeeded by General Kawabe. As we were boarding I was told to my dismay that one of General Sakurai's two suitcases was missing. I asked the ground crew to search and send it on the next flight, and told the General with regret, but he received the bad news calmly. General Iida also heard it and consoled me saying, 'It will be sent on soon.' General Iida usually seemed dignified and hard to approach but this time he was kind and gentle. We met General Iida again in the plane from Singapore to Japan. He asked me about the missing suitcase, and I told him that it was found. He said, with a kind, considerate smile, 'That was very good!' I felt that one's impression of high-ranking officers differed according to circumstances.

In Tokyo I was invited to stay in his house in Setagaya, and was given a detached room which seemed to belong to his daughter. As I was sleeping comfortably, a training air-raid alarm siren was heard, so I got up and put on my uniform. His daughter came to get her anti-air-raid hood and bag and told me kindly, 'You don't have to come.' But I thought it desirable as a military man to take part in the air-raid drill, and followed her and went out. To my surprise the General was in plain clothes and was standing in a line with the neighbours. At the end of the line I answered roll call; my officer's uniform seemed to have impressed the leader. I was amused that the leader did not know that the lieutenant general, as he now was, who commanded a distinguished division was in line and was calling out his number soberly, when military officers were highly respected in the society. He lived as a common citizen at home.

I returned to Burma to continue the job of adjutant to the commander of 33 Division, General Genzo Yanagida, and then General Nobuo Tanaka until the war ended.

After we were defeated in Imphal area we again went through Kalaw in April 1945: I was told that one of the two mixed-race ladies was standing by the road with a baby in her arms looking at retreating Japanese troops. The baby was said to have been the child of a Japanese military doctor; I did not know whether she could find her loved one among the exhausted, retreating Japanese troops.

40 · Chasing Chindits

Lance Corporal Shinsaku Honma, 2nd Machine Gun Company,
2nd Battalion, 215 Infantry Regiment, 33 Division

Monywa, Tamu, Shan

While we had been enjoying a peaceful occupation in Monywa, we were told that a British force had penetrated into Burma, and our 2nd Battalion arrived at Kanbalu railway station (about 100 kilometres south-east of Pinlebu) from Monywa on 28 February 1943. It was on 3 March that our battalion commander, Major Ichiro Nasu, was killed in an unexpected clash with Gurkhas in the jungle. In order to trap the enemy ten men, including myself from the Machine Gun Company, were attached to 7th Rifle Company and advanced towards the Yu River.

We arrived at the village as ordered, but we found no sign of the enemy and the village people welcomed us and showed us dances by Burmese girls. When we woke next morning there were no girls or children in the village and soon all the village people disappeared. At that time we did not suspect that our move had been disclosed to the enemy. It was when we were taking a sleep wearing only underpants that we heard the noise of British planes. I did not mind the sound as I thought they would go to bomb our rear. But then I noticed something strange and went outdoors and found the planes were circling over the village. I cried 'Air raid!' and everybody dressed only in underwear ran out of the village.

At that time a plane came diving on us, so I cried, 'Quick, escape to the jungle as you are now!' We left our rifles and kit in the house. Before we could run 50 metres two bombs fell in the centre of village and exploded. The second plane was already diving which caused a fire in a house and a palm tree fell down. We all sat still in the jungle. The fire was terrifying as well as the bombs. When the bombing by the fourth plane was over we carried our guns, ammunition and kit from the house. As soon as we entered the jungle, the planes started raking the ground with 20mm machine guns, but fortunately without any damage. The planes left and half the houses in the village were burnt down.

A messenger came from 7th Company telling us to move to a jungle one kilometre north-east. Arriving there, we found the traces of camping and horse droppings. They must have been the enemy's. The place was suitable for camping with a water source and big trees. As the enemy were on secret mission they must have avoided entering villages and tried not to be informed on to the Japanese army. We spent the rest of the day building toilets and putting up tents. Another plane came and flew low over the village but did not attack it. We judged the plane came because the enemy was nearby.

Next morning suddenly we were ordered to fight. We carried mess kits wrapped in camouflage nets, canteen and fifteen rounds of ammunition. We came to a place where there was a river 50 metres wide with water 30 centimetres deep because of the dry season. To the right was a wide marshland with reeds, and beyond it tall palm trees where probably there was a village.

The leading section suddenly started to run and we heard someone cry, 'Enemy!' It was so unexpected that we had no time to fire. The enemy poured into the marshland. I assembled the gun so that it could be carried by four men, though the platoon leader did not order this. We did not know the strength of the enemy. Lt Takizawa, Commander 7th Company, ordered us to encircle the marshland and our machine gun was located in the centre on a cliff above the river. A few minutes later I heard the noise of reeds being broken about 40 metres ahead. Our plan was to fire at them with machine-gun and grenade launchers and to threaten them that we were a large troop, and then the rifle sections would pursue them. My machine gun fired five rounds into the area where we had heard the noises. Grenade launchers also were fired. Enemy soldiers came out one by one; all were captured without any bloodshed. The plan of Lt Takizawa had been successful. We took them to the ox-cart road and examined their belongings. The senior man was a medical officer who had more than 200 one-rupee silver coins in a cotton bag.

We moved our camping site to a foot of a mountain 1.5 kilometres from the former position. For the next two or three days we had no information of the enemy. Probably on the fourth day about fifteen enemy soldiers came in a single file at a leisurely pace on the road at which our machine gun was aiming. All of us were tense. Distance, 200 metres. The enemy had not noticed us. On one side of the enemy was a river, the other was reed bushes. Our rifle units were ready to charge. I did the accurate aiming and awaited the order of the commander.

I pressed the trigger as soon as I heard Lt Takizawa's order, 'Fire!' Before I had fired one round, all the enemy lay flat on the ground. There happened to be driftwood nearby and the enemy hid behind it. While I was consulting with the section leader whether I should fire to intimidate them, Lt Sakamaki came running to us holding his Japanese sword in one hand and ordered me to cover the charge of the rifle units. As five or six men who were still on the road started to move, I fired about twenty bullets. A white cloth tied to the top of a stick appeared behind the driftwood and was waved. The rifle platoon advanced with bayonets on rifles. There were only eight men behind the driftwood; all were captured. It was the officer who held out the white flag. The remaining fifteen men ran into the reeds. I thought there should be seven or eight there. Around midnight I heard men walking in the river about 50 metres below our gun, so everybody took up their positions. But it was so dark that we could not see ten metres ahead. They were lucky: they must have returned to India safely.

Because our sleep was disturbed we slept well after breakfast. At about 10 o'clock I was roused by the sentry's alarm. Again seven or eight enemy soldiers came walking leisurely with rifles on shoulder straps. I knew that I should not let them escape into the jungle again. If they reached the driftwood it would be the repeat of yesterday. I aimed exactly at the waist of the man in front, so that even if he lay flat the bullets would hit the men in the rear. I reported, 'Aiming OK!' but the order to shoot did not come. I am supposed to fire by the order of the platoon leader. I made up my mind that I would not care to be scolded later, and pressed the trigger. The leading three men fell down one by one. Then I moved my aim to the remaining men who lay flat and fired another thirty bullets; 7th Company ran to the enemy and found two men killed and five wounded. I was impressed by the excellent performance of the Type 92 medium machine gun. Enemy soldiers captured yesterday and today's wounded (British) were delivered to battalion headquarters at Mawleik.

4

ARAKAN OPERATIONS

January 1943 to March 1944

41 · To Akyab

Sergeant Naoyuki Aikawa, 2nd Machine Gun Company,
2nd Battalion, 213 Infantry Regiment, 33 Division

China, Rangoon, Donbaik

We left China in the last group of 33 Division, arrived at Rangoon by boat from Moulmein, and spent a week at Pegu where we received ammunition and rations. We left by lorries of a transport company in the afternoon of 14 April 1942, with 5th Company, a platoon of engineers, a platoon of airfield ground service and a radio unit.

After a pause at Prome we started to cross the Arakan mountain range in the dark night, and found the road very narrow, steep and winding. At about 3 a.m. on the 15th the lorry of our company commander, Lieutenant Abe, plunged over a cliff and he was killed instantly. We arrived at Taungup in the afternoon, and began a long and hard march across wild country. There was a small path along the telephone line but we had to rely on a guide from a local village. As we were carrying ten days' rations and had to cross many small streams and marshland in the severe heat, we were really exhausted.

In the evening of 2 May we crossed the River Kaladan in local boats. As the river was about 4 kilometres wide, it took time to row across, and horses and ammunition were still being unloaded when four enemy gunboats came up the river. We hid our boats in the riverside grass and fortunately were not found by the enemy. Early next morning the gunboats again showed up, seemingly with no precaution. We were ordered to aim below the mast of the leading boat and began firing with our four medium machine guns, six grenade launchers, light machine guns and rifles when it came within 150 metres. Much smoke and flame came out of the boat which turned back and steamed away at high speed. Later in the day Japanese bombers and fighters flew over us and went south to attack Akyab; a huge black cloud of smoke from bombs indicated to us where the airfield was. Later we were told by a message from our scout plane that the gunboat had sunk a few kilometres downstream.

In the early morning of 4 May we moved into Akyab airfield fully armed but met no enemy; we only saw eight burnt British planes and empty, paved runways. Then we entered the town of Akyab but saw no residents; everybody must have evacuated by sampan to avoid the fighting. Our platoon stayed in a hospital building in the centre of the town and enjoyed the freedom of walking around. A group of Burma Independence Army arrived at the town by boat; they were not well trained and could not march with us like soldiers. The next day several Japanese scout planes and fighters landed at the airfield. We were told that the chief of staff of 5 Air Division had flown in and encouraged our commander. In a few days the famous Kato Fighter Squadron arrived and was stationed at Akyab to our delight.

Local people came back to the town one by one. They showed no resentment of the Japanese army although some of their houses were occupied by us. They seemed friendly to us. A few middle-class people understood English but most residents spoke only Arakan dialect, so it was very difficult to communicate with them. In June one company of engineers and our 6th Company flew in to Akyab. It took only three hours for them to come from Toungoo, compared to our twenty-one days' hard march. The engineers built concrete bunkers for us on the sandy island.

42 · Donbaik

Senior Private Takeo Kawakami, 12th Company,
3rd Battalion, 213 Infantry Regiment, 33 Division

China, Arakan, Tiddim

Our 3rd Battalion moved from Allanmyo to Akyab in October 1942 and built defence positions on the west coast of the island. After we had celebrated New Year with rice cake and drinks, my platoon was pulled out from the company and became a part of the mixed company together with a platoon each from 10th and 11th Companies, a machine gun platoon, a section of guns with a mortar and a 47mm automatic gun (both captured from the British), a platoon of anti-tank guns, a doctor and a radio, about 250 men in all.

During the night of 4 January, we landed at Angumaw, on the southern tip of Mayu Peninsula, covered by our leading platoon, and advanced towards Donbaik. At about 1 p.m. we encountered an enemy force of company strength with several armoured carriers, and after one hour of fighting they retreated when two carriers were destroyed by our close-range attacks. Our commander, Lieutenant Watanabe, was shot through his throat and killed, and 2nd Lieutenant Asano took the command. We reached a small river as Forward Defensive Line (FDL) and our commander decided to build defensive bunkers along its south bank. Our platoon was at the western end of the line, close to the sea. The river was about 5 to 8 metres wide and our side was a steep bank 2 to 3 metres high while on the other side was an open field up to about 600 metres wide. We had made many bunkers in China, but this time we made stronger ones by the working day and night as we expected the British would have many big guns.

From sunrise of 7 January, the enemy shelled our positions heavily for about two hours: we were covered by sand dust and explosion smoke, then enemy infantry approached and attacked us. We brought our full firepower to bear, followed by grenades and hand-to-hand fighting and repulsed the attacks. Later, one shell fell on the trench of our section, and two men were killed, two badly wounded and one lightly wounded. These were the first casualties in our platoon, a big loss of five men! It was mortifying to lose our comrades, who gave their young lives while calling to their parents in Japan. We were frustrated that we could do nothing against the enemy shelling. What were our mountain guns in the rear doing? They should have fired one shell at least the enemy positions. What had happened to our planes? There seemed no way out of our critical situation. A shell exploded four metres in front of us, but this time everybody was safe including our section leader, Sergeant Kojima.

That evening we received new orders for defence: 1. During the concentrated shelling of the enemy, each platoon will leave one sentry in position, and the majority will take shelter in nearby caves. 2. When enemy guns extend their shooting range, everybody will move to the front bunker and await the signal for everyone to begin firing simultaneously. 3. The leader of the machine gun platoon, 2nd Lt Kayano, will judge the timing when the enemy approaches close enough to our line, and order his medium machine guns to fire. All rifle platoons will then start firing. The enemy attacked us strongly on 8, 9, 18 and 19 January, and 1, 2 and 3 February. Each time they shelled us for two to three hours and then their infantry approached; we rushed out of the caves, and after severe close-range fighting forced them to retreat. Also, attacks by the enemy in small groups were repeated almost every night, possibly to recover dead bodies. We also went out to collect rations and ammunition from them at night.

Our transport unit led by Sergeant Nagatsuka cooked rice in the rear and carried it on their shoulders along the beach at low tide; a mess-tin full of rice and a bottle of water were delivered to each of us every night, which we received with heartfelt thanks. This mission was also very dangerous as the beach was regularly shelled and the enemy had occupied some part of our rear. Every night we were very busy repairing and reinforcing our bunkers, camouflaging them with fresh leaves and sometimes going to Angumaw to send our wounded and to collect grenades and biscuit rations. Also, we set up fake positions with loopholes in the rear area to attract enemy shelling and bombing.

On 16 February, enemy shelling began once again. I hurried to the sentry bunker as Private Nishino was hit. A bullet came through the loophole and penetrated his helmet and head. So upsetting that we had lost one more man. At about 10 a.m. I cried, 'Enemy armoured carriers on the beach!' Senior Private Odano directed his machine gun towards the sea. One carrier, then another, then four carriers came sweeping towards our positions, followed by infantry of about platoon strength. As Odano fired the machine gun at them, they hid behind the carriers. The weary riflemen of our section kept up their fire. Suddenly the leading carrier burst into flames, and other carriers turned around and retreated; the infantry also withdrew and the attack was repulsed. The carrier had been hit by a first shot of our automatic gun. We thanked our machine-gun platoon who repulsed the repeated enemy attacks on our beachside bunkers every day with their machine guns and automatic gun. The faces of our comrades were all black and we silently rejoiced in our good fortune.

We did not know why, but the enemy seemed to shell us heavily on Fridays and days involving the numeral 8. I thought, 'Tomorrow is the 18th so I may have to die and be consecrated at Yasukuni Shrine.' Suddenly I recalled the face of my mother who was far away in our homeland and tears poured out. I wished her well.

Early on 18 February, Sergeant Kojima was on sentry duty. Because of the shortage of men even the section leader had to stand watch. As 5 o'clock was the time of the change of sentry I went to him five minutes early. Just as I arrived, the first shell exploded in a village to the rear and volley firing begun. The shelling by British–Indian artillery was really fierce, impossible to express in words, which only those who participated in the battle of Donbaik could appreciate. Later I took part in 'Operation Imphal', but the shelling there was not comparable to the fierce bombardment at Donbaik. It was like hitting innumerable drums at the same time. Nothing at all could be seen in our rear, which was covered by heavy clouds of dust. We estimated that we were receiving 500 to 600 shells in an hour. Together with the shelling nine British fighter-bombers shot up and bombed our positions. We could not liaise with other sections in our platoon and several enemy carriers and infantry came from the beach and penetrated our lines. We fired the machine gun at them but it did not help. I called other bunkers of our section but there was no reply. I cried, 'Platoon Leader!' but all I could hear was the sound of shooting. 'What has happened to our platoon? Are we three in this bunker the only ones alive in our platoon?' Lance Corporal Ishii, Odano and I looked at each other. We called again to the other bunkers, but got no reply.

As soon as the shelling ended, enemy infantry attacked us. We fired at them relentlessly with the only machine gun we had and threw grenades, and just managed to repel their attack. 'Kawakami,' Odano called to me, 'What?' 'Double charging!' As we put down the machine gun on the ground to fix the trouble a mortar shell exploded just in front of us. I saw that Odano was bleeding on his cheek and left eye; fortunately a slight injury, yet he could not see. If we were late in lowering the gun just for a second, all three of us would be enshrined at Yasukuni. I saw two metres in front of our bunker a British sergeant lying dead; a silver watch on his left arm reflected the sunshine. Still we could not contact other sections and the platoon leader; they might all have been killed, but it was a relief to see the machine-gun platoon fighting hard with enemy carriers.

The defence line of our platoon was broken, the enemy were in our rear as well as in bunkers to right and left. Odano said, '130 bullets left for the machine gun.' So I counted mine and Ishii's, a total of 45 bullets and four grenades. What should we, the remaining three, do? If the enemy charged us tomorrow morning, it would be our end.

The glowing red sun went down on the horizon. We heard no sounds of guns and rifles; it was really a quiet time. We three discussed what to do, and decided that if the enemy attacked, the machine gun would fire until the last bullet, and if the situation was still no better we would kill ourselves with grenades. With this conclusion I felt somehow carefree. Ishii asked if I had cigarettes; I searched in my pockets and found only two, so we smoked them in turns. I can never forget the taste of the cigarettes. Tomorrow I am really going to die; to think of this was a strange feeling. I thought of my mother back home and a teardrop rolled down my cheek. It was a tranquil night; the hard fighting during the day seemed incredible. I wondered how the enemy soldiers were feeling at the time.

As Odano and I were watching the front and Ishii the rear, I fell into a deep sleep as I was completely exhausted by the continued hard fighting. I do not know how long I slept, but Ishii kicked me and silently pointed ahead to where a crowd of soldiers was advancing with their bodies bent low. Odano had his machine gun ready to shoot. Now our last moment had come. I handed a grenade each to Ishii and Odano who nodded without a word. I thought that when the enemy crossed the river we would start firing and I would throw the last grenade. Ishii fired a shot and shouted, 'Odano!' Then voices, 'Friendly army', were heard. The three of us looked at each other, and could not hold back tears; we just stood still in the bunker for a while.

A warrant officer of 55 Division came close and asked, 'How many are defending here?' 'Three!' Ishii answered. Now help had arrived. The joy when I heard the words 'friendly army', and the feeling of absolute euphoria that followed is difficult to describe, my sense of being alive after having thought I would die. This I will never forget.

When the eastern sky turned bright, all the enemy began to retreat. Taking the chance, Odano fired the machine gun at them, and I threw all the grenades, killing enemy soldiers. We gave thanks for the reinforcement. We had done very well, and prayed that our comrades and platoon leaders were alive.

The warrant officer brought us an order to return to the original company. We waited until sunset and walked along the beach back to Angumaw. It was a strange feeling then to turn our backs to the enemy; we were devoured by anxiety that enemy shelling might be resumed at any time. Anyhow, we were back to the company and Lance Corporal Ishii reported the battle situation to the leader of the Command Unit. An end to an operation.

43 · Fighting for Indin

Apprentice Officer Satoru Inazawa, 1st Company,
1st Battalion, 112 Infantry Regiments, 55 Division

Arakan, Pyinmana, Mawchi

I graduated from a commercial college in December 1941, and after working with the Bank of Japan for only three weeks, I was drafted into the army on 1 February 1942, and graduated from Toyohashi Reserve Officer Training School in October 1942 as an apprentice officer (equivalent to second lieutenant in the British Army). Twenty-four of us graduates were transferred to 112 Infantry Regiment on 19 December, and after a long voyage via Singapore, Rangoon and Taungup, arrived at Akyab on 4 March 1943. The Japanese offensive 'Operation 31' (First Arakan) had just started. That night we went to our regimental headquarters and were impressed to see the regimental colours under candlelight.

After being briefed for three days in a group I was assigned to lead 1 Platoon of 1st Company which was under the direct command of regimental headquarters. The major part of the company was still awaiting boats at Kyauktapiu Island. As there was no company commander or battalion commander to guide me, a green officer with no actual experience, I felt under great strain.

On the evening of 9 March I walked alone with a simple mimeographed map and was met at the entrance of Sabahta village by a soldier of the platoon. I met my men in the village and took command. As I was so new I kept Sergeant Yamamoto, who had been the leader, as my adviser for the time being, instead of transferring him back as the first section leader. The enemy position, surrounded by a barbed wire barricade, was located on Hill 105 one kilometre north-west of Sabahta village. Our three sections were in trenches dug under the biggest house in the village, and the second section was on a hill opposite the enemy position Point 105 across the River Sabahta.

Next day I went to the second section with two men carrying some supplies. As we were climbing the hill, we were suddenly fired on by our own men. We had lost our way and were approaching the hill from the slope facing the enemy, for whom we were mistaken. We lay flat on the ground and cried 'Friend!' My own men gave me my baptism of fire! As I reached the hilltop the enemy mortar began to fire on our position, probably alarmed by our shooting. Although the men there had their own foxholes, I had no place to shelter. I lay down in a small depression as low as I could and felt more dead than alive. Gradually I could distinguish the sound of firing, with the added fear that in few seconds the shell might explode on me, but there was nothing I could do. The shelling did not last long, and I felt very relieved; it was my first encounter of enemy shelling.

On 11 March, six British light bombers flew over and dropped a concentration of bombs on Sabahta village. Fortunately the bombs did not hit our house but the neighbouring house was smashed to pieces. Then eight fighters came and repeated firing from a low altitude. Empty cartridges dropped from the planes made rattling noises as they hit the tin roof, and their 20mm cannon shells penetrated the poles of our house and caused a lot of dust to fly up which made it hard for us in the trenches to breathe. For about an hour this small village with only six houses was bombed and shelled. Nobody was hurt as we were crouching low in trenches, and we really appreciated them.

On 12 March my platoon was ordered to attack the enemy to the north-west of Sabahta at twilight. For me, the first battle! But there was no company commander nor leader to teach me what to do. I made up my mind bravely that I would end my young life here, and advanced in a basic formation which I learned at school. Following the last round of grenade launchers, I pulled out my Japanese sword and cried 'Charge!' But as I ran into the enemy position I found no one there. I felt relieved as well as disappointed. I left the first section there and went back to Sabahta with the rest of the platoon.

On the following day, 13 March, we were ordered to attack Hill 105 at night, and one radio section was attached to the platoon. After sunset engineers of the River Crossing Material Company came up the chaung in a folding boat. We landed the boat and, carrying it on our shoulders, went north until we hit the Sabahta River, and put the boat in the water. The boat carried us to the other bank in several journeys, and the engineers took it back. Then we advanced quietly in umbrella formation towards Hill 105. At 3 a.m. we came to within 200 metres of the enemy position and fired one grenade as a trial but there was no reaction. We ran up the hill without a pause, but again the enemy had already gone. This was the hill from which I was mortared four days ago. Thus my initial two battles met no enemy resistance, and my life was spared. But in the same period two of my comrade graduates had already been killed in action.

At 2 p.m. on 17 March we advanced individually while the enemy planes were flying over us, and entered Htizwe on the River Mayu where we found a lot of food in warehouses. As I had not eaten anything sweet for a long time, I drank plenty of condensed milk.

On 22 March, as we were preparing to cross the River Mayu at a hill south-east of Prindaw, the major part of the 1st Company arrived, commanded by 2nd Lt Tsukuda. So I was placed under a commander for the first time. It was lucky that no one in the platoon had so far been wounded.

Note

Out of twenty green officers who arrived at Akyab with me, eleven were killed in action, five were badly wounded and were sent back to Japan; and four, including myself, were wounded and treated at military hospitals and went back to the front line. To sum up, every one of us twenty was hit, but just a small difference in the part of the body that was hit decided his fortune. (I have no information about four persons not included in the above.)

44 · Horseshoe Hill

Corporal Shouhichi Namikoshi, 1st Company, 1st Battalion,
112 Infantry Regiment, 55 Division

Indin, Arakan

On 5 April 1943 we were on the Horseshoe Hill (which was about 500 metres north-west of the village of Indin) and were shelled continuously by mortars. I was the leader of 3rd section, a brand-new leader who had finished NCO training school just three months earlier.

We crossed the River Mayu on 24 March and climbed the steep Mayu mountain range through jungle and arrived at its western foot on 31 March. In the morning of 3 April 2nd Lieutenant Tsukuda, who was then commander of 1st Company, was sniped, and Apprentice Officer Inazawa, who was now the only active officer in the company, became the acting company commander. Late in the day we arrived at Horseshoe Hill and next morning we were shelled all day. It was dangerous to leave our foxholes. On 5 April we ran out of food and were very thirsty; the River Indin which flowed to our north was salty and unsuitable for drinking.

In the afternoon of 5 April, while we were being attacked by the enemy, a messenger arrived and said 'Section Leader Namikoshi, report to the platoon leader.' I ordered Corporal Okuda to take charge of the section and crawled over to our platoon leader, Sergeant Yamamoto. He told me that our regiment was going to attack the Indin area before sunrise on 6 April and my section was ordered to be the leading troop of the attack. Our 1st Company was attached to the 3rd Battalion.

At the moment I received the order, I gave up hope: 'As God wishes. Tonight will be the end of my whole life', and I came to accept my death. Then I thought over and over how I should give this order to the men in my section. Even though I was above them in army rank I was the youngest, with the shortest period in army service. Among Japanese soldiers the number of army meals one had eaten counted much more than the rank!

As the order came to our 3rd Section I could accept the situation but still could not wipe out the thought, 'Why us?', which would never be understood by those who were not at the critical stage. I was sorry for my men who were sure to think, 'If our leader was not such a green guy, we could have avoided being the dangerous leading section.' Also I was inclined to think that a section in the 3rd Battalion should be leading, not ourselves temporarily assigned to them for the attack. Was this Fate?

I hurried back to my section. As my men were spread out in individual foxholes in fighting formation, I could not collect them at one place. So I took the chance of an interval in the shelling, crawled to each one and told them of the coming night attack, the checking of equipment and the wearing of night signs. The enemy shelling continued and I felt it became more severe as the evening approached. Then enemy soldiers advanced. Our grenade launchers fired. The first volley was short, but as the following ones landed close to them, they withdrew to their positions.

Trees and grass on the slope facing the enemy were blown away and the hill seemed deformed. Our wounded men and corpses were gathered under the shade of the few remaining trees on the other side of the hill. In the Indin area there were three rows of houses extending north to south in straight lines, which we tentatively called East Village, Middle Village and West Village. Our target was the north end of East Village.

Just before it became dark, I collected all the men in my section in a foxhole, and spoke to them: 'Listen carefully! In tonight's attack we are ordered to rush the enemy position as the leading section. Although it is not long since I became your leader, you have all followed my orders and fought very well. I thank you. The success or failure of the coming battle depends on the performance of our section.'

After a pause, I continued: 'Please trust your lives to me

tonight. If you think that there is no hope of returning alive in the coming attack, it is already a defeat. Once in the fight, we must win! And to win, do not waste your life carelessly. So obey my instructions. It is most important for us to approach the enemy position undetected. When we charge, the major part of the regiment will follow us. There is no one wishes to die. If possible I would trade my life with all of yours. I don't wish to see any of you killed. Our names will be recorded in history if our section paves the way for the whole of our regiment. The secret of winning is the strong unity of everyone in our section, as we have learned. We will charge into the enemy like a fireball!' As I talked, my men seemed to have made up their minds, and felt easy and bright even though they were facing a life or death battle within a few hours.

Before it got too dark we attached a white squared cloth or paper to the back of our helmets to distinguish ourselves from the enemy, and I ordered my men to check equipment for the night attack. Leather shoes were replaced with sound-proof socks, and scabbards of bayonets were wrapped around with cloth; those who did not have socks wrapped their leather shoes with cloth; everything was done to reduce noise. We confirmed to each other that the password for the night was 'Fukuro – Nezumi' (bag and rat).

Lastly I explained the attack formation: 'We, being the leading section, will advance 200 metres ahead of the major part of the battalion. I will lead the section and men will follow me at an interval of about three steps in a single file until we are 100 metres from enemy positions. Lance Corporal Okuda will be at the tail end in advance. When I raise my arms, you should spread sideways in a line in utter silence, and when I cry 'Charge, rush in!' all of us will run forward with bayonets. Never stand up in front of the enemy until I shout, 'Charge!' Keep crawling all the way. You will be shot if you stand up. The enemy must have fixed their guns in the directions where they expect us to come. So it is absolutely necessary that we crawl on the ground. Do all of you understand? Even if bullets are coming like a shower, don't stand up; if you do it will be the end of your role. If you crawl the bullets will fly above you and meanwhile we can think of our next move. It is a waste of your life to be killed before attacking. If you are to die, thrust and thrust with your bayonets. I trust you will do this.' I repeated this several times so that everybody would fully understand these instructions.

The time of our fate was approaching moment by moment. It was a long day on the hill facing enemy attacks. After 10 p.m. we started to move to a gathering point near the beach. A new moon of six days old had set in, and it became so completely dark that a friend one metre in front could hardly be distinguished. We awaited an order. At about 2 a.m. we received the order, 'Advance.' Our company was to attack East Village of Indin in two groups and my platoon was to advance to its north end.

As we advanced toward the village for about thirty minutes, I received a relayed message, ' The lance corporal is not following us.' On hearing it I thought that I had made a mess of it, but now it was too late to turn around, and I could not spare my men searching for him. I told the tail that we would advance as we were, and we moved forward with the utmost caution step by step.

About one hour after we started, when we could see the East Village faintly under the dim starlight, someone must have turned aside from the single file and was caught by the enemy's detection device. As soon as it made a rattling sound, concerted firing of enemy automatic rifles and other guns started up. Though the situation was serious, strangely I became calm and ordered my men to take a cross-line position in crawling, and on the order of our platoon leader I cried as loud as I could, 'Charge! Charge! Charge!' My men responded to it and rushed forward, striving to be the first, and fighting at close quarters continued desperately for several hours. I was in ecstasy after we charged; if I did not kill them, I would be killed on the battlefield!

I did not know how long we had fought but enemy resistance got weaker and weaker, and finally it became quiet. As it was now really dark I suspected that the enemy might have been hiding somewhere in the village. We were ordered to assemble at the south end of the village, where I saw our platoon leader carried unconscious on a makeshift stretcher. We moved towards the south-east for a kilometre and came to a hill of about 20 metres high just as the sun came out. While we were digging foxholes on the hill, the enemy shelled us intermittently and then British soldiers came and started to climb the hill. We fired at them with our light machine guns and rifles until the barrels got too hot. They retreated but shelled us with so much mortar fire that we felt that the shape of the hill must have been altered.

In the afternoon, as we watched from the hill, the enemy moved in a grand parade on the beach towards the north. They were far beyond the range of our grenade launchers, and even if we came out to attack them, we would be killed soon by the severe shelling. We hoped in vain that our mountain guns would have arrived. It was really frustrating that we could do nothing to prevent the enemy escaping from our trap. In the evening the shelling ceased and we moved to a new position near the beach and joined our battalion.

45 · An Enemy Officer's Surrender

Apprentice Officer Yoshiki Saito, 4th Company,
2nd Battalion, 112 Infantry Regiment, 55 Division

Indin

Late in the night of 5 April 1943, we moved from Horseshoe Hill to the assembly area near the beach, where I saw Inazawa of the 1st Company for a moment. As the leading platoon of the 4th Company, we were to attack the West Village of Indin, together with the 6th Company who were to go on our left. I was the platoon leader.

Just after midnight we were ordered to advance and moved along the beach quietly towards the village. I had no idea how long we walked; it might have been a long time or short. I had no accurate information about the enemy, so I was leading tensely in the pitch dark.

Suddenly, tracer bullets came from the left with the sound of shots from a medium machine gun. I thought that the enemy might have spotted our attack, but the firing soon ceased, and I felt relieved for a while. As we advanced about 50 metres more, we were spray shot, as severely as we had experienced in past encounters. Grenades in abundance exploded to our front and bullets flew above us. Some of our men fell down screaming 'Ah!...' I cried, 'Machine guns forward! Infantry guns forward!' and our commander sent them up to us. The guns fired shells with fuses set on zero time. It was lucky for us that darkness and the close distance between us and enemy made it impossible for enemy tanks and big guns to attack us. We lay flat on the sand and moved steadily towards the enemy positions. An inexperienced soldier got excited and threw a grenade which flew short and a fragment hit my right hand. As we struggled in the close-range fighting, the morning light came up and I could vaguely discern enemy positions in the mist. We were afraid of British tanks, but I figured that in the village several tanks (as I thought then, but they were in fact carriers) had been left unattended; probably their crews were dead or had escaped. With sunlight on us, I was worried that British planes would come to attack us at any time.

By sunrise it seemed that we had controlled most parts of Indin, but my dried-up brain could not judge the enemy situation correctly. Even though it was past 8.30 a.m. enemy planes did not come.

We had used up almost all of our ammunition, but the enemy fire had also became sporadic. Then a messenger brought me an order from the company commander: 'Advise enemy to surrender.' At the moment I heard this I hesitated, being more shy to speak broken English than to stand up in front of the enemy.

137

I lifted my upper body slightly and spoke as clearly as I could: 'This position has fallen into our hands, give up your attack...' The sound of firing had completely stopped, and the strong sun shone down on us.

From a defence bunker on our left, a group of men came out quietly with imperturbable calmness. They came towards me: a tall officer in neat tropical uniform who seemed like a commander in the centre, an officer with a British flag covered with newspapers on his right; and several soldiers. They stopped 20 metres in front of me and answered that they would accept my request and then came closer to me. I stood up.

The tall British officer looked down on me with sincere eyes and offered his hand. I asked sternly with bloodshot eyes, 'Are you the commander?' He answered calmly that he was, and handed me his pistol, a watch and two compasses. I thought he might be a major or so because of his age and attitude, not recognising his rank badge. My men came and surrounded them. Then our company commander arrived so I handed them to him. The tall British officer asked my commander his rank and he answered 'Lieutenant Kuroda.' The lieutenant then took them to the regimental headquarters.

My mind was fully occupied during the enemy counter-attack. We had to defend the area by all means, so we were busy preparing the abandoned bunkers and foxholes for our use. In a bunker a British soldier lay dead with his earphones on.

After a while heavy firing on our positions started and British armoured cars came to attack us. Five soldiers who went out of the bunker to attack them with portable mines were killed almost instantly by their shelling. A shell exploded and destroyed the bunker and I was hit by more than ten pieces of shrapnel. I was covered all over with blood and fainted.

It was after I recovered my senses next day that I knew that the dignified officer was Brigadier Cavendish, the Commander of the 6th Brigade, and the officer who held the flag was his adjutant, Captain Fanshawe.

46 · Killed by Friendly Fire

Lieutenant Tadahiro Ogawa, Medical Unit,
112 Infantry Regiment H.Q., 55 Division

At daybreak on 3 April 1943 we arrived at Horseshoe Hill (U-shaped hill, about 15 metres high and 100 metres long) with the regimental headquarters and 3rd Battalion. My unit consisted of myself, Doctor 2nd Lt Ishikawa and two assistants. From 9 or 10 a.m. of 3 April severe mortar shelling fell on the hill for about eight hours until sunset. Strangely, the firing ceased suddenly and at that moment we saw British soldiers near the ridge. Our soldiers charged up the hill and after a severe close-range fight, the British retreated leaving behind many dead bodies.

After the attack we suffered from thirst, as we had not filled our canteens since the morning of 2 April. The Indin Chaung just close to us was salty and we tried hard but in vain to find a drinking water source. All the soldiers were dehydrated and could not move around actively. Someone even tried to scoop a drop by drop of morning dew on the leaves. In the afternoon of 4 April a pond was finally found north of the chaung, but there our soldiers often encountered British soldiers who also came to get water. The water was available to us at the risk of men's lives.

Late in the night of 5 April, the regiment started to attack Indin. The regimental headquarters followed the 2nd Battalion, while most of the 3rd Battalion remained to hold the hill securely and to protect injured men.

When we reached the south end of West Village, we saw many British soldiers on the beach retreating towards the north. Colonel Tanahashi, the regimental commander, did not order us to attack them but instead he ordered us to dig trenches there.

As several soldiers of the 4th Company were wounded we put them in a dry pond and treated them. Then several British POWs were brought from the 4th Company and found to be Brigade Commander R.V.C. Cavendish and his staff.

Soon afterwards a carrier came at full speed from the direction of Kwason, two men sticking their heads up to look around. While we were watching them, amazed, it ran between Middle Village and East Village and returned by the same route.

Soon afterwards shells fell on us. The commander decided to move the headquarters and Signal Company and took the lead in transferring to Middle Village, headquarters men and POWs following him. I had to take care of the wounded so I arrived a little later and stumbled into Middle Village not knowing what I was doing while shells kept exploding around us. I could not see the commander though I looked around, and machine-gun bullets started to raise clouds of dust round my feet. I found a trench on my left and hurriedly jumped into it, where there were two visitors from 2nd Battalion. Although I planned to take emergency shelter there, the severe shelling prevented me from joining the commander. The powder smoke and dust covered all Indin. The shelling at Horseshoe Hill had been very severe but this one was much more frequent. First, field guns from the south and mortars shot at us; moreover, heavy guns from Kyaukpaund joined in the shelling. I thought it inevitable that one of these shells would fall on my head, but I prayed that such a moment should come as late as possible.

Late in the afternoon a hut just behind us started burning; if the fire reached our wood-covered trench it would burn completely. I peeped out cautiously, and saw smoke shells which looked like briquettes with holes lying around us. I was tense, judging that the enemy was going to attack us under cover of smoke, but nothing happened. On the beach enemy soldiers and vehicles were marching in column towards the north, which looked picturesque against the evening glow.

I went around to look for the colonel, and found him at East Village. A bullet had penetrated his right forearm which was roughly bandaged. He was happy to see me alive. Among men in my unit I met only Master-Sargeant Kasahara who was wounded; the whereabouts of 2nd Lt Ishikawa and Medic Tanaka were not known, which worried me.

The battle was over. After such continued strain I felt wholly spent, but there was a lot of work to do for the medical unit where I was the only active man. With the help of two capable medics (nurse soldiers) of the Signal Company, I treated the wounded soldiers one by one.

Late that afternoon I went around to look for the two missing men. The whole of Indin village was completely devastated; almost all the thatched-roof houses were burnt down, trees were split with their broken branches hanging down, and here and there on the ground were many shell craters. Corpses of our men and the British lay scattered, not yet recovered. A crowd of vultures that had been attracted by the smell of the dead were circling in the air. An awful sight. A hell on earth!

I found the corpse of Ishikawa, whose head was smashed through by a piece of shell; his helmet had a hole. Close to him the British brigadier lay dead. In the Middle Village my medic, Tanaka, was directly hit in his abdomen and lay 10 metres north of where I took shelter. According to our custom at a critical battlefield, we cut off the little fingers of both men, and cremated them. Their corpses were buried in nearby trenches, and I put up small wooden plates on their graves with their names written with pencil. I made the offering of lighted cigarettes to the graves of those who had enjoyed smoking. It was a pity that I could not offer even a grain of rice to those who died while being hungry.

Accompanied by the regimental commander, I examined formally the corpse of Brigadier Cavendish who lay about 10 metres away from our Ishikawa. He lay flat in a paddy field which was 20 metres west from the centre of East Village, with his head turned slightly to the right in a south-east direction. His only injury was a great gash through the lung from a piece of shell which apparently had damaged his heart and lung. As he was lying in the same direction as Ishikawa, both must have been killed by the same shell. I judged that he had died about noon (Japan time) when he and the colonel were moving from Middle Village to East Village.

On 9 April a Dressing (Interim Accommodation) Station of the 4th Field Hospital which arrived from Akyab was opened at Indin, where we transferred all of our patients. Colonel Tana-hashi refused our recommendation to be hospitalised, because of his strong sense of responsibility, and continued to command while treated by us, until the 112 Regiment occupied the But-hidaung–Maugdauw line in mid-May, when the First Arakan Operation was finished. Then he contracted malaria and was admitted to the hospital at Akyab.

We had no accurate information of casualties of the 112 Regiment at Indin. I roughly estimated that about 150 men and 10 officers were killed and 300 men were wounded in Indin area from 3 to 6 April, approximately half of the total casualties of the regiment in the 'First Arakan Operation' which totalled 301 killed and 560 wounded.

47 · A Secret War

Lance Corporal Toyoichi Katou, 1st Company, 55 Transport Regiment, 55 Division

Arakan

I was despatched to Hikari Kikan at Akyab in mid-1943 togeth-er with Sergeant Matsuo. Hikari Kikan was an organisation to support military operations and assist the independence of India, and its branch at Akyab was headed by Captain Shingo Hattori who had graduated from Waseda University and was an expert on Indian operations. His staff were Holy Priest Maruyama Gyoushou, two interpreters, five Burmese assistants, the sergeant and me. The holy priest had been engaged in Buddhist missionary work for a long time in Burma. 'Hadji' Kayabuki, who graduated from the Islamic University at Mecca, lived in a separate house and worked with Captain Hattori. Also 200 men of the Indian National Army (INA) led by Major Misra arrived in late 1943. The INA was organised mainly of Indian Army volunteers who surrendered to the Japanese in Malaya and Singapore and was under the command of Subhas Chandra Bose ('Netaji').

On 3 February 1944 I was ordered to go with Captain Hattori on a very dangerous mission. We began to climb Point 1800 after dark with Major Misra, an interpreter and a few INA soldiers. The hill was covered by dense jungle and we encountered groups of wild monkeys. We were told that a message from 'Netaji' had been delivered to the Indian troops at Point 1800, whose reaction seemed favourable, and that their British commander had left for his headquarters and would not be there that night. The captain told me that my job was to guard him to get out if the negotiations broke down and then find my way back to the base. Sergeant Matsuo with ten INA soldiers would be waiting on the way to help our return to the base. In case of failure, three shots of a pistol would be the signal.

We walked on and approached the advance post of the enemy. An Indian soldier said, 'Pani' and offered me an aluminium cup with water in which I saw mosquito larvae. I looked at the captain who briskly said, 'Drink!' Speaking the only Indian words I knew, 'Bahut Merbany' (Thank you very much), I emptied it in one gulp. Indians at the post clapped hands and pressed my hand, and we went on to their headquarters. There we were met by Lieutenant Gajardalcin. At first Captain Hattori talked through the interpreter, and was followed by the earnest persuasion of Major Misra. I kept close watch on the Indian commander but as the talk went on I felt that I could relax. Lieutenant Gajardalcin said that all of his men would join the INA and called his leaders who confirmed the decision. We told them to leave their position soon as the Japanese were about to attack it. They then went to a Japanese base guided by one of our number.

I went to the headquarters of 55 Division with Captain Hattori and others where the Divisional Commander, Lieutenant General Hanaya, thanked us for our distinguished achievement. The surrender of a superior army to one man had never before been recorded in history.

I enjoyed my twenty months at the Hikari Kikan which was very interesting and unique, living together with such kind individuals as Captain Hattori and Holy Priest Maruyama.

48 · Sinzweya – the Turning Point

Lance Corporal Toshiyuki Sakano, 4th Company, 1st Battalion, 214 Infantry Regiment, 33 Division

Taung Bazar, Buthidaung, Tiddim

We were ordered in the coming big operation: 'Advance straight into the enemy key area. Keep going ahead and do not take care of the fallen comrades. Carry seven hand grenades and as much as possible of other ammunition, but only three days' rations. If the food is not enough, get it from the enemy.' This was a harsh order, which meant that I might not be able to return home. We cut our nails and hair, wrapped them in paper and sent them back to the rear in case our bones were not recovered and could not be sent home. I put pictures of my family in my helmet.

At 8 p.m. on 3 February 1944, we left our positions, assembled at the company headquarters and prepared for the fight. We fixed bayonets on our rifles and pasted mud on them so that they did not reflect light. Sound-proofing was done on all metal articles. Company Commander Marukawa gave an address of instruction: 'Let everyone toast their lives to me in this operation...' He was speaking in tears. Then about ten porcelain cups were brought in, filled with Japanese sake, and circulated among us. After we all had a sip the cups were thrown at a rock to be broken in pieces – a ritual before going into a hard battle.

We moved to a hill with a withered tree on it, located north of Buthidaung, where other units were also arriving. We lay flat on the south slope and waited. The enemy mortars shelled the hilltop at intervals of about 20 minutes with explosions on the other side of the hill but sometimes shells burst behind our rear. A shell burst where our machine gun company was and caused severe damage. We waited for almost seven hours. It was really torture to be kept waiting under the threat of shelling. In fact a shell exploded in our rear and shrapnel fell near my feet.

I felt relieved when I heard a low but stern voice, 'Prepare for departure!' The moon was still shining above the western hills, and I wondered whether we would be able to penetrate through the enemy line. We lined up where our comrades fell and smelled blood.

At 3.00 a.m. we started to advance towards the enemy in four lines. The moon was still slightly above the hill, and we hoped that it would go down soon. Fortunately the usual morning mist came flowing and covered us. Sixth Company led the advance followed by our 4th Company and then other units. We were worried about the sound of our army shoes treading the grass.

We came within 100 metres of the enemy front line, then 50 metres, but heard no enemy reactions. We advanced quietly, praying that nothing would happen. We advanced between two long hills, both about 70 metres high and stretching from north to south. I wondered why the enemy did not find us, so many troops advancing in a column of four lines.

As we advanced about one kilometre in the enemy area, we saw a light on our left. The sentry there seemed to be sleeping, and was killed by men of the advance platoon by bayonet. We walked or half-ran at a very fast pace without resting, and when we came to 2 kilometres from Taung Bazar, where we assumed the enemy headquarters would be, the dawn came up. We were really tired and kept tripping over for several hours. Our battalion commander ordered us to be the leading company, and we had to run fast to pass the 4th Company.

In front of Taung Bazar was a branch of the Mayu River, into which we jumped and waded through as the water was low. While we were climbing its steep north bank, we heard the sound of many planes. Instantly we thought they must be enemy planes, but this time they proved to be Japanese; we saw the red round marks clearly on their wings. The enemy stopped shooting and shelling all at once and we realised how helpful the powerful planes were. However, we seldom saw our planes. We got into Taung Bazar and captured many weapons. Then we chased the enemy retreating towards Sinzweya. As we came close to Sinzweya and looked down from the surrounding ridges, we saw enemy anti-aircraft guns in the tiny basin. We fired all our weapons at them and saw enemy soldiers running away here and there. After a while we were shelled heavily from the direction of Sinzweya; the shells exploded in our vicinity, wounding our battalion commander and company commander.

Our company went back to a Japanese position north-west of Buthidaung and received rations and ammunition, and then went up the winding river bed of the Ngakyedauk Creek to a western ridge surrounding Sinzweya, while the enemy mortars kept shelling on us at random.

As I looked down from the ridge, the enemy in the basin seemed wholly surrounded by our troops. In the night hundreds of tanks and armoured cars took position all around a small hill in the centre of the basin which formed a solid defence circle. Big transport planes flew over the basin and dropped plenty of supplies. After dark on 13 February, we arrived on the ridge of Point 1033 and rested until the moon came up as it was too dark to recognise our route. I lay on the rugged hillside and slept with knapsack on and rifle in my hands. After a while I woke up as it was very cold and when I tried to sleep again I heard three sounds of firing which were followed by deafening explosions and flashes. We lay flat in depressions preparing for the next development. I thought that some of us must have been hurt, but it was still very quiet. Then our medic Hayashi shouted out, 'Any men of the 4th Company around? The Command Unit has been wiped out.' A shell exploded in the centre of the headquarters of our company, killing nine men and badly injuring five; only the company commander and the medic were not hurt. I helped to bury the dead just as the moonlight came up. I missed Sergeant Nagao, whose home was close to mine.

The wounded soldiers were sent back to the rear, and we started moving and soon were met by men of Matsukihira (1st) Battalion of 112 Regiment. We were surprised to hear that Point 1033, where our Command Unit perished, was a fake headquarters where a Japanese flag had been hoisted intentionally to attract enemy shelling. This was a favourite tactic of Major General Sakurai, our infantry group commander. We were sorry that we had halted at a most inappropriate place! We took over the roadblock, the only outlet to the west from the basin. I was impressed to see such a fine road in the mountain area which must have been built in a very short time. We built our positions on the slope, and small raiding parties were sent out under cover of night but were repulsed by the strong formation of tanks.

On 16 February we were shelled heavily by mortars from the rear of our positions. Somebody cried, 'Enemy attack!' Enemy soldiers came very close to us, so we threw hand grenades to daunt them and fired our machine guns and rifles with the utmost ferocity to defend our positions. After a long fight the enemy finally retreated, but our company was surrounded, whereas we thought the Japanese had been encircling the British–Indians in the basin. Many of our men were killed or wounded, and the second toe of my right foot was injured by a mortar fragment.

On 19 February, after transferring our positions to Matsukihira Battalion, we moved eastward. I could not wear shoes as my right foot was bandaged, so I tied my shoes at my waist and kept up with the march. The wounded were carried on makeshift stretchers.

When we came to a ridge south of Point 1033, we heard a buzzing in the northern sky which turned out to be a formation of about twenty planes. We prayed that they would pass over us, but they dived and dropped many black objects with a whirring sound. They were coming towards us. We had been identified, and I covered my ears and lay flat on the ground as they exploded with a huge noise, dust and blast around us. I heard moans here and there in the thick dust. I thought I was saved. The severely wounded were carried on stretchers and the lightly wounded walked with sticks.

While we were crossing Point 1033 at high speed, again we were shelled by mortars and two men were killed. Stretchers formed a longer line. We had run out of our food, and had not eaten for the past two days. It was very difficult to go down the mountain carrying stretchers when we were so exhausted and hungry. The line of stretchers was a miserable sight of defeated men.

At last we broke through an enemy advance post, and returned to our base in Buthidaung. After a brief rest, we moved to Kaladan Valley where 81 West African Division was advancing from the north.

49 · A Hard Road to Buthidaung

Second Lieutenant Satoru Inazawa, 1st Company, 1st Battalion,
112 Infantry Regiment, 55 Division

Arakan, Irrawaddy Delta

We kept walking from 3 a.m. on 3 February 1944 and arrived at Point 1070 around noon on 6 February, where my platoon was ordered to block the Ngakyedauk Pass on its south together with a half platoon of Engineers.

Early in the morning of 7 February the Engineers blasted the road leading to Sinzweya and we dug foxholes on small hills, painstaking work as the earth was very hard. At 10 a.m. to my great surprise, five tanks came down from Point 935 towards us, followed by twenty foot soldiers. They stopped at the blast and the men looked down the blast hole. Lance Corporal Ohno sniped and killed one Indian and wounded one. They did not know from where they were shot. Tanks shelled here and there on the hill not knowing our position, and withdrew after firing all their shells. None of us was injured.

Our positions were shelled by tank guns every day for fourteen days until 20 February, a terrible experience. One man kept watch on the enemy and others hid low in their holes. We did not fire unless the enemy came over the blast hole.

On 18 February a bridge-laying tank came and laid a bridge over the blast hole. On 20 February about ten tanks came and shelled our position, heavily aided by machine guns. My hole was half blasted and my rucksack was blown to pieces. Shelling continued all day, so after dark I moved our positions 500 metres east on the road.

On 21 February tanks were still shelling our former positions. I thought it was lucky we had retreated a little. At 3 p.m. we could contact our company and were ordered to go to the south slope of Point 1033 where the major part of the 1st Company was in position. We were told that Division had ordered Sakurai Column to retreat on 26 February and hence we went down mountain tracks counter-attacking after British assaults. Before dawn on 1 March we crossed the Buthidaung–Maungdaw road undetected by the enemy, and arrived at the Japanese position 2 kilometres west of Buthidaung, where we felt relieved and talked out loud with friends. Until now we had only whispered, as we had to be very careful not to be detected by the enemy.

5

IMPHAL AND KOHIMA

March to July 1944

50 · The Battle of Singgel

Sergeant Kazuyoshi Nakahara, 4th Company, 1st Battalion
215 Infantry Regiment, 33 Division

Monywa, Tiddim

In October 1943 our battalion moved from Monywa to the Kalemyo area, and then to Dolluang. From 4 March we moved secretly to Mualbem on the Manipur River. We crossed the river with our engineers' rubber boats before sunrise on 9 March and hid in the nearby forest until dark; meanwhile, a British plane flew around over us for twenty minutes without finding us. Each of us, including officers, carried a heavy knapsack with rations for twenty days, ammunition and other equipment.

We walked day and night in the mountains west of the Manipur River. Our 4th Company, with a platoon of medium machine guns and a radio unit, led the advance on 13 March and attacked a hill south of milestone 100 and captured it with little resistance. The company commander ordered me to take charge of all grenade launchers in the company and their concentrated shelling proved effective. I was a sergeant in charge of weapons in the Command Unit of the company. While our 3rd Platoon stayed at Point 5197, we left there in the early morning of 14 March via the west valley and came up to the road to Imphal at milestone 100 where we met a small number of the enemy, defeated them, and went north on the road. We saw a hill to the west of the road and thought it would be the Point 5708 that we were ordered to take. (In fact it was a hill south of Point 5708.) We spread out on the hill and dug foxholes in a hurry.

Late evening of 15 March three tanks came up on the road and proceeded south without noticing us. The company commander planned to attack the tanks on their way back and ordered me to organise a close-range attack team. I volunteered to be the leader and two privates, one each from 1st and 2nd Platoon, were assigned to the team. We carried two anti-tank mines and four magnet mines and waited at an appropriate place. I explained to the privates that we would succeed if we made good use of the terrain and our lives would be safe. I stuck together two magnet mines to be sure to destroy the armour-plating of the MkIII tanks.

Soon the tanks came back from the south. I aimed at the leading tank and had the privates attack the second and third tanks. I threw the mines which stuck to the rear part of the tank by magnet, and the tank was immobilised but our attack on the other two tanks failed. The second tank went forward and protected the destroyed tank, and the third tank went on north. The second tank fired its tank-gun and machine guns in all directions. I took an anti-tank mine and moved position to attack the tank, and had two soldiers sent back to the company to report the situation. At that time there was still some light. I moved to a hollow and waited until the shooting stopped. Meanwhile it started raining, and it became completely dark with only thunderous flashes from the shooting. After a long wait the firing stopped, and the sound of a wireless key was heard from the tank. Then it became silent in complete darkness. I approached the tank and by finger touch alone I attached the mine between the caterpillars and returned to the company. I reported the situation to the commander and proposed firing at the tank with a medium machine gun, but as everybody was sleeping it was decided to do this in the morning.

Next morning I approached the tank and found several enemy soldiers outside it; our medium machine gun started firing at them. As I expected, shooting came from the tank and as soon as it started to move it was immobilised by the explosion of the mine. But it kept firing, while we were heavily attacked from the front. On my proposal the commander ordered me to attack the tank with two men.

As I approached, the inside of the tank was quiet. Suspecting that the enemy might have ran away, I struck the turret with my gun-stock but there was no reaction. I ordered a soldier to report the capture of the tank to the commander, and as he walked in front of the tank, the turret swung. I told two men to throw the magnet mine at the rear and lay flat. With the explosion of the mine six crewmen, including two British, bailed out of the port hole and lay down in a ditch just in front of me, not noticing me. I took my rifle and shot five of them one by one. While I was reloading the rifle after five shots, a Gurkha jumped out with a submachine gun but he also was shot dead. I climbed up the tank and saw its inside was burning from the engine room due to the explosion of the magnet mine; I understood the reason that its crew tried to escape. Thus we captured two tanks.

Our positions were shelled heavily by mortars and howitzers, and surrounding trees and grass were burnt by mortar incendiary shells. We heard construction noises in our front and were shot at by machine guns and rifles. Even during the night the enemy fired light flares and shelled with howitzers. Very fortunately for us, the enemy howitzer slightly overshot us and all the shells fell in the valley to our rear; only their shrapnels fell on our positions. Had the concentrated shelling come directly onto us we would have been decimated.

Soon we got a report that our 3rd Platoon at Point 5197 had suffered heavy damage, and was nearly decimated. As we were attacked continuously and casualties increased, we could not go down to the river to get water and boil rice. So we ate uncooked rice for four days. We made contact with battalion headquarters who sent us boiled rice in mess kit once a day, but it was just enough for one meal a day divided among us. We got a good supply of ammunition and also one mountain gun reached our position.

As I was wondering what would likely develop as the enemy shelling became more intense, enemy infantry with tanks came to attack us. I thought it essential to separate the infantry from the tanks, and gathered all grenade launchers in a hollow below the position of the Command Unit, and had them fire at the tanks as long as the ammunition lasted. The mountain gun could not shoot at the tanks, being too close, so I volunteered to attack and approached the tanks carrying two magnet mines. I looked at the tanks in a hide twenty metres apart. They were rotating their turrets and shelling the position of 1st Platoon. I wondered how I could get close to them, while I lit a cigarette to calm myself down. As I thought that the tank crew would be looking at their targets and their dead angle could be judged by the direction of the tank gun, I moved close to a tank when the guns were firing away from us, tossed two mines stuck together at the rear of the tank, and ran back to my former position and watched it. As the mines exploded, the tank raised its gun high and rotated the turret, probably to relay the situation to their comrade. With this, another tank went back. I reported to the commander that I had destroyed a tank; he seemed very happy to hear it as the tanks were the imminent threat. I was afraid that the tank would be in a defensive position and volunteered to attack it with petrol bombs. I approached the tank in the same manner as before, ignited the bomb, climbed on the caterpillar and threw straight into the aperture. The tank started burning with black smoke but the crew did not bail out. Afterwards no enemy tanks attacked the positions of 4th Company.

The reasons why we could successfully destroy tanks without any casualties of our own were first, that the terrain was uneven, and secondly that we could separate the accompanying infantry from the tanks by liberal use of our grenade launchers. Later, at Ngarangial (north of Kokaden) near Imphal, we encountered enemy tanks but then we could not use the grenade launchers as we wanted and were beaten off.

We had been attacked persistently by enemy infantry and artillery, so our casualties increased, creating a lot of gaps in our position. We were in a critical situation and could be destroyed easily if the enemy were to attack our positions. On 25 March we received the awaited order to retreat and moved in darkness to regimental headquarters. The number of fighting men in our company was reduced to a little more than twenty out of the ninety that had crossed the Manipur River two weeks earlier.

51 · Sangshak and Kohima

Captain Shosaku Kameyama, 3rd Battalion, 58 Infantry Regiment,
31 Division

Thai border, Irrawaddy River

Almost all of my comrades in the unit I belonged to, 58 Infantry Regiment, died in those battles. What I, one of the few survivors, can and should do is not to forget those dead comrades. My sincere wish is that 'how the dead comrades lived through the war and how they died' should be remembered not only by myself but by as many people as possible.

My unit came from Niigata prefecture, where Buddhism is widely believed in and almost every house has a small but fine family Buddhist shrine to worship their ancestors. However, those drafted into the regiment were young and unmarried, and could not be ancestors. Their parents had died and in their family there are only the uncles whom the younger generation has not met and who are going to be completely forgotten.

Most of those who died in the war were twenty to twenty-two years old. They fought for their country, to save their country in the national emergency. They believed that the country was in a serious situation, on the brink of survival in the face of the foreign invasion. It was natural at that time that the younger generation should go out and fight in such a national emergency. Moreover, when they left their home town, many schoolchildren and local people cheered their departure, singing songs and waving flags. This had greatly impressed the soldiers, who had a strong obligation to families and local folk.

Nobody wants to die, but soldiers dare to fight bravely to pursue their duties and to fulfil the wishes of the people at home. It is not easy to suppress the wish to live, and they charged at the enemy line in trepidation. Nobody dies smiling. Such brave comrades are now almost forgotten. I wish more people know how they lived, how they fought and how they died.

I was an officer in the first reserve. At that time, late 1930s, those graduated from middle schools (at age seventeen or eighteen) were eligible to apply to become army reserve officers. As graduates of the formal Military Academy were too few as the war in China extended, the middle-school graduates were in fact forced to apply to be reserve officers. I was drafted in December 1938, and after twenty months' training was commissioned as an infantry officer, starting from the rank of Apprentice Officer. My first assignment was as an infantry platoon leader in 58 Regiment which had four sections of thirteen men each. In the Japanese army three platoons made up a rifle company, three to five companies formed a battalion, and three battalions with supporting units made up an infantry regiment. In these organisations, I was successively a platoon leader, commander of a transport unit, adjutant to the battalion commander and a company commander.

I took part in 'Operation Imphal' as we called it: the Japanese official name was 'Operation U-Go', which we were told a necessity was for the defence of Burma. However, we thought that it would not be easy to win, as we had to cross the rugged Arakan mountain range for about 200 kilometres from east to west. As the supply of food, ammunitions and many others was crucial, we had to carry by ourselves two weeks' rations, ammunition, shovels and clothes; a total weight of 40 to 50 kilograms. This was so heavy that once we sat down to rest we could not stand up by ourselves; we had to be pulled up by someone. The top brass came up with the idea of using oxen for carrying supplies, but Burmese oxen were used to pull carts, not to carry heavy loads on their back. About 700 oxen were allocated to our 2nd Battalion, and one of the four rifle companies was transformed into a transportation unit using oxen. Soldiers of the company had a hard time training oxen for carrying loads on their backs, for oxen did not budge when they were tired. These ideas of our top brass proved to be wishful thinking which disregarded the harsh reality.

Sangshak: on 15 March 1944 our 2nd Battalion crossed the River Chindwin and started to advance westward at the same time as other units of 31 Division and 15 Division. We climbed up and then went down the steep mountains, undisturbed by British troops or planes. After six days' hard march we poured into Ukhrul, a small village on the road from Kohima to Sangshak. British troops seemed to have evacuated it only a few hours before and the village was burning. We then realised that the enemy had destroyed all their food and supplies, to our great disappointment, but a sergeant brought a bottle of whisky he found and wanted me to give it to Major General Miyazaki, commander of the Infantry Group accompanying us. He seemed pleased to receive the bottle. We were very tired because of the long march and also as we had to run uphill to reach Ukhrul, so we were very eager to get a good rest. But to my disappointment when I went to General Miyazaki, he ordered our battalion to pursue the retreating British and to occupy Sangshak. At that time I did not know that Sangshak was in the operational area of 15 Division where we, in 31 Division, were not supposed to attack. This caused a problem later, as in such a big operation the area in which a division ought to deploy had been defined on maps and any departure from it should be approved by the Army Headquarters. As adjutant I was told that our target was Kohima but did not know the scope of the operation.

In the evening of 21 March, we occupied the village of Sangshak and found that it was not the main position of the enemy, so we then attacked a hill north-west of the village and occupied the enemy's south front position. The enemy mounted a heavy counterattack on us after sunrise. This was the first time we had fought with the British–Indian forces, which was very different from our experience of fighting the Chinese army which had inferior weapons to ours. Our battalion commander observed the enemy positions and ordered an attack during the coming night: 8th Company to lead the attack, followed by 5th and 6th Companies. From our experience in China we were confident of the success of the night attack, but we had to expect that a mass of bullets from the overwhelming enemy automatic weapons would result in much greater casualties. When 8th Company broke through the enemy front line, 5th and 6th tried to advance, but very fierce enemy firing made their progress impossible. Under a strong counter-attack the commander and most soldiers of 8th Company were killed or wounded. Though we wanted to advance we could not even lift our heads because of the heavy fire which we had never before experienced.

Major Nagata, the battalion commander, insisted: 'The bones of 8th Company men should be recovered by all means and all the battalion should advance.' He was then shot through his neck and was bleeding, so I took out a bandage cloth, but he cried, 'Don't mind me. It's a trifling cut. Adjutant, organise the attack!' So I asked a soldier to bandage him and crawled to the commanders of 5th and 6th Companies and asked their opinion. Both said regretfully, 'We should retreat and try again. If we continue, we shall all be annihilated.' I agreed with them and went back to the battalion commander. Hearing my report, the commander finally realised that the attack could not be carried out and he broke down in tears, a man weeping in front of his subordinates, saying, 'Too shameful not to recover the bones of Lieutenant Ban and soldiers of 8th Company.' I tried to calm him down, 'Please be patient, we are not running away.' So we retreated back to a slope facing the enemy hill, under cover of the morning mist. It was the morning of 23 March.

During the day of 23 March, the enemy attempted to capture our position and fighting continued. We had then five medium machine guns, but our guns with air-bursting shells had not yet arrived due to the bad road, so we could do nothing against the enemy mortars which threatened us. The mortar shells came down from above, so we could not shelter behind obstacles, as against bullets which fly low. The battalion commander and I were in a trench dug by the enemy. In the late afternoon, I had to visit company commanders to convey orders for the coming night attack. I went by way of a communication trench and saw five soldiers crouching in it. On the battlefield soldiers feel forlorn and tend to stick together. Just as I told them to disperse, a shell exploded between me and them and all five were killed. I was facing the enemy so my face was injured. I could not see, I could not open my mouth and because of the wound I could not apply styptic treatment. If I tried to press my blood vessel closer to the heart I would be choked. So I put my towel on the wound and held it there. A machine gunner saw me and ran up and wrapped his towel around my face, which slowed my bleeding. As the enemy was near at hand I sent him back to his gun, which fought well and halted the enemy advance.

Next night, 24 March, firstly we charged into the enemy flank-defence position which had been hindering our advance. The battalion commander, commander of 5th Company and I were together. As adjutant, I had to be with the commander. Two grenades came tumbling down the slope towards us. As the distance between us and the enemy was so close, there were still some seconds before they exploded. The battalion commander picked up one grenade quickly and threw it back at the enemy. I kicked the other grenade at the enemy as I had my sword in my right hand and had no time to pick it up and throw it; otherwise it would have exploded in my face. The one I kicked back must have killed an enemy soldier. The rule of the battlefield is 'If you do not kill the enemy you will be killed.' This is why war is a vice. It is war that forces us to do the killing. In the war my comrades were killed in rapid succession and I may happen to be killed next. Despite that we had to advance towards the enemy. If we didn't, we would never win a war. If we advance we have to face determined men. It is the war which forces human beings into such a dreadful environment. In the human mind, there exists Buddha as well as demons, and natures vary. But the environment of the war turns human beings evil. As I said, I kicked the grenade at the enemy, but it had been set to explode within seven seconds and he had no time to kick it aside.

As the grenades we threw into the enemy position exploded

continuously with much noise, some of the enemy seemed to be getting rattled. Taking this opportunity, the battalion commander stood up crying excitedly, 'Charge! Charge!' and took the lead in dashing at the enemy position. We secured the position and 6th Company took up formation to prepare for the counterattack. After a while, when the situation seemed settled, I ventured an opinion to the commander. 'On the next charge, please follow the company commander and platoon leader. Your presence is the basis for morale of all soldiers of the battalion.' He thought for a while and then looked up at me gently: 'I understand your opinion. I do hate the need to urge soldiers to fight more vigorously. But I must respect the pride of my commanders.'

On 25 March, 5th Company charged the enemy from the position we had captured the previous night, but failed and suffered big damage before reaching the enemy line, due to the fierce fire from automatic rifles.

At 4 a.m. on 26 March, the remnant of 6th Company, about 50 men, together with 100 men of 11th Company, attacked the enemy position around the church, led by Lieutenant Osamu Nishida, commander of 11th Company, and secured a part of it. Due to the heavy counter-attack Lt Nishida was badly wounded and many men were killed one by one, leaving only twenty fit men by evening. So we were pathetically preparing for the final night assault with all the remaining men of the regiment.

We attacked every night from the 22nd to 25th and every night many soldiers were killed. Despite that, we went forward. In war it is hard to comprehend the real situation. We felt that we were badly off as we knew our situation well, while we did not know the state of the enemy. But it happened that the enemy at Sangshak escaped. As we attacked on five consecutive nights, the enemy could not sleep and their nerve must have broken down. That's why they retreated. They left many things for us; shells, big horses and also wounded Indian soldiers. A few men were left behind having been sound asleep, sedated, and when they woke up they were in Japanese hands.

I was very much impressed to see that the corpse and sword of Lt Ban had been buried neatly packed in a blanket. Our men were all moved by this. As the enemy treated our company commander respectfully, our regimental commander ordered that enemy wounded should be treated and prisoners of war (those captured) should not be killed. After fierce battles when many comrades were killed, men were excited and felt strong hatred against the enemy soldiers and were provoked to kill even helpless prisoners. At that time our commanders had a conscience and controlled our men. The badly wounded enemy soldiers were sent to a Japanese field hospital.

Eight hundred and fifty men of our battalion crossed the River Chindwin, but now after twelve days, active men were reduced to half, 425 men. It was very heavy damage and in a normal situation the fighting power of the battalion would be regarded as almost lost, so we ordered the Oxen Company to leave the animals and join the main unit. They were far behind as oxen carrying supplies cannot negotiate steep mountains. We were reorganised and supplemented with captured weapons and headed for our target, Kohima.

Although my commander was shot through his neck he did not agree to be hospitalised. I wished to treat my own wound as I could hardly open my mouth and eyes. But as the wounded commander said he would proceed to the next battlefield and asked me, 'How about you?' I had to say, 'I will accompany you', against my personal inclination. So both the commander and I were bandaged like monsters and went to Kohima. Because of my wound I could not chew, so my only food was milk poured into my mouth as I looked upward. Fortunately, we captured canned milk from the enemy.

Kohima was a big village of about 4,000 people and was located 140 kilometres by road east of Dimapur, which was linked by railway to Chittagong. There was a good paved road from Dimapur to Kohima and then south to Imphal. Also a road ran from Kohima to the east, so it was located on a three-way crossing. There were British Army warehouses in Kohima. The village of Kohima lay to the east of the road and British defence positions were on a range of hills west of the road. We advanced along the road and occupied enemy barracks (at GPT Ridge) on 5 April, as the enemy retreated to positions north-west of the barracks (Pimple), which we also occupied that day, but this time we suffered a high casualty rate of 110 men. One hundred and ten men killed just to break through a position! I named the hills of Kohima from the south, as Goat (Jail Hill), Horse (Detail Issue Store), Ox (Field Supply Depot), Monkey (Kuki Piquet) and Dog (Garrison Hill). We attacked the hills one by one. The village of Kohima was occupied by our 3rd Battalion on 6 April.

On the evening of 6 April Captain Nagaya, battalion commander, went ahead to scout the enemy positions of DIS and happened to come out in front of one. Being in imminent danger, the commander and his men rushed the position and captured it, but a grenade struck his head and he was killed. At that time I remained in the rear to organise arriving units for the attack. When I ran to him, he was dead, lying on a makeshift stretcher, a tent sheet tied between two poles. A small bundle of white wild chamomile was laid near his nose, which was the only offering to him. As we were to charge the enemy that evening, I could do nothing for him as my duty came first. I asked someone to take care of the corpse; to bury him in earth and cut off his finger and cremate it. The finger bone would be sent to his home.

I really felt that the commander was a respectable person. There would be few such as he, a battalion commander who could weep in front of his subordinates crying, 'I should go to pick up the bones of my men. Forgive me for not going to pick up your bones.' Such a genuine man! I had felt that I could go with this man without hesitation. Many of those who talk about the crime of war may have a feeling that the military is somehow inhuman, insidious and cunning. But that is not true. If it were so, we could not charge at the enemy. We went together, trembling, in a scrum-like formation! This could be done only when an excellent human relationship was established among us.

As I have said, war is like a vice, but armies differ. I belonged to the army whose men performed their duty saying, 'We do not mind the danger, after all, if we have to do it,' and risked their lives for the mission. We captured Barrack Hill on 6 April, where our commander was killed, and another unit took Goat Hill on the same day. Then, on 7 April, our battalion attacked DIS. We left our knapsacks on Jail Hill, went down the valley and moved secretly to the west slope of DIS. On the slope there were supply warehouses, ammunition stores and an automobile parking area. We went undetected by the enemy, surprised them, broke through the position, and captured the warehouses. We were very delighted. Such good news also pleases our superiors, so this was relayed to the regimental commander, who was happy and impatient to see the result and to report to his superiors. He went to the battalion headquarters. This caused a problem later. So far the situation looked OK, but there were several defence lines still before we could get to the top of the hill. Though we advanced steadily, destroying positions one by one, there were still more to go. If the sun rose before we took the top, our position would be exposed and we would be shot in the back from FDS; a real danger. We heard the noise of grenades near the top, which meant that not all positions were secured. I was worried about it, as were the battalion commander and regimental commander. I expressed my opinion to them that, though we hoped to take all positions by the sunrise, in case we could not, we should dig foxholes and prepare to fight in daytime. If one is involved in fighting eagerly, 'Secure quickly, advance quickly', one tends to forget the alternative preparations. I set out by myself to tell this to our commanders.

The enemy on the hilltop, cornered like stags at bay, kept up their heavy gunfire. We were unable to find even a gap to advance by crawling, and it seemed we had reached deadlock. I made use of all available shelter and ran into the position of Hashiguchi Machine Gun Platoon at the ration warehouse, which faced the enemy at FSD. There I saw about ten Indian soldiers sitting down in a dazed condition. I ordered Warrant Officer Hashiguchi not to kill these POWs and not to let them run away.

As dawn came, shelling from FSD became more and more intense and under its cover enemy soldiers came crawling up from the valley and threw grenades at us; a strong counter-attack. If they took this position and climbed up the hill, our men on the hill as well as the regimental commander and the battalion commander would be wiped out. So we had to prevent them getting up the hill at any cost.

I ordered the Machine Gun Platoon, 'Defend this position to the death.' So I had to say, 'I will do the job with you. Fight with me to the death.' My mission was to tell the men in the front line to dig holes if we did not capture the hilltop. But the situation I saw there was so critical that I was obliged to stay there. I fought on, sometimes throwing grenades.

The Machine Gun Company, with two guns, fought very well in a calm state of mind. They waited until the enemy soldiers came very close and fired accurately at them, followed by grenades, and several attacks were repulsed while enemy corpses were heaped up in front of us. Section Leader Kawase was shot through his head and another section leader fell down as his right thigh was cut through by a shell fragment. But all men remained bravely in position. Our men near the hilltop were fighting with grenades, but were also shot from behind and the sides from FSD and were in a critical battle. By 9 a.m. on 7 April, 6th Company was decimated after its desperate 'Banzai' charge.

From 10 a.m. the shelling became more severe, especially on the clothing warehouse and ration warehouses. As a result more than ten POWs and our guard were killed instantly. POWs were killed by their friendly fire. This is war! The shelling mixed with incendiary shells burnt the clothing warehouse where the regimental and battalion headquarters were located. Then the west ration warehouse, where the Machine Gun Platoon was, started burning and flames licked the roof, setting the whole warehouse ablaze.

I decided to move our position to the east ration warehouse, which I thought would not be shelled and burnt, being so close to the enemy. If we did not move we should be incinerated. But the enemy on the hill was waiting to snipe as we jumped out and crossed the parking space. Our soldiers were well experienced on the battlefield; removal of wounded and guns was done promptly and neatly. Although it was very dangerous to carry wounded men on their shoulders and to cross the open space, they did it in an orderly manner.

The fire moved to the ammunition storage and shells in it started to explode. Platoon Leader Hashiguchi was shot through his head at about noon. Men were moving around here and there trying to find a better place. It was clear that anyone who left his position would be sniped at from both DIS and FSD. In a critical situation everybody tends to think that his position is the worst. This mentality on the battlefield drives men to panic, disregarding the actual situation. At this stage the only method to defend this place was to stand united. And what we needed was a dependable commander. As I was the only officer there, I pulled out my sword and cried, 'Battalion Adjutant Lt Kameyama will command you, men here!' 'Survivors of every unit! Come here with your wounded men.' So about thirty fit men and about thirty wounded men gathered around me.

I ordered them to build a circular position under the eaves of the warehouse, and two medium machine guns were set upon each, facing the tops of FSD and DIS. Wounded men were placed in the centre of the circle. Bags of sugar and soybeans carried out from the warehouse were piled up around the circle and covered by soil dug by bayonets. This was not easy work as the soil was very hard and digging had to be done lying down; anyone who stood up was sniped at immediately. I told all the men: 'If you move out of here, you will be killed by the enemy waiting for you. We must hold this position to the last man, in order to protect our wounded and also the headquarters.' Trucks parked close to our position caught fire and flames set alight bags of sugar and beans which we were using instead of sandbags: we put them out with milk from cans. It was unbearably hot; my face had a tingling pain and I almost fainted. I ordered every soldier to quench fire-flakes falling on the back of the man next to him while lying down.

The enemy came attacking from the hill to the east side of the warehouse and started to throw grenades over the roof, but because of the distance they bounced on the roof and fell on top of us. We spread a tent-sheet over our bodies and the grenades falling on it bounced away before they exploded. I told men that 'attack is the best defence', and when we heard enemy footsteps, or their voices, 'Hurry up, hurry up!' I let a selected soldier throw grenades, or ordered the grenade launcher to fire. As we were lying down it was not easy to throw grenades such a distance; the grenade could be lobbed back at us if it did not travel far enough. Actually I was wounded by a grenade thrown by one of us. So I designated Lance Corporal Tanaka to throw grenades. He gripped a grenade pressed against his forehead and prayed, 'May the shrine of my village help me', and threw it over the roof. Everybody asks God's help in case of emergency, and he threw the grenade uttering a prayer because of his sense of responsibility. All our eyes followed the flight of the grenade. In this way we could hold out until the evening, but the number of fit men was reduced to eighteen. I wrote a report of the day's fight and had a messenger deliver it to the battalion commander. It was very fortunate that the enemy did not come charging at our position. If they had, as we Japanese would have done, we might have been decimated as we were far fewer in numbers. I told the men, 'Our commander will come to help us. Hold out! Show your nerve!'

The battalion commander called my name and came crawling to our position, while we threw grenades at the enemy to cover his move. He asked me, 'How's the situation?' I answered, 'As you see now. We have not the power to charge the enemy.' So the commander gave up and allowed us to retreat.

I still told the men that we would keep fighting, but in order to lessen our load we should first send back the wounded and then the bodies of the dead soldiers for their bones to be sent home. On the battlefield if a man feels 'I should do this' or 'I should defend here', he thinks of nothing other than his mission. If he is told to retreat, he feels that he is saved and wants to stay alive and loses his courage. When about half of the dead were carried down, I told the men regretfully that we should not try again as we would not win even if we charged the enemy. So we went down with machine guns and the remaining corpses. I carried on my back a dead soldier. A dead man is heavy, in the same way as a sleeping baby is heavier. When I carried him on the back, his head bumped against my neck. When I changed his position, his cold head stuck to the other side of my neck. Painful feeling of sorrow!

When I came back to headquarters the commander, with only a messenger, was waiting for me. It was almost the dawn of 8 April. The soldiers were allowed to sleep until the evening, but the officers had to prepare plans for the next attack. It is true in war that when we are suffering, the enemy is also suffering; and as the defender should be suffering mentally more than us, our commander decided to attack the hill that evening. But our battalion had lost most of the men and had not enough soldiers to charge the enemy. So the regimental commander ordered his Signal Company to attack the hill with us. It was a critical decision; if the soldiers of Signal Company died, the regiment, without communication, would not be able to continue fighting as a systematic unit, which was like burning our own boats.

From the bitter experience of the last attack, we realised that we could not win against the strong enemy, who had many automatic weapons, by surprise night attack as we had done successfully in China. So we laid out all available anti-tank guns, medium machine guns, light machine guns and grenade launchers (2-inch mortars), and assigned each gun a specified target. I commanded these support weapons on Jail Hill, while the battalion commander went to attack DID with the Signal Company and the remnant of our battalion (mostly 5th Company). After breaking through several defence lines we finally captured the hilltop by noon of 9 April. But our strength had been exhausted.

On 15 April our 7th Company, who had been despatched to attack a retreating route of enemy, returned. In the night of 16 April we shelled all the enemy's firing points with all of our guns and additional mountain guns, and 7th Company with a platoon from regimental headquarters charged towards the top of FSD shouting 'Wasshoi! Wasshoi!' (Rush forward). The enemy was startled by this dashing cry and fled towards Kuki Piquet along the ridge. We chased them and captured FSD as well as Kuki Piquet. After sunrise persistent shelling from Jotsoma fell on the captured hills. Enemy incendiary shells covered all our positions in flame, and even the roofs of positions started burning and many of our men were lost quenching the fire. British planes bombed us repeatedly and the enemy counter-attacked us fiercely several times. From these we suffered greater damage after the occupation of hills than during the attack.

On 19 April enemy tanks came attacking us for the first time. Our anti-tank gun shells hit the leading tank but without any damage. Our close-attack teams threw fire bombs (glass bottles filled with petroleum) onto the tank from the top ridge of the cliff, and as the tank faltered a soldier dashed up with an explosive and cut the caterpillar tread, but he did not come back. All the tank crew, who bailed out or remained to fire the machine gun, were killed by sniping, and two tanks which followed turned back.

On the night of 23 April the remnant, thirty men of 7th Company, attacked Garrison Hill supported by machine guns and only a few shells of the mountain gun, and captured the front line position. But when a company of 138 Regiment went ahead to the hilltop, petrol drums stored by the enemy caught fire and all advance routes were blocked by the spreading flames, lighting up the battlefield like daytime. As the attackers were shot at from the hilltop, the commander had to give up the attack.

After the attack our rifle companies which originally had 180 men each were reduced to four in the 5th, four in the 6th, sixteen in the 7th and none in the 8th. Machine Gun Company had thirty-five and Battalion Gun Platoon fifteen. With such small numbers of men we were not able to attack any more. As our mission was to prevent the enemy reaching Imphal as long as we could, we went on the defence.

It was fortunate for us that the enemy respected human life. They came attacking our position, but when we sniped at them they retreated. And next morning they bombed us from planes and shelled us or surrounded us, and after most of our position was destroyed the enemy infantry came climbing up the slope. But when we shot them 'bang, bang', they went back. If they came close we were sure to be killed. But as they did not charge like Japanese, we had little fear of being killed; as long as we were in the foxholes we would survive unless we got a direct hit. However, if we had been on the plain, none of us would have been alive under attack from tanks. In such circumstances we continued fighting in foxholes until 31 Division ordered us to retreat, from the Kohima hills on 13 May, and from the Aradura hills on 3 June.

Although we kept fighting it was very lonely and miserable to stay isolated in a foxhole on the mountain in the situation when a chance of winning seemed too remote. We ran out of ammunition and food, so sometimes we went out to attack an enemy position at night, and when the enemy ran away after firing several rounds, we collected rations, bullets and grenades, and used them the next day. In this way we held out stoutly day by day, but inevitably someone got hurt or killed, so only a few, maximum seven to eight, men defended a position. It was heartbreaking that even if one did his best, nothing could help. And it was even more heartbreaking that one's comrade had to do more work if one became unable to move. If he were heavily injured he would regret over-taxing his mates. Those men passed away saying, 'Excuse me. I regret dying.' They died apologising and weeping. The battlefield takes the life of such brave men, and there is no way of helping them.

We were short of food, but most distressing was that we did not have bullets. Still we did not give up and never thought of running away. In fact, our unit was not beaten off in the fighting, but by the bold strategic decision of Lt General Kotoku Sato, Commander 31 Division, we turned back towards Burma. We walked over the muddy mountains, drenched in rain, exhausted and hungry, and got back to our base on the River Chindwin in the latter part of July 1944.

52 · Feeding a Battalion

Probational Account Officer Masao Hirakubo, 3rd Battalion,
58 Infantry Regiment, 31 Division

Kohima, Myotha, Mawchi, Bilin, Thaton

The 3rd Battalion of 58 Infantry Regiment fought at Point 7378 and at Shangshak, and then worked around to Kohima from Mao, while our 2nd Battalion went on the Kohima–Imphal road. I was the accountant officer of the battalion who was responsible for 1,000 officers and other ranks, when any supply from behind seemed impossible.

We went into Naga Village north-east of Kohima Ridge (which the Japanese called Kohima Village) in the early morning of 5 April 1944 with complete silence, the enemy being surprised. To my great delight there were twenty warehouses in which a lot of rice and salt were piled up.

I thought it essential to secure the food and asked the battalion commander to lend some men to carry out rice from the warehouses during the night. The adjutant bluntly refused, as all the soldiers were fast asleep after the hard march in the mountains and the work could be done on the next day. So I argued and fought hard with him and the commander finally supplied me with 50 soldiers. I took command of the men and carried as much rice and salt as possible to a valley. Next morning many British planes bombed the warehouses and everything remaining was turned into ashes. I regretted not to have carried out more.

While the battalion was attacking Kohima Ridge from the fork road, my unit with fifteen men cooked rice and boiled water for drinking all night after sunset. We put two big rice balls in a mess kit and water in a canteen per person, and carried them to the front line. They ate them, breaking them into small pieces.

My problem was that there was nothing to eat with the rice balls. We purchased pigs from a village about 20 miles away and collected edible wild grasses from the field which were boiled with salt and put in the mess kits. Sometimes I went to the divisional depot and got a tiny but satisfactory allocation of rice, thanks to my securing the warehouses.

When we were to retreat on 1 June, we had still some rice left which we divided among all the men in the battalion.

53 · Drifting Down the Wild Chindwin

Senior Private Manabu Wada, Transport Section, 3rd Battalion,
138 Infantry Regiment, 31 Division

Kohima

In July 1942 I was to enlist in the 138 Infantry Regiment. Against my wishes my father accompanied me to Nara, where I had spent my childhood. We stayed for the night at the home of a friend of mine, the Yamadaya Inn, close to the Sarusawa Pond.

The next morning father and I set off for the regiment's depot at Takahata. At the gate I handed to my father my possessions wrapped in a *furoshiki* – a cloth used for wrapping clothes. Three days later my unit marched to Nara railway station on the first stage of our long journey to the central China front. I had been ordered to tell my parents of our departure date and obediently sent them a postcard. Near the station I saw my stepmother and stepsisters, but I could only glance at them due to the crowd of people.

The train took us to Kure, in the Prefecture of Hiroshima, where we embarked on a troop transport. The crossing to China was very rough, the ship pitching and rolling and tossing so that many of us were seasick and longed to be on dry land again. We steamed up the wide Yangtse River to Daitsu, a dirty, run-down port where we disembarked. In the gathering twilight we could see gun flashes on the mountainside across the river, and knew we had arrived at the frontier with China.

For the next three months we underwent an intensive training course in the area around Daitsu. In January 1943 we set out in a troop transport, taking on supplies and water at Keelung, in Taiwan, en route to an unknown destination. We spent many hours guessing where the ship would end up. If we carried on southwards we should arrive at Java in Indonesia, we agreed – but if we turned to the west it must be Singapore, for the Burma front. The ship turned westwards and towards the end of February we were disembarked at Singapore before travelling to Kelang in Selangor State. We fought once against the Communists' Anti-Japanese Corps, and then the regiment moved towards Burma.

One day in May 1943 while we were advancing on Burma we heard rhythmic shouting in Japanese by British prisoners: 'One! Two! Three!' and then we met a working party carrying rails and sleepers and wearing only loincloths in the burning heat. All of them were wet with perspiration. A British soldier came up to me and said, 'Japanese master, please give me a cigarette.' He was a very tall man, perhaps about 1.8 metres tall. Owing to the hard daily work he was skinny but well shaped. He had brown hair and I thought that he was 22 or 23 years old. These men were working to build a bridge on the Burma side. A similar wooden bridge was to become famous as the film *The Bridge on the River Kwai*.

I gave him a few cigarettes from my chest pocket, and we each lit one and smoked together. He smoked with great enjoyment and blew out great puffs of smoke. Although we could not understand one another clearly we managed a dialogue with gestures. After a little while he threw out his chest and said, 'Japanese Army will be defeated. The British Army will finally win without fail.'

I was displeased at his words because he was actually smoking my cigarettes and I questioned him closely. 'Japan will win definitely,' I said heatedly. For a short while he kept silent then said, 'The Japanese Army can never defeat the British Army if the Japanese continue to construct railway by human power like this. The British Army would not use human power in this difficult construction work, but with mechanisation.'

I could agree with this opinion although I had no feelings about the way the work was done as a Japanese operation. We continued the conversation and at last parted with a handshake and a smile, telling each other to be careful about health, and to be tenacious although there was no telling when the war would be ended. All this took place in about twenty minutes. (But later, I remembered his words when the Japanese Army was smashed to pieces in the Imphal Operation.)

Because he spoke with such confidence of the virtues of his mother country I bore him respect and at the same time I had an affection for him. As the Japanese proverb says, 'Yesterday's enemy is tomorrow's friend.'

I SHALL NEVER forget the date of 15 March 1944. This was the dry season, and the great Chindwin River was now so shallow that we were able to walk across it at Tamanthe on our first steps towards the Imphal Operation. The regiment was to spearhead 31 Division's rapid advance to attack the British and Indian forces beyond the Arakan Mountains and capture Kohima in India's Manipur State.

We began the operation with twenty days' rations and a herd of cattle, and marched towards the border with India. It was absurd that we should have been ordered to go into battle hampered by cattle, but no more food reached us from the rear as the days went by and we struggled up the Arakan Mountains. At that time we thought only of victory, never of defeat, and soon the path was opened as we brushed aside enemy resistance.

Conditions were hard, well-nigh impossible. At 3,000 metres the mountains were shrouded in freezing cloud, and the rocks and trees were covered in moss and lichen. Matches struck at this altitude went out immediately, so we could not light cooking fires or boil water. Our cattle and horses fell down the mountainside, taking our provisions with them; the slopes were so steep we couldn't go down to retrieve anything. The bodies of enemy soldiers lay along the track, corpses blown up with gas gangrene as they decomposed, but at last we reached the summit and could see, to the west beyond the boundless sea of clouds, Tibet and the Himalayas.

We complained bitterly to one another of the incompetence of our generals who had sent us into the mountains without any proper climbing equipment or clothing, and hampered by large herds of cattle which could not climb the steep, rocky paths which even we soldiers found hard enough. To make matters worse, medical orderlies had to do their best to walk alongside the sick and wounded, slipping, sliding, falling, time and time again.

In mid-April, after many days of bitter fighting we captured ridges north of Kohima but 138 Regiment now had no rations left. The British had burned their food and supply depots so that not even a grain of rice or a round of ammunition was left for us. The best my comrades and I could do was to find three tins of corned beef in the enemy positions. How could we be expected to fight on in these circumstances? By April 5 our three weeks' rations were exhausted. As April entered its third week, we had to stave off the pangs of hunger by eating meagre supplies of biscuits and the corned beef.

The enemy's heavy and medium artillery opened up on us as a prelude to their infantry attacks. For our part, we were limited to reply with just a few shells each day, while the British shells rained down on us in hundreds and thousands in great barrages. In this storm of fire we had to run to seek shelter and could barely hold

Kohima. It is not possible to express our terror as shrapnel burst upon us with tremendous force so that officers and men were cut to pieces by jagged splinters that tore into the head, the abdomen, arms, legs. We watched as enemy reinforcements arrived by truck with more and more arms and ammunition to be thrown immediately against us. It was only at about three o'clock in the afternoon when they took a tea break, as we could see through our telescopes, that we had a respite from the shells, but we could not use our rifles on them because the range was too great.

Throughout our long siege of Kohima enemy fighter aircraft flew along the face of the valley in front of us and cargo planes dropped arms and water to their leading troops. Without meat, rice or rifle and machine-gun ammunition we could only watch. Occasionally our own fighters, marked with the Japanese Sun, flew in support of us against heavy anti-aircraft fire but quickly disappeared again beyond the Kohima Mountains.

It was during the battle that our Commanding Officer, Major Shibazaki, was killed by a hand grenade. That was on 18 April, a month after the commencement of the Imphal Operation. Sadly, we cut off his hands and cremated them so that his bones might one day be consecrated at the cemetery back home. One day when we were walking on a jungle road, leading men hit a piano wire between trees, causing the connected grenades to explode. Then we were fired on by machine guns and a number of our comrades were killed. I was not hit as I was in the rear.

It was not surprising that in the middle of May the British 2nd Division found it possible to recapture the hills of Kohima Ridge from us. Our losses had been dreadful. Our soldiers fought bravely, but they had no rations, no rifle or machine-gun ammunition, no artillery shells for the guns to fire. And, above all, they had no support from rear echelons. How could they have continued in such dreadful circumstances? The monsoon season had started and the Kohima region is notorious for having the heaviest rainfall in the world. In the unceasing rain there was no shelter. If one hid beneath a tree the enemy's shells would destroy not just that tree but everything around it. There was only one consolation: the rains reduced the firing but it resumed as soon as the rain stopped.

It was impossible to cook rice in the rain. Sometimes we made a fire from undergrowth and boiled vegetable matter as the only means we had of staving off our terrible hunger. When the shelling began again we entered our 'octopus traps' – holes dug in the ground to a soldier's height – but the rain flooded in so that we were chest-high in water and had to climb out. We felt we had arrived at the very limit of our endurance.

At the beginning of the Imphal Operation the regiment was 3,800 strong. When our general gave the order to withdraw to the east we were reduced to just a few hundreds still alive. Without shelter from the rains, with boots that had rotted and had to be bound with grass, we began to trudge along the deep mud paths carrying our rifles without ammunition, leaning on sticks to support our weak bodies. Our medical corps men slipped and slid as they carried the sick and wounded on stretchers or supported the 'walking wounded'. Some of the orderlies were themselves so weak that they fell to the ground again and again until their physical and moral endurance was at an end, so that when a sick man cried out in pain they simply said, 'If you complain we'll just let you go, and throw you and the stretcher down the cliff side.'

Icy rain fell mercilessly on us and we lived day and night drenched to the skin and pierced with cold. I remember how we longed for a place, any place at all, where we could take shelter and rest. Once we found a tent in the jungle; inside it were the bodies of six nurses. We had never imagined there would be female victims, especially so far over the Arakan Mountains. Why, we asked one another, had the army not taken the nurses to a place of safety? In another tent we found the bodies of three soldiers who had killed themselves. How could one ever forget such terrible, distressing sights as the dead nurses, and the soldiers who had taken their own lives? All I could do was to swear to myself that, somehow, I would survive.

Our path to safety lay beyond these Arakan Mountains covered in dense jungle. In the rain, with no place to sit, we took short spells of sleep standing on our feet. The bodies of our comrades who had struggled along the track before us lay all around, rain-sodden and giving off the stench of decomposition. The bones of some bodies were exposed. Even with the support of our sticks we fell amongst the corpses again and again as we stumbled on rocks and tree roots made bare by the rain and attempted one more step, then one more step in our exhaustion.

Thousands upon thousands of maggots crept out of the bodies lying in streams and were carried away by the fast-flowing waters. Many of the dead soldiers' bodies were no more than bleached bones. I cannot forget the sight of one corpse lying in a pool of knee-high water; all its flesh and blood had been dissolved by the maggots and the water so that now it was no more than a bleached uniform.

In my thirst I looked for clean water as I struggled to catch up with the division's remnants. Once I found what I thought to be a spring whose water rippled out of a fissure in the rock. Filling my cupped hands, I was about to drink when I saw maggots floating in them and in disgust I threw it down. It was then that I found it was a stream where ten or more soldiers had come for water and were now no more than bones. Upstream beyond the skeletons I at last found water that I could drink. It was where the water buffalo drank.

We walked and walked endlessly along a road littered with corpses. With almost nothing to eat and our feet aching and legs weary, we used sticks to support ourselves until at last, several days later, I don't know how many, we reached Tonhe. Although there were three or four houses there we found no villagers and assumed they must be hiding somewhere.

While Accountant Lieutenant Sasakai and his men would make their way by land, four of us, Sergeant Masuda, chief of the transport section, Fukushima, Kano and I decided to build a raft and float on it down the Chindwin to Thaungdut, where we hoped to obtain food. My companions were all older than me

178

by seven years or so and had more experience than I had.

It was already three o'clock in the afternoon and there was hardly time to make a raft and leave Tonhe before sunset. Hurriedly we went into the bamboo and cut about thirty lengths, each five to seven centimetres in diameter and five metres in length. By five o'clock the raft was ready for the water. It was already dark. This was the middle of the rainy season and the red-brown river was running fast and rough with white-capped waves in the shallow, turbulent rapids. We launched the raft and scrambled aboard. 'Let's go!'

Immediately, though, the raft sank beneath our weight until we were up to our waists in the water. Jumping onto the riverbank we cut another twenty bamboos which we lashed to the raft and at once set off again. Pushed along by the strong current, we manoeuvred to the middle of the rapids, our feet continually under water. None of us had a watch and we soon lost track of time in the darkness but it must have been about ten o'clock when rain began to fall. The clear sky and the stars disappeared and now the monsoon rains fell in torrents to drench us. With no shelter we had somehow to survive the bitter cold. Hours seemed to pass as the raft was carried along and we huddled together, soaked to the skin and shivering wildly. Suddenly I spotted a red light ahead of us on the right.

'That fire is the first sign that we are arriving at our goal,' said Masuda. 'We have arrived very quickly,' said Fukushima. 'It would take us a week by land!' At once we prepared to try to bring the raft to the riverbank, as close as possible to the fire. As we approached a number of soldiers ran towards the shore to help us land. 'Here you are!' they shouted, but the raft was pushed away from the shore by the strong current and carried back into the middle of the river. Still we floated on and on, hungry but with almost nothing but a few grains of rice to eat, our legs deep in the water. I told myself that walking was difficult enough, but much easier than sitting motionless on the raft, afraid to move an inch for fear of capsizing. I took some rice from my waterlogged bag and began to gnaw it like a rat. It was soft and water-saturated, but it was food and we shared it.

'There is no way we can manoeuvre the raft to the shore in order to land,' said the chief. 'When we see land close enough, will you swim to the shore?' 'Kano and I cannot swim. I will tie a rope to you so that once you are on land you can pull the raft to the bank.' I lengthened the rope and tied one end around me. Soon we were about ten metres from the shore but we couldn't get it nearer and the rope was not long enough. 'I'll jump in here,' I shouted, 'but pull me in on the rope if I sink or I shall drown!.' Wearing only my loincloth I threw myself into the water, looking for the nearest place to land. With all my strength I tried to swim against the current but it was useless and soon I began to sink beneath the surface, swallowing quantities of water as I struggled to stay afloat before they pulled me back to the raft.

'Now it's my turn,' said Fukushima, and untying the rope I handed one end to him. Quickly he jumped into the river, going under at once before coming to the surface seven or eight metres ahead of us. I began to feel that he might be all right and shouted, 'Swim across the rapids towards the shore while we paddle hard behind you!' He found it very difficult to swim the last two or three metres but somehow managed it. We were now almost at the shore and Kano shouted to Fukushima, 'Bind the rope to a tree!' But as Fukushima scrambled onto the bank he stumbled and let go of the rope which he had not tied around him. Wearing only his loincloth, he could only watch as the raft went spinning out into the middle of the river once more. On it were his clothes.

'Wada,' he shouted, as he ran along the bank to keep pace with us, 'paddle the raft to the shore!' It was no good, and we watched as he turned away and disappeared into the jungle.

We all were sad that there was nothing we could do to help him and gazed at the surface of the water in sad thought. Then Kano broke our silence. 'He will have a hard time of it. All he has is a loincloth and he will need clothes in the cold night. Where will he find food? he asked. 'Well,' he answered himself, 'somehow he will muddle along.' The chief was silent for a while. Then he said, snapping out of it, 'He will put on the clothes of dead men.' I prayed to God that Fukushima would survive his ordeal and soon catch up with our division. (Much later I learned that he had died of sickness in the jungle near Sagaing on the Irrawaddy. It was a miracle that he had managed to travel as far as he did.)

The heavy rain continued and in the strong currents the raft's speed was ever-increasing so that we shot along as fast as an arrow, piercing the night. Wordlessly the three of us crouched together, arms folded against our curled-up bodies for a little protection against the cold. Kano told us that villagers had warned him not to float below Sittaung because there was a great swirling current the width of the river which would seize the raft and drag it to destruction and we would surely die. He went on, 'If we continue as we are we shall see a white pagoda at Yuwa, the junction of the Yu and the Chindwin, where the river becomes a maelstrom due to the monsoon rains, and the sound is so great that it is like that of the Niagara Falls in America. We must somehow land upstream of the junction.'

It was pitch dark. We had no idea of the time, nor even whether the sun had set, but the rain had stopped at last and a weird silence fell with only the sound of the water splashing against the raft. It could have been midday or midnight; all we could make out was a dark rain-filled cloud above the river. Then we heard a deep, rumbling noise, something like an earthquake shaking the earth or a mountain. Was there a waterfall ahead? We panicked at the thought, our stomachs tightening in terror. Was this to be our fate? Again the raft increased in speed as we approached the waterfall and the noise grew ever greater. Somehow we must stop the raft before it was too late. But how? Now we could make out the white pagoda over to our right. This was Sittaung and we were at the mercy of the current. Very soon we would be at the junction of the two rivers the villagers had warned about. Suddenly the raft was stationary! Kano threw a piece of wood into the water. It floated beside us, motionless!

Almost at once, though, we began to move again and I saw a big log nearby which I thought I might be able to tie our rope to as a drag-anchor. With the rope around me I jumped into the water and swam to the log which I then pulled to the raft and lashed to the side. In an instant we were careering through the wild white water, the bamboos creaking and groaning and the raft turning, turning, turning in the chaotic currents. We prayed that the raft would not break in pieces. Then we were too tired and fell asleep. When Kano woke me up we were through the terror, and all fell quiet as we looked at one another. We were tired to the point of exhaustion and once we had rejoiced at our deliverance we dozed off as the raft floated safely down river. We were safe.

I asked Kano whether we should untie the log which was slowing the raft down. It had done its job. 'Yes,' said Kano, 'we must arrive at our destination as soon as possible', and in a moment the log was released and floating away behind us. In the growing light of dawn the dark green of the jungle was changing to a lighter colour as it began to give way to the plains. No longer could we see the white pagoda which in the darkness had appeared like a great cliff beside the river. It was as though we were now awake following a nightmare.

Now, though, we felt a great uneasiness: could we get the raft to the shore without being attacked by enemy aircraft? We gnawed a little water-saturated rice. A knife and a stethoscope I had with me on the raft had been lost over the side; parts of the stethoscope were of ivory. Both had been given to me by Dr Kajitani and the loss upset me. The sun grew hotter and hotter as though we were in the South Seas, I thought. I took off my canvas shoes and as I did so the entire skin of the soles of my feet came off with them. Both the chief's and Kano's feet were all right but mine were very painful and for a while I put my feet in the sun to dry them after so long in the water.

A miracle happened! The raft was drifting to the shore, towards the grass on the right bank! Forgetting the pain in my feet I jumped over the side with the rope to tie one end to a tree only

10 metres away from us. At once I went beneath a mat of fallen leaves and withered trees lying on the surface which mistakenly I had though was solid land. Fortunately the water was still and I struggled to the shore but I had not the strength to haul myself up the metre-high bank and Kano helped me back onto the raft.

After about an hour's rest I crept across the floating, leafy mat and was able at last to tie the rope to a tree. Removing several of the bamboos from the raft I laid them to form a bridge which we could walk across to the bank. 'Out of the frying pan, into the fire!' We now found we were trying to walk through a thicket of cane – the cane which chairs are made of – with its sharp thorns. It was impenetrable.

'Wada,' said Kano, 'you wait here. The chief and I will go to see what we can find', and off they went with a 'ra', a sword that villagers use to cut vegetation. In an hour they were back, dripping with sweat.

'We searched for a path,' they told me, 'but there is nothing, only water, and we can't reach the other side without swimming across the stream.' They added, 'We shall carry you on our backs to the water and then you can swim across.' I thanked them for their hard work in trying to find a way through the jungle in such heat.

We rested a short while and then Kano carried me on his back along a path cut through the jungle. Forty minutes or so later we came to a large pond, or lake, which had trees growing in it; the rains had flooded the land here. The water was so clear that we could easily see the bottom. To get to the far side we would need a raft, or perhaps two – one for the chief and the other for Kano – which I could pull over once I had swum across.

As soon as the little rafts were built I swam across with the rope around my body and the other end already tied to one of the rafts. We put what few things we had on the raft which I then drew towards me and unloaded so that they could pull it back to them. Next, the chief came over on his raft, then it was Kano's turn. He tried to get onto the raft but because he was heavier than the chief there was a danger the raft might capsize and he shouted, 'Don't move at all once you are on. If it leans over cling to it and we will keep pulling!' Slowly we dragged him over to join us but now I was exhausted, so tired that I could do nothing more that day.

As darkness fell we gathered leaves with which to make a bed and lay with legs and arms outstretched. In the daytime the jungle was chokingly hot but at night it grew cold and we longed for a fire to warm us. The chief took a cartridge from his bag, together with three matches and a piece of black paper one centimetre square – the paper on which matches are struck. Kano and I looked on in hope and wonder at a tiny bunch of dried leaves in the chief's hand as he struck a match and held the flame to them. They caught alight! Immediately we had a vigorous fire going which shone on our happy, cheerful faces.

'Is there any rice left, Wada?' asked the chief. 'I think I have a little,' I answered. 'Let's boil it into a thin gruel.' Soon it was ready, without any salt but juicy and hot so that its heat soaked into our stomachs. Thanks to the fire we slept soundly until the following morning. We walked through the jungle, eating tree buds as the only food we could find. Now we began to hold different opinions as to our future plans. Kano insisted on returning to the raft, but I preferred to stay in the jungle and look for a village and this was what we agreed.

Around about midday the three of us began to descend a valley stream of about two metres' width. We were so tired and weary that we had to hold on to one another as we staggered and slipped on the rocks; where the obstacles were too big we left the stream and walked in a roundabout route to rejoin it. On and on we pressed until the stream widened to ten metres or so with a sandy shore-line which made our walking much easier. Suddenly there came the sound of a dog barking. We listened intently and heard somebody cutting bamboo. Then we saw two villagers with a dog digging up bamboo shoots. At the same time they saw us and smiled, asking, 'What is the matter with you? We had not expected to see Japanese here.' The chief said, 'Is there a village near here?' to which they answered, 'If you go on another four kilometres you will find a village but it has no villagers. They have all run into the jungle for fear of the aeroplanes.'

We explained that we had not eaten for many days and then they told us that we would find plenty of rice and sugar in the village, and they would show us the way. With that the two villagers began to walk very quickly, saying that soon the sun would set. Somehow Masuda and Kano managed to keep up with them but for me it was impossible.

'Follow on as fast as you are able, Wada,' said Kano. I replied that I would but I felt my feet were too heavy and painful to catch up with them. Soon, in the gathering gloom, I could only dimly make out their figures and almost lost sight of them. It must have been about eight o'clock when I found the village and called out, 'Where is the chief? Where is Kano?' To my relief they shouted, 'Here we are!' and I tried to stagger to the house with a roof where they and the two villagers were sheltering.

The house was built on stilts; the area underneath was for keeping pigs and cows. I picked up a ladder with notches cut in it for footholds, but each time I tried to climb it I fell down so that then my companions had to pull me up to join them. Almost the moment I was safe and lying on the floor of the house I lost consciousness through malaria, dysentery and malnutrition.

THAT EVENING Kano cooked the rice we had so much longed for. With raw sugar the taste was not good, but the rice was hot and that was important. All the same I could not eat any of it because of my malaria. By the following night I was semi-conscious with a high fever and hovered between life and death; my bowels were loose with dysentery, and I was weak through starvation. With no blanket to cover me and with nothing but the bare floor to lie on, I lay there shivering uncontrollably. 'You must eat,' said Kano, 'without food you will die.' And he put rice in my mouth but again I lapsed into unconsciousness. For several days – I don't know how many – the chief and Kano fed me with gruel but I couldn't swallow it. My eyes saw nothing, I could not hear, nor was I able to speak. Then a miracle! Suddenly my senses were restored! I stood up unsteadily. My malaria was gone. Dizzy, I looked around me and saw the hot sun shining on the fields and the trees. The next thing was to try to walk and I took a few steps supported by a stick. Maybe I walked thirty or so metres before I had to lie down on the grass near the house.

I had no idea how many hours I slept. When I woke I found beside me a portion of rice on a banana leaf lying close to my mouth. A villager or a priest might have put his ration actually to my mouth because I found a grain of rice stuck to my lip. As I slowly ate the rice I gave thanks to the Burmese for their kind deed.

A few days later Kano said to me, 'We can't stay here until you recover from sickness. We have to go. I will get you to a field hospital even if I have to drag you!' But it was no good; my health and strength did not return and I found it impossible to keep up with him and the chief. Now Kano took me by the scruff of my neck and forced me to walk. All I could think was, 'Leave me alone. I want to sleep in the jungle as long as I need.' But when I asked him to let me rest he said, 'How foolish you are! If I let go you will sleep immediately, and if you wake up you will find you are dead! You must keep walking.' And he continued to drag me along.

Once he picked up a piece of wood and hit me with it so that I should not fall asleep. I hated him then but at the same time I was thankful for what he was doing to save me. Ten days later we entered Kalewa where there was a field hospital. I was so grateful in my thanks to the chief and Kano for all that they had done for me.

54 · Horses and Oxen

Captain Seiryo Yamashita, Veterinary Department, 15 Division

Pinlebu, Indainggyi

In March 1943 I was transferred to the Veterinary Department of 15th Division headquarters at Nanking in mid-China. This was a slight disappointment as I was hoping to go back to Japan, having been in China for three years and I had not worked in headquarters. Upon arrival at Nanking I presented myself to Lt General Masabumi Yamauchi, commander of the division and to Colonel Kiyosi Sakata, chief of the Veterinary Department. As I was told, General Yamauchi had graduated from the Army Staff Academy first on the list, then graduated from the US Army Staff School and was military attaché in the Japanese Embassy in Washington. He was slender and relatively short, and was not a husky fellow. Because of his career he was not deemed as a fighting commander, but I felt he was really a soldierly man. I came to respect him (after the war I married and named my first son Masabumi, the same as the general). While in Nanking guns and trucks of the division were increased, and I was happy as the horses were fully replenished, and in June 1943 we were told that the division would move to Thailand. But the division moved bit by bit, as only several ships that carried rice from French Indo-China to Japan were allocated to it. After the ships unloaded rice in Japan, they made a berth for soldiers and space for horses and loaded some army supplies, and came to Shanghai to pick us up. After the soldiers disembarked at Saigon berths were disassembled, rice was loaded and the ships went back to Japan. It took a long time for all the division to move.

In August I went to Saigon by plane, and was ordered to buy iron shoes for oxen, as oxen would be used to carry supplies toward Imphal over the steep mountains of the Burma–India border. There were no ready-made shoes in Saigon, so I had to go to the local iron works, show them a sample and have them make the shoes though they had never made them before and it was not efficient. Then I went to northern Thailand by train, and in November was ordered to move to Burma as quickly as possible. I got on a truck which ran during the night, and slept in a jungle during daytime. Oranges that a supply base gave us tasted so delicious, and I could see cherry blossom here and there which reminded me of Japan. I spent New Year Eve's in Maymyo where we were blessed by British bombing. Next afternoon I passed through Mandalay and arrived at the river-crossing point of the Irrawaddy. Sagaing, as seen over the river, was beautiful with white pagodas standing on the green hills. While I was enchanted by the scenery, a sudden air-raid brought me back to the reality of war. We crossed the river during the night, as the bridge over the wide river had been constantly bombed and never reconstructed. We drove from Sagaing to Shwebo and then along a new dirt road cut in the jungle, blowing up a lot of dust. While we were sleeping a big group of monkeys moved on the trees, making a squeaking noise.

I arrived at divisional headquarters eight kilometres east of Pinlebu on about 10 January 1943. Departments of headquarters were in bamboo buildings with roofs of palm leaves and were widely scattered in the forest to avoid air-raids. One evening I went to the chief of staff to receive orders and on returning I bumped into a big tree and dropped my candle light, which I could not find in the pitch dark. As I thought my house could not be far away I searched around all night in vain, and when the sun rose the house was just in front of me! The night in the jungle was really awful. At that time only half of the troops had arrived due to the long and tedious trip from Thailand, so priority was given to transportation of troops. Supplies had not accumulated, so we were faced with a shortage of food. Each department was allocated a part of the nearby mountains where we dug deep in the earth to get yams. This was quite different from my war experience in China and I felt that I might not come home alive.

One of the important jobs of the Veterinary Department was to buy oxen for the coming Operation Imphal. Lt Colonel Sakata went with soldiers to an area designated by the 15th Army, visiting village by village, and bought 1,000 oxen, though the quantity was much less than the 20,000 that the army had expected. The plan was that the oxen would carry food on their backs and after the food was consumed the oxen were to be eaten: the unique idea of Lt General Mutaguchi, commander of 15th Army, derived from the expedition of Genghis Khan of Mongolia. Around the end of January, I was called to Lt Colonel Sakata and told that I was transferred to the Veterinary Department of the 15th Army and should report to Maymyo as quickly as possible. I protested that I was busy preparing to cross the River Chindwin for the important operation and that I had been with the division less than a year. He tried to calm me down, and I returned the way I came three weeks earlier.

I was back in Maymyo which I thought would never see again when I had stayed overnight about a month before. Maymyo was a beautiful resort just like Karuizawa in Japan with a lot of flowers blooming in a pleasant climate, and was very different from the front line of my former assignment. I just wished good luck to 15 Division. I lived with the veterinary staff in a nice white building, and was busy preparing for Operation Imphal, when it decided that 15 and 31 Divisions should start crossing the River Chindwin on 15 March, while 33 Division should advance from the south on 8th March.

I was ordered to inspect the river crossing of 31 Division and left Maymyo by train again for the front with Major Yasuda who was to visit 15 Division. From Sagaing we boarded a train with the 3rd Battalion, 114th Infantry Regiment (18 Division), which was on a way to attack British paratroopers in Katha area. (It was the large-scale British airborne expedition into Burma commanded by Major General Orde Wingate which began on 5 March, but the Japanese did not know the extent of the British operation and the attack on Imphal was started as scheduled.) I sat near a door of the carriage as it was cool to feel the outside air, but I happened to move inside to talk with Major Yasuda. Then suddenly the train shook violently and the carriage fell, side down, and two men who were near the door were crushed and killed; I was lucky that I had moved a few minutes before the crash. Soldiers got out of the train to the defence position, but no enemy was sighted; it must have been rail demolition by British paratroopers. Major Yasuda was lying unconscious with his ribs broken and was sent to base hospital at Kinu together with many soldiers wounded by the crash. I felt a pain in my waist but walked to Kinu because of my duty. From there I caught a truck to go to the front line and arrived at Homalin and heard about the river crossing from 31 Division staff. After the crossing by infantry was completed, horses and then oxen entered the water, guided by soldier-drivers from the steel boats (operated by engineers) and the animals swam alongside the boats. But although oxen were able to swim, some were frightened and stampeded. Some tried to turn back in midstream and others were exhausted and drifted downstream; it was really hard work for both men and oxen as the river was 200 metres wide. Some oxen were too tired to move after crossing the river. Horses performed much better.

After watching the crossing of the animals, I boarded a truck after dark and started my return journey. I saw a big group of bombers and towed gliders heading west with an impressive whirring. During daytime British fighters with ominous machine guns sticking out in front flew low over our road very often. Fortunately our truck was not fired upon by fighters and I was able to return to Maymyo safely and reported that the veterinary staff there were in high spirits despite the difficulties.

About a week after my return, army headquarters were moved to Indainggyi. I went by trucks with others, passed through Sagaing again, then went west and crossed the River Chindwin at Kalewa where I saw many trucks which the British had abandoned when they retreated to India in May 1942. British planes flew over Kalewa very often and supplies accumulated there were bombed and were destroyed here and there, as there was not enough flat land to keep the supplies well dispersed. From Kalewa we had to drive 80 kilometres on a narrow road, during the night with only one dim lamp as a precaution against British planes. Our trucks arrived at Indainggyi without much trouble and we settled down in a bamboo house with a palm leaf roof. The houses were in a dense forest with a lot of distance in between, and the radio station was more than four kilometres away, in order to avoid detection.

Despite such precautions British scout planes started to circle over us from the day we arrived, and 14 Tank Regiment, who happened to be around, gave a concentrated shooting to the planes. Later in the day a big group of bombers, escorted by fighters, came over us and sprayed petrol on the forest around our houses and then dropped incendiary bombs, which burned the forest and most of the houses. Then fighters came low trying to shoot us, as we ran around to avoid the fire. Fortunately, as they were, covered by smoke, none of our team was shot. We could build a new bamboo house in the forest by the late evening of the same day as it was so simple to erect. Most of our supplies and papers were on the way and were not lost. So the damage was relatively light.

Lieutenant General Mutaguchi, commander of the 15th Army, lived in a simple bamboo house. Although I did not have a direct contact with him on military matters, he seemed to be a good-natured old man. When I got promoted I did not wear the ensign of new rank, as it was not possible to buy it in the isolated mountain area. One day I was called to see the general. I wondered why he wished to see me, and then he gave me the new ensign; I was impressed by his considerate feeling. Near his house he had a special place for prayer in Shinto style, a flat narrow square area covered with white sand with bamboo poles on four corners. Every morning he sat there and recited Shinto prayers loudly. As the Japanese advance was beaten back by a strong British counter-attack, he spent more time there; he was praying for God's help for victory.

I was ordered to go back to Kalewa to take care of the iron shoes for the oxen that I had ordered at Saigon nine months ago. They had arrived delayed by inefficient manufacturing and poor transportation. From Kalewa I was able to return to Maymyo before Japanese troops retreated to the River Chindwin miserably defeated.

In Operation Imphal 12,000 horses including mules, 30,000 oxen and 1,030 elephants were used by the 15th Army, crossed the River Chindwin and went into the rugged mountains. All the horses died in the mountains but several mules that survived arrived back at the river. Japanese horses died earlier than mules. The average time that Japanese horses survived from the beginning of the operation was 55 days against 73 days for mules. It was remarkable that almost all the elephants were able to survive despite hard work in such difficult jungles and they returned to Burma.

55 · Naval Guard in Irrawaddy Delta

Sub-Lieutenant Hiroshi Yoshida, 12th Coast Guard, 13th Naval Base Headquarters, 10th Southern Fleet, Japanese Navy

Rangoon, Pegu, Sittang River

I graduated from a mining course at college in September 1943 and was drafted into the Navy, underwent busy and quick training at the Tateyama Naval Gunnery School for eight months and was commissioned on 31 May 1944. I arrived at 12th Coast Guard in Rangoon with my classmates Onishi and Sato on 16 July 1944.

To my disappointment I was made the divisional officer in charge of ten motor boats, of which I had little knowledge. At the school I received only several days' training on the operation of boats, practising rowing and how to arrive and depart in a motor boat at a pier, as I was specialised in anti-aircraft guns. But my face was saved as I was made responsible for the training of the operators of the 13mm machine guns which were being fitted to all motor boats. I performed the job well.

Twelfth Coast Guard had four platoons consisting of the landing party, six platoons of 25mm machine guns (each with four double-barrelled guns), a battery of anti-aircraft guns, one gun boat, seven torpedo boats, two launches and fifteen motor boats (length 15 metres, load capacity 24 tonnes). As these guns and boats were located at various places in the delta, one of the important jobs of my boat unit was to supply food, water and ammunition to their locations.

Cruising in the network of rivers in the delta was very interesting. I once saw several hundred water snakes raising their heads up from the mud in a mangrove forest. One late night I saw a kind of pillar of fire in a distance. None of the crew had seen such a sight. I thought that it was not fire as the colour was different and I moved the boat towards it, in fact it turned out to be a great many fireflies swarming around a big tree, lighting the creek as bright as daylight. Curiously, there were no fireflies on other trees.

A few weeks after my arrival, I was ordered to transport a boat-ful of mines from Rangoon to our base in the south-west tip of the delta. The mines were to be laid in the Bassein River, a big branch of the Irrawaddy. As the rainy season was not yet ended, I thought that the danger of enemy air attack was small and cruised during the daytime. On the second day of the trip I heard the sound of shooting and the noise of a plane flying low, which I thought would be attacking army boats cruising in a creek. I ordered the coxswain (captain) of the boat to shelter under an overhanging bamboo bush. I covered the boat with cut bamboo leaves and I stayed on the boat with Leading Seaman Sugimoto, an ammunition loader, while the rest of the crew landed and hid in the bush. As the boat was fully loaded with mines, they would explode immediately and the boat would be torn to pieces if hit by the plane. However, it was vexing to run away from the boat, so I put my finger on the trigger of the 13mm machine gun and directed it towards the approaching sound of the plane. At this time the training of machine-gun operators had just started and nobody was yet able to operate the cobweb sight.

Soon I saw a twin-engine Mosquito coming towards us along the creek. I said, 'Sugimoto, lie down!' and he lay flat by the side of my foot. The Mosquito was approaching as if gliding over the creek at an altitude of 30 metres. I aimed at its centre, ready to shoot. But as I waited I realised the enemy plane had not found us. If I could not shoot it down with the first round, we could lose the battle. I could see the face of the pilot, but still he did not notice us. I turned around the gun quietly, and after it was turned 180 degrees and the Mosquito disappeared, I removed my finger from the trigger. Although I did not think I was so strained, I panted for breath and told Sugimoto, 'A narrow escape from death!'

Later I reported this to our commander, Captain Kawano, who asked me: 'Didn't you feel confident in shooting down the plane?' So I answered, 'I would have fired if we had not been carrying the mines. Also I have heard that a Mosquito is a plane which is hard to shoot down.' And he nodded without speaking.

Captain Kawano was an obstinate man, not as clever as many of the other naval officers were, and he was an uncomfortable presence for us young, selfish officers. But when any young officer returning from the front reported to him, he welcomed them with a smile, saying, 'You young people do a good job,' which impressed us greatly.

Sub-Lt Onishi became the commander of the anti-aircraft gun battery at Dala, and I envied him a lot. As it was on the other side the river from Rangoon where our boat pier was, I visited him often. The battery had one 8cm gun and two British-made 4-inch guns. The 4-inch guns did not have their sights, which the British had destroyed when they retreated from Rangoon, so the 4-inch guns were fired by the measurements transmitted quickly from the 8cm gun.

On 17 December 1944, I took lunch at our barracks in Rangoon, and while a banana was still on my table, I heard engine noise and the sentry's warning, 'Air raid!' I thought it not urgent and ate the banana. Then, as the whirr approached quicker than I expected, I ran out to the road in front. But I had no time to go to the shelter, so I lay face up on the road and watched the sky. A formation of big, shining, silver wings came towards me from the direction of the Dala battery. I thought they were different from the usual B-17; I guessed they were 4,000 metres high. Then a high-pitched sound of firing specific to the 8cm gun was heard and at the same time a bright flash was seen near the leading plane, and after a moment the second and the third planes exploded, induced by the leading plane. Our 4-inch guns and also the army anti-aircraft gun battery fired almost at the same time.

I judged that the first shot from the 8cm gun directly hit the front plane in the big triangle formation. I did not see any explosion of anti-aircraft shells before the leading plane exploded. I could enjoy looking at the spectacular show. It was the first time I saw a big bomber crash. Though the leading plane was hit, flashed and belched out a big flame and dark smoke, it seemed as if it was gradually descending to land. The next planes exploded, induced by the explosion of the second and the third planes. A kind of chain reaction occurred above the Rangoon River. As other planes dropped their bombs in order to avoid exploding, the sound of bombs falling in the air was heard, mixed with the firing of the anti-aircraft guns and the explosion of their shells.

From the planes which dropped out from the formation, blowing out flame and smoke, the crews baled out and then their parachutes opened and continued to fall, blown by the wind.

A plane in flames crashed to the ground, and four or five planes reduced altitude and disappeared from my view. Another four or five planes blew out white smoke but stayed in the formation and flew away in the direction of the Pegu River.

They were eleven Boeing B-29s. We did not know how many planes were shot down, but we were delighted to hear the radio broadcast from Delhi, received by our telegram room: 'The

Japanese used a new weapon and they caused great damage, but the British are not afraid of it.' For a while enemy planes did not fly over Dala.

It was natural that both Army and Navy batteries claimed to have fired the shot. Finally, the Army battery got a letter of citation from Lt General Kimura, Commander of the Burma Area Army, and Sub-Lt Onishi and others of Dala Battery got a letter of citation from Vice-Admiral Tanaka, Commander of 13th Naval Base Headquarters.

56 · Those Forsaken by God

Staff Sergeant Yasumasa Nishiji, 20th Independent Engineering Regiment

Hong Kong, Singapore, Burma, Java

During the last stage of the Pacific War, for four months from March 1944, the Japanese went on to the offensive at Imphal, north-east India. The counter-attack of the British and Indian Allied Armies, supported by the air force, was powerful, and in July 1944, the Japanese Army received the order to retreat through Burma.

It was the beginning of one of the worst and most disastrous retreats ever witnessed.

From March 1944 the platoon to which I belonged was in the front line on the Palel road. When all Japanese troops retreated in July I and ten relatively healthy men selected from the company operated boats and ferried soldiers across the Yu River which was flowing with great turbulence due to the heavy monsoon rainfall.

When all the soldiers had crossed the river we struggled through muddy mountain passes to make our way to the east of the Chindwin River. In our position at the very rear of the retreating troops I saw many exhausted men unable to keep up with their units, and their comrades too weary to help them.

Numerous soldiers whose regiments were unknown trudged along the road; those who were wounded in battle and were trying to get to a field hospital and those who had fallen ill and were unable to remain at the front. During the retreat these men were joined by many others who were unable to keep up with the main body and were left to look after themselves. Almost all of them, tens of thousands, perished.

We called the road the 'Human Remains Highway'. What happened here was beyond the bounds of acceptable human behaviour. It was a vision of hell.

Those struggling along this road were almost all in their twenties yet they stooped like old men. The sight was one of total misery. Nobody could have believed that these men had once possessed the strength to survive a series of intense battles.

Many enemy soldiers were deterred from pursuing us on this road; they did not want to witness such an atrocious scene; they made a detour instead.

Hard as I tried, after the war, to recount my experience, I failed to bring it home to many people; there was always something missing. I stopped talking about it and tried writing and showing some photographs but this proved no more successful. Then I thought of drawing and some acquaintances encouraged me to follow this course.

I am uncertain if my drawings are expressive enough for people to understand the position we were all in. However, I am happy if they can even catch a glimpse of how things really were.

While I was drawing these pictures and writing the script, I shed a tear several times.

When confronted by the actual scenes I was not moved to tears, perhaps owing to my youth or the fact that I had an unsentimental view of the war in those days.

But I do not have the same unsentimental view now, nor am I young any longer. Now I can freely cry over my friends who died.

I could not imagine that this was a man who had fought successfully in battles in Hong Kong and Singapore.

He looked to be deep in thought; in fact, having been exposed to the monsoon, he had reached the limit of mental exhaustion and was merely gazing intently at the water trickling down to his feet.

Though I prayed he would make it to the river-crossing point, he passed away at the roadside only a short distance from it.

One of the soldiers carrying a stretcher perished – then the soldier on the stretcher died. No one could help them and they could not help anyone. In the end every one of them perished.

We gradually became acutely aware that there was nothing any of us could do.

Taking one's life seemed the only way out. Soldiers who had no chance of recovery were increasingly pressured to take this path.

In increasing numbers our soldiers fell, physically emaciated and crippled, yet mentally alert. I had heard the locals saying that they exiled their serious offenders to this region in the knowledge that the environment would surely kill them.

We could not simply abandon our dying comrades in a place like this. In our desperation to help them we often ignored orders.

This soldier gave his money to his mates and, light-heartedly, told them to buy something to eat when they got away from the front.

After a while, he crawled to the foot of a tree, holding a grenade.

Without any sign of hesitation, he activated the grenade and ended his life.

Some of his mates who had witnessed the incident cut off a part of his body and left. They probably tried to catch up with the rest of their unit.

'I feel much better today, I'll move on now; you can catch me up later.'

After saying this, the soldier went off alone.

We came across him dead. He had committed suicide in the middle of the road. Since he knew that we would walk past he must have been hoping that we would attend to his body. As he had still been able to walk we all felt dismayed at his decision. However, knowing his nature, he probably did not want to become a burden to his unit.

In tears, some of our young soldiers held on to him.

He was married, with children, and was good-natured and amicable; even more so when he had been physically healthy and strong.

I had the bewildering thought that perhaps married men were more decisive than single men.

Having witnessed what had happened while resting, a sick soldier told us that he saw the man pull the trigger of his rifle with his big toe.

It became a routine that a soldier who was emaciated and crippled, with no hope of recovery, was given a grenade and persuaded, without words, to sort himself out.

This soldier was so outraged at being given a grenade that he put on his boots and puttees and crawled after his officer screaming, 'You've lorded it over me; what have I got in return? I'll bloody kill you.'

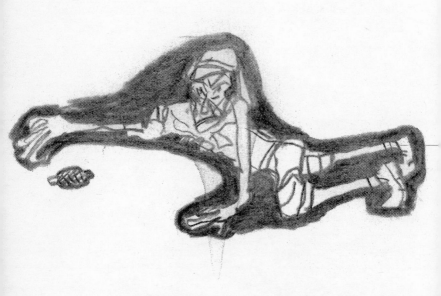

It often occurred that soldiers took their own lives in pairs. They embraced, placing a grenade between them. We called it double suicide.

This scene reminded me of the painting of 'The White Tigers' stabbing each other at Mount Iimori.

At dawn, at our encampment alongside the road, some rifle fire was heard. As it was most unlikely that enemy troops were near-by, I ordered one of the privates to go and check it out.

After half an hour or so, he came back. He reported that there had been a double suicide. I asked him why he was carrying a pair of boots and he told me that he had taken them off one of the bodies. For quite a while we had not been provided with any clothes or shoes so we had to manage with what we had; there was already a hole in one of my boots.

Although the private who returned with the boots was older than many of his fellow soldiers he had only been in the army for a short time. I was astonished that this quiet and unassuming man should have removed the boots off a dead comrade and, although I understood that he had done it for me and appreciated his good intention, I certainly could not bring myself to wear them. I do not recall who used them.

The sun managed to shine through a band of cloud. The wet clothes, soaked with rain, were put in the sun to dry. I noticed that some military tokens were placed neatly and carefully on the rocks where the sun was drying them. I was much disgusted as I felt that this man's will to survive was ruled by greed. However, I gave him the benefit of any doubt. I did not think it necessary to remove my wet clothes as I knew they would dry gradually while I was on the move.

I thought that there must be some good reason for this man to take such care of his possessions; perhaps he was just the sort who found it unbearable to be untidy. A few days later I passed the same spot again, expecting to see him looking dry and neat. He was clinging to the rock – lifeless. In my surprise, I realised that he had been preparing for his end.

A man met his death on the road; he had exhausted all his energy. The portable tent which now covered his body was his only possession. It was clear that no one else had covered his body; he had surely done it himself, anticipating his early death.

A few days ago there had been only one corpse there, now two – then three. Each of the dead men had covered his face in this way; perhaps they all wished to avoid others seeing their decomposing faces.

When death is near, one seems to want to come closer to the dead; as if the dead were beckoning or one dreaded the loneliness of existing on the edge of life.

I saw a sick soldier snatch a rucksack. The owner was a dying soldier lying at the roadside; he had been using it as a pillow. I assumed that the snatcher was after a bag of rice in the rucksack. He staggered away awkwardly under the extra weight but he did not look back.

The dying soldier could no longer utter a single word, merely raising his emaciated arm as if asking somebody to catch the thief. I might have been able to catch him and rescue the rucksack but something discouraged me from doing this.

I stood still, astounded by the scene and amazed at the fierce tenacity for life of both the snatcher and the victim.

During the retreat, my unit came across a field hospital in the jungle. Hundreds of sick and wounded soldiers were lying on the ground, under the trees on both sides of the road. Among them, an army surgeon was working frantically.

We recognised our sergeant who had an injured arm following a severe battle north of Palel. I had anticipated that, provided he was treated quickly, he would recover completely and return to us. In fact, the skin from the elbow up to his neck was coloured purple and was infested with maggots. It was obvious that he would not survive. Although he looked blank, he realised who we were and gave us a faint smile – but he could not speak. I have no knowledge of what happened to him after this.

The condition of the hospital, towards which wounded men were dragging themselves with walking sticks, was absolutely appalling. I could not blame the patients if they felt despondent.

A barefoot army nurse came into a section of the field hospital, took a syringe from his rucksack and gave injections to those who were on the verge of death. They would all be dead in about seven seconds.

The nurse said that he was carrying out orders, clearly trying to convince himself that he was morally right in freeing them from pain. Having completed his task, he turned his back on us and moved on.

'Isn't he a member of your unit, lying dead over there?' a soldier from another unit asked us. He was; there was no doubt about it. He was lying under a portable tent, the four corners of which were tied to branches of trees.

Suffering from malnutrition and diarrhoea while fighting at the front, he had been sent back behind the lines; one of the luckier ones at that time.

I assumed that, on reaching this point, he had sensed his imminent demise, put up his tent and waited to die beneath it. In his rucksack there was a postcard, a toothbrush, toothpaste and a pipe made of ivory.

Before we buried him next to others of our unit, I managed to cut off one of his fingers to send to his family. It was not at all easy and bloodless pieces of flesh fell off. Just then, the moon appeared in the sky. As it shone down on his face, he seemed to be smiling slightly. Having had to die alone he would be buried by his close friends. We felt that his smile showed his appreciation.

At the river-crossing point, having tired of queuing for the boat for three days or more, many soldiers ventured to cross the river using a rope strung across it.

Those who managed to reach the middle of the river found that their weight and the looseness of the rope combined to lower them into the river. The strong current prevented them from holding on to the rope; they were swept away and eventually drowned. This scene was repeated again and again.

Although everybody saw exactly what happened, why did so many follow suit? And nobody tried to stop them. Every single one of them was driven to lunacy.

Unlike the Allied forces whose practice it was to create ceme-
teries near to the battlefields and bury their dead as soon as possible, it has long been the custom for Japanese warriors who fell in
battle to be cremated and their remains returned to their native
land. However, due to the circumstances of the Second World
War, the Japanese Army did not have either the resources or time
to do this. To compensate, it became the practice for comrades of
the fallen to cut off their dead friends' fingers and return them to
their families for burial in Japan.

'THE WHITE TIGERS'. At the end of the Edo Period, battles broke
out between those who supported the Shogunate authority and
those who wanted to restore Imperial power. The Alzu clan
backed the Shogunate authority and many young men volunteered to be trained as fighters. As they saw their castle burning
down and their defeat became imminent, the surviving members
of 'The White Tigers' killed each other on Mount Iimori.

6

RETREAT

August 1944 to August 1945

57 · The Battle on the Irrawaddy River

Second Lieutenant Kazuo Imai, 12th Company, 3rd Battalion,
215 Infantry Regiment, 33 Division, 15 Army

Irrawaddy, Shan

In late November 1944, I reported to 3rd Battalion at Gangaw, 110 kilometres south of Kalemyo, and was fighting with Lushai Brigade and East African 28 Brigade. On 10 January 1945 we were bombed seven times by a strong British air force and all our positions were destroyed. On orders from the regiment we left there secretly on 12 January and went to Yesagyo, 53 kilometres south of Monywa. With the defeat of Imphal Operation, our battalion had lost more than 80 per cent of men and weapons. By that time some of the lost weapons, medium and light machine guns were replaced and a few men who had been wounded or sick came back from hospitals, but still rifle companies had only twenty to forty men each.

In late January we moved to Kyigon, opposite to Myinmu and 15 kilometres downstream. Our mission was to deny the British–Indian force crossing the Irrawaddy River.

In the late evening of 15 February, our 12th Company with Yokoyama Machine Gun Platoon were ordered to attack the enemy, who had crossed the river two days earlier and were at the northern end of a sandy, dry river beach 3 kilometres long north to south, and 600 metres wide.

Corporal Ishizaka, who was crawling behind me, pulled my foot, came close and whispered in my ear, 'You are going too fast. We may lose contact with the men following us.' I was crawling for more than thirty minutes on the warm sand along the bank of the Irrawaddy River, leading the attack team of forty men. A lamp at the enemy's crossing point, which was our target, seemed to be very close, but I felt that I could not advance as planned. I was impatient to be there by the time agreed with our mountain guns for support shelling.

I sent a sign to halt and rested for a while. I looked back and saw signs of our men creeping silently. The moon had just gone down and Orion was shining beautifully. I saw a sturdy boat, that would carry ten men, pulled up on the beach and the sand well trodden. So I judged that we might meet an enemy sentry and paid attention to a plateau on the right.

The crossing point seemed close at hand. A bright light flashed high in the dark and we heard the high-pitched tone of an engine, probably a generator. The point was still 200 metres away, so I placed the grenade launcher section at this spot. We kept crawling and stopped in a gully, 70 metres from the crossing. I was very thirsty. The crossing point was at the end of the plateau, where the sandy beach became narrow. I saw men moving to unload cargo and a pile of square packages. Red lights were flashing that looked like communication with the other bank. I signed Corporal Ishizaka, the section leader, to spread out to the side. So far we had not been spotted by the enemy. All I had to do was to wait for the shelling of our mountain guns and then charge the enemy. I relaxed, feeling I would like a smoke, and awaited the advance of Lt Midorikawa, our commander.

A small low heap in front caught my attention; it marked the end of the enemy position. I approached it to check whether there might be an enemy sentry. There were sandbags. As the situation seemed serious I pulled out my sword. When I got close and was almost touching the sandbags, I heard the sound of a shell over the bushes on my right, followed by an explosion flash. The shell exploded on the plateau far short of the crossing point. Then I heard 'bang, bang', the sound of firing and the noise of flying shells. Again the shells fell far short of the point. What had happened? It was earlier than the agreed time. The light at the crossing point was turned off after the second explosion. Enemy positions were surprisingly quiet. At the flash of the third explosion I saw an enemy soldier rise up in front of me, glance at the point of impact and turn towards me. As I thought I was seen, I stood up and rushed at him, raising my sword. I ran over the sand-bags and struck my sword down against his neck; I felt the shock of hitting him. He roared and came to grab me; a big fellow. He had detonated the grenade, which exploded near my right foot as I fell down entangled. I was blown back and lay flat. I felt I should charge again quickly, but I could not hear or see. I might have been unconscious for several seconds.

Seeing a bright red flame, I came to myself. A flare bomb was in the air, and tracer bullets flew over me in red arches across the river; I thought these very beautiful. I found myself lying on my back in front of the sandbags. I saw Corporal Ishizaka lying on my right. He stretched his hand towards me; he seemed to be badly wounded. I saw a soldier behind me and ordered him to take care of the corporal. My senses came back and I noted that my right leg did not move. I had a pain in my left leg and felt that my thigh was wet, probably from bleeding.

I saw the shadows of two men running when there was a pause of tracer bullets. They went around to the other side of the position and stuck their rifle bayonets in the trench crying, 'Ya! Ya!' I saw a terrible face in the flare; it was Sergeant Takahashi of our Command Unit. He ran towards the plateau on the left; I did not have time to call him, but nobody followed him.

'Enemy in the river!' someone cried. By the light of the flare bomb I saw several silhouettes of boats moving towards the beach from upstream. I could not judge whether they were boats that had drifted from the crossing or those of the enemy trying to attack us, and I called, 'Light machine gun.' The black figure lying on ground on my left front answered, 'Machine gun, out of order.' So I cried back 'Disassemble and clean the gun.' Then I contemplated what I should do. Mortar bombs began to fall around us and I smelled burning powder. The mortars seemed to be beyond the plateau.

A medium machine gun commanded by Lt Yokoyama was set down five metres to my right. The gun began to fire aiming at the river and over my body. It was really unbearable to lie flat so close to the front of the medium machine gun. From the shock of firing that blew up sand dust, I felt as if my internal organs would be blown out. I turned my face and tried to endure the torture. I saw the silhouette of a man fall from a boat which came close to the beach. I thought the boats were carrying enemy reinforcements. Because of the continuous shooting of the machine gun near my ear, I was deafened again.

The medium machine gun switched its aim to the plateau. I thought this an excellent time for a change and tried to raise my body but I could not stand up as my right foot was too painful. 'Platoon Leader! What are you doing!' Commander Midorikawa threw himself down, and asked, 'Are you hurt? Foot?' He sat on the sand cross-legged and watched the enemy lines which were well lit by the flare bombs, while tracer bullets flew here and there. The enemy had several firing points on the plateau just in front of us, which our machine gun was sweeping. So they were in chaos; some men ran up the slope, some slipped down to the sand, and some stood up raising both hands, probably as a sign of surrender. It was a good opportunity to charge the enemy line. Our commander cried to them twice, 'I will help you!' He said to me 'Imai, lend me your sword. My sword is ruined. I will rush in.' I gazed up at the coughing commander and saw something like blood coming out from his mouth, and tried to call out to him. Then a mortar bomb fell very close to me and I buried my face in the sand to cushion the explosion. When I raised my head, he was not there. Before I could ask how he was, tracer bullets came buzzing around me.

I noticed that bullets from our medium machine gun were hitting the sand in front of me. The machine gunner was dead with his head down, still pressing the trigger knob. A shadowy figure pushed aside the gunner and started to fire. A very bright flare shone on him and the enemy machine guns targeted the gun; our second gunner was shot in his face and lay prone. Undeterred, a third gunner took the position and fired, and soon the ammunition ran out. I heard the voice, 'No bullets!' and the voice of the commander, 'Machine gun, retreat!' I felt relieved to know he was well and strong. The gunner lifted and held the barrel; a very quick action. Another man who held the tripod fell down as if in a slow-motion movie.

Somebody came crawling to me. It was Lance Corporal Shimada who said, 'Platoon Leader, I got hit.' He stretched out his arm to me. His entire arm to the fingers were burning, as he said, having been hit by a flare shell. It could not be quenched even though he pushed his arm into the sand. I hesitated for a while but then told him, 'You may retreat.'

The medium machine gun had been withdrawn and we were left alone to stand fast in the sand. All light machine guns in the company, one Type 11 and two Type 99s, were jammed because of the sand. The battlefield was as bright as in daytime due to flare bombs. Unless we destroyed enemy firing points by supporting guns, it would be impossible to rush the enemy. Enemy firing became more fierce and I could hardly lift my head. By chance I remembered our Grenade-launcher Section, and called, 'Command Unit. Master Sergeant Morohashi.' This was relayed by several people and from 30 metres on my right the reply came, 'Master Sergeant Morohashi here.' As I was about to say, 'Grenade-launcher Section' several of my grenades exploded together. I was choked by the terrific explosion and lost consciousness.

When I came to myself, it was dark all around. It took me some time to understand the situation, but I realised that our troops had retreated and felt suddenly alone. I moved to my right. Though I felt several dead bodies, I could not tell who they were. Here and there cinders of flare shells were burning with blue-white flames. I saw a corpse lying face up and burning, possibly hit by a flare shell. I crawled to him and recognised him, 'Ah! Master Sergeant Morohashi.' I called out, 'Twelfth Company, Twelfth Company!' A flare shell lit around me, and tracer bullets flew. I moved backward saying, 'Anyone wounded? We are to retreat.' Nobody reacted to my call. I could do nothing to these many dead soldiers. Suddenly I felt that I could no longer stand the fear.

I reached the beach and stepped into the river which was shallow for some distance, and lowered my body into the water. A gulp of water tasted so refreshing although it had looked dark red and turbid, and I recovered my senses. I moved along the beach downstream, half floating in the water. After a while I was almost dragged into the main stream and could hardly get to the shore. I met two soldiers limping; one was Private Iijima. A mortar shell exploded near us. I was told, 'Your sword is shining.' Indeed, I was gripping the drawn sword in my right hand.

It was about noon when I returned to the bunker near Kyigon. Commander Midorikawa, who was wounded in the chest, was there. When Commander Aoto of the mountain gun arrived, I told him angrily that the supporting shots were 30 metres short. He repeated, 'I have no excuse for it.' Commander Midorikawa did not say a word, just sternly staring ahead. In this battle fourteen men of the 12th Company and nine men of the Machine Gun Company did not return.

As the 3rd Battalion was to continue the night attack to the crossing point, commanders of the 9th, 10th and 11th Company came one by one to hear the situation at the crossing point; all of them were the experienced warriors who got hurt in the Imphal Operation. In a bunker of about 10 square metres, I did some explaining and Lt Midorikawa complimented me. I felt sorry for myself. I had not fought well and was now not able to participate in the battle, due to my aching wounds. From then until 24 February, the battalion attacked the crossing point, and many officers and soldiers were killed.

The attack to recapture Meiktila by 18 and 49 Divisions failed, so 215 Regiment broke off from the enemy in the dark night of 30 March 1945 and retreated eastwards.

58 · Mawchi Road

Lieutenant Satoru Inazawa, Guard Platoon, Headquarters,
55 Division

Arakan

After the hard battles in the Mayu Peninsula, 112 Regiment moved to Taungup by boat in September 1944, and settled down in the Irrawaddy Delta. Headquarters of 55 Division were at Henzada (Hinthada), and 112 Regiment were at Hegyi.

On 24 October I was appointed to the chief of defence unit at Danubyu, 45 kilometres south of Henzada on the River Irrawaddy, and went there with Sergeant Hayashi and six men. My main jobs were collection of information and pacification works. So I wore the Burmese lungi instead of military uniform and walked around freely among Burmese people.

One day, when I was at Pantanaw, 32 kilometres south of Danubyu, about thirty British planes passed over there. One of them dropped out and emergency-landed on a plain 4 kilometres north-west of Pantanaw. I ran to the place with a soldier but found that the pilot had been taken to the county office in Pantanaw by Burmese people by boat. So I walked back and met the pilot who was unable to move because of a fracture of the hip-bone. I called a local Indian doctor to treat him. When he felt comfortable, I talked with him casually for some time and got to know that he was a British sergeant pilot and was on the way to attack Rangoon from Chittagong. I assigned a soldier to attend and nurse him, and gave him the same meal as ours.

Next day, after my work there was finished, I went with the pilot to my base in Danabyu by ox-cart, and after resting there for three days we went to Ieji and I handed him over to regimental headquarters, whose adjutant was happy as I submitted a one-page report of him: he did not have to call an interpreter. I also handed the radio and parachute from the plane to him and got the pistol for my own use, which was very helpful as I had lost mine in a night attack in Arakan and could not get a replacement. In late November I was replaced by an elderly second lieutenant, and went back to the 1st Company as a platoon leader.

After we had celebrated the New Year happily except for a minor air-raid, we took part in large-scale manoeuvres against an airborne attack which involved all vehicles of the division. After the manoeuvres we paraded through Bassein led by three tanks in order to impress the inhabitants.

In February 1945 I was transferred to divisional headquarters as the officer in charge of its guard platoon which had about 50 men with three light machine guns and three grenade dischargers. There always had to be sentries at entrances and near the commander, and an anti-aircraft watcher. When the British–Indian forces occupied Meiktila in March 1945, the headquarters with about a third of divisional forces moved hurriedly to Pynmana, partly by trucks and the rest by trains, but the British tank corps easily broke through our defences and we were left behind the enemy. So we moved south-east, forded the Sittang River and arrived twelve kilometres west of Toungoo on the road to Mawchi on 27 April; 114 Regiment was at milestone 3 to defend against a British advance. Our headquarters was in a forest on a wide plain; we dug trenches as we might be shelled or bombed at any time. One day at 3 p.m. an enemy observation plane flew over our position at a very low altitude of about 20 metres at a slow speed and the pilot leant out of the seat to look down. As I looked up his eyes met mine. I felt an instant chill, a rare encounter. I thought it possible to shoot down the plane by killing the pilot or shooting through its fuel tank, but I dared not order our three machine guns to fire at the plane. The reason should be well understood by those who were in Burma in 1945. If we shot at the plane we were sure to receive heavy shelling and bombing in return. I just hid behind a tree trunk. Nobody blamed me for not shooting, even though many top brass were around me. A few days later the enemy must have noticed the smoke of our cooking and started shelling our headquarters area. As they shelled at random at night, we had to sleep in narrow foxholes. Even General Hanaya slept in his trench, which was unusual for a divisional commander. So we moved to milestone 12 on 5 May and stayed there until 10 May and then at milestone 23 until 30 May; meanwhile men moved rations and ammunition from a depot in the eastern suburbs of Toungoo to milestone 23.

We arrived at Mawchi, 150 kilometres from Toungoo, on 8 June, marching on a road which had been used by the tungsten mine. From there, carrying twenty days' rations, officers and soldiers alike, we walked over rough terrain, climbing up and down three mountain ranges, on muddy paths soaked by rain. The 31 and 33 Divisions had passed the same route a month ago, possibly before the rainy season. We struggled through it at the worst season. On the way an officer who was walking a few metres behind me stepped on a mine and was killed instantly. I was lucky as I was walking on the right-hand side of the narrow road and he was on the other side. Our scout in a mountain region saw parachutes dropped from a British plane, but could not find the base of the guerrillas.

All men of the guard platoon arrived at Moulmein on 12 July, completing the hard march of 500 kilometres in 44 days, and rested in rain-proof buildings. Unfortunately Senior Private Ueda died in military hospital at Moulmein although he had completed the hard march. On 16 July we got on a train and crossed the Burma–Thai border, heading for Phnom Penh in Cambodia. where we heard the Emperor's order for a cease-fire.

59 · The General and a Soldier

Lance Corporal Masao Kojima, 7th Company, 3rd Battalion,
55 Mountain Gun Regiment, 55 Division

Arakan, Mawchi Road

We were broken through by British tanks at Pynmana and Toungoo, and were ordered to retreat to Moulmein via a mountain route between the Sittang and Salween Rivers. We marched along a good road to Mawchi. There we were told that we had to walk over rugged mountain paths to Papun, our next supply point. After only a day's rest we climbed the mountains on 30 May 1945 carrying the heavy load of fifteen days' rations on our shoulders. It rained every day, being in the notorious rainy season, and our going was extremely hard, slipping and sinking in mud. Our 7th Company had been allocated six oxen for carrying rations and ammunition, but their legs sank deep in the mud and soldiers had to pull them out which was exhausting. I walked at the tail end of the company, encouraging tired soldiers to go on. An elderly private, an assistant medic, was really exhausted and almost dropped out. I let him throw away everything, medicine bag, rifle, bayonet and duffel bag, except one grenade (for suicide), and hit his hip with a bamboo stick saying: 'A little further to go. Stand up and advance. It will be the end of your life if you do not keep up with us.'

'I don't mind dying here. Let me stay here as I cannot walk any more.'

'Remember, you have a wife and children. Do you want to be a white skeleton left in the wild mountains.'

'It's my body. Leave it alone. You hit me with a bamboo.'

'If you are angry for being beaten, stay alive!'

At that time Lieutenant General Hanaya, the divisional commander, riding on a horse, passed by and saw me beating my tired comrade. He turned to me and called, 'Soldier, come to me.' I saluted him, standing at full attention and surprised by his call. His adjutant, Captain Eiichi Eguchi, spoke to me: 'Are you the tail end? The General is worried about you. Look out for guerrillas. Shells won't fall but watch out for the buried mines. Our goal is not far. Get a move on with him.'

I dared to say: 'The soldiers have been more and more exhausted as they have to pull out the oxen. May I leave the oxen while you watch?'

'Don't be foolish. It was not easy to get these oxen. They will surely be useful. Pull the oxen for as far as their bodies last.'

I repeated: 'I entreat you. I beg your favourable permission.'

He was moved by my sincere request and went to the General who was drenched in rain. 'The General will directly instruct you. Go to him.'

The General said to me: 'You are trying hard to get the dropouts to walk. Never let them be a prey for wolves. How far are you from your company? Even though oxen are useful for transportation and as food, they should not be at the cost of human life. There is a limit that a man can do. If you feel they are at their limit, get rid of them. Hanaya grants it.'

'Thank you, General. We are saved.'

'You are not yet saved. You have to go a little further. If you get over the mountain range, boats are waiting for you. When the time comes, you can go home. So stick it out. The rain won't kill you. Are you the last? Is there anyone left behind?'

'No one is left behind though many men are very tired.'

'Well done, you may retire.'

Seeing me talking with the General, Second Lieutenant Harada, platoon leader, and Sergeant Ohi came running and said sternly: 'What were you talking about with the General?'

'As the soldier pulling an ox was exhausted and unable to walk, I told him the situation through his adjutant. If my judgement was wrong, I will report it to the company commander.'

'Understood. I will tell this to the commander. You bravely said what was in your mind.'

When we came to a plain after crossing the mountain, the company commander told me: 'I heard the outline from Harada. I understand your situation well.'

Three oxen were completely exhausted by the evening of the day I met the General. As I reported it to the commander, he ordered me to discharge the remaining three oxen. As I went to the battalion headquarters to receive daily orders, Adjutant Nitta told me that the battalion commander wanted to see me. He was sitting on a mat-rush chair in a local hut and asked me: 'Did you present your view to the General a few days ago?'

'I know well that as a soldier I should not talk directly with the top brass. But as the General happened to pass by I dared to mention the situation to him. If I was wrong, please punish me.'

'You have done well with your deep concern for the soldiers.' My talk with the divisional commander became a popular topic in the company, and the medic came to thank me. It took eleven days to cross the mountain area by hard marching through mud. At last we reached Papaun where we received two pieces of dark sugar which was refreshing.

After we arrived at Moulmein I received a letter of citation from the battalion commander, for my endeavours in getting through the mountains, not for asking permission from the General.

60 · Nurses Escaped from Hell

Nurse Hideko Nagai, 490 Relief Squad (Wakayama),
Japan Red Cross

Rangoon, Paungde

I graduated from the Nursing Training Course attached to Wakayama Red Cross Hospital on 30 October 1943. I was 18 years old and was hoping to be a midwife or a military nurse. However, soon afterwards I was drafted as a member of 490

Relief Squad (Nursing Team) which was composed of a leader (Mr Ikematsu), chief nurse (Miss Toshiko Nakao), twenty nurses and a male assistant. We were given new uniforms and left Wakayama by train on 4 November seen off by our families. We were advised not to look sad but tears flowed continuously.

We boarded *Arabia Maru* on 6 November together with nine other relief squads and many soldiers, cramped into the narrow hull. As we sailed south in a convoy of eleven ships, one which was closest to us was torpedoed by a submarine and sank immediately; it was very frightening to see the disaster. We landed at Singapore on 1 December and worked about a month at the 3rd Southern Military Hospital as assistants. Most of the patients there had been transferred from Burma and gave us information about the local climate and conditions.

We left Singapore by train on 16 January 1944 and arrived at Chumphon in Thailand where we stayed for a week and had time to wash our clothes. We went by truck to the west coast of the Kra Isthmus, where we embarked on a ship of 400 tons for a port in southern Burma. Our eight teams were loaded on fourteen open trucks. Though we could stand getting wet in a storm, we were really depressed to find that our baggage was gradually getting soaked and our white clothes were stained by red dye from our flags.

From Iye we went by trains which ran only at night and were often delayed due to air-raids and the destruction of the track. We disembarked at a station short of Rangoon at midnight on 20 February, as Rangoon station had been often attacked by British bombers. Our team and the Kumamoto team went to Rangoon Military Hospital while the other six teams went north to Maymyo.

We worked busily at the hospital, but many of us were infected by dengue fever and had to rest with high temperatures, waist pain and loss of appetite. Our male leader and assistant cooled the heads of the sick nurses and took their temperature which was very unusual. It was our first unpleasant experience when one of our members, Shimizu, was flown back to Japan due to tuberculosis. I went to see her off at Mingaladon airport.

We were transferred to a newly established Hlawga Branch Hospital in October, and then, on 18 January 1945, we were transferred to 118th Base Hospital located at Paungde, a town on the River Irrawaddy 30 kilometres south of Prome, close to the battlefields. Everybody felt sad by the transfer, as we knew the miserable situation of the front lines from the conditions of patients carried into the hospital. The wounded were extremely undernourished, in poor spirits, just like living skeletons and their uniforms were worn to shreds with sleeves hanging down. I was often shocked and wept secretly in sympathy with these new patients when they asked in solemnly, 'May I eat all of this?' as I put boiled rice in their mess kit.

At Paungde we worked with eighty Burmese assistant nurses who had been trained by the hospital. I was really impressed with how they worked hard and faithfully. One morning I saw a Burmese girl was lying on the floor with a high malaria fever, but soon afterwards she was measuring the temperatures of patients as usual. When a bed pan of a patient's faeces was splashed on the leg of a girl she did not change her composure. There were almost one thousand patients in the hospital, but medicines and medical supplies were scarce. We had to put on a small amount of cotton gauze on wounds and cover it with a thick layer of dried banana leaves.

In late February, we were ordered to camouflage all hospital facilities. Even the Red Cross sign on the roof was covered by tree leaves. As we heard, 124 Base Hospital at Taunggyi in Shan States was attacked by planes on 20 February and then heavily bombed by 50 or more bombers on 25 February, disregarding the Red Cross sign, and many patients were killed. Fortunately no nurses were injured except Chief Nurse Sono Shimodaira, who suffered a penetrating cut on her right arm. Senior Burmese nurses had been transferred from Taunggyi and knew her well. We hoped for her quick recovery.

We were told that the Burmese National Army, who were

trained by Japanese, had rebelled against us on 27 March. Many Japanese soldiers were attacked and injured by Burmese swords or shot by rifles, and were brought to the hospital, emergency operations had to be done day and night, which made us very busy. All medic soldiers had to go out with rifles to guard the hospital and the town, so we, with the Burmese nurses, had to take care of all the patients, and we could not leave the hospital. We had to do a bamboo spear drill just in case of emergency.

The hospital had been preparing to send chronic patients to its Moulmein branch via Rangoon. But trucks did not arrive as planned. Finally thirty or so trucks came in the evening of 26 April and about 350 patients were escorted by Medical Second Lieutenant Ide to Rangoon, where they boarded several small boats and headed for Moulmein. One of the boats was sunk by enemy planes and sixty patients were killed while 2nd Lt Ide was saved by a civilian boat and came back to Paungde: it was not a safe trip. We had been advised to get on the trucks and go to Moulmein but we preferred to stay with the remaining patients and did not go.

On 28 April, 220 hospital staff, including nurses, and 700 patients who could walk, started to move on foot towards the eastern foot of the Pegu mountain range. We wore open shirts dyed by teak leaves, small Red Cross badges, skirt pantaloons, canvas shoes and dyed triangle cloths to cover our hair, so that it was difficult to recognise us as women from a distance. (We did not know that this would cause a disaster.) We walked in the group silently. There was no light in the night, so we followed eagerly not to lose sight of the person in front of us. When we came to an open space and were ordered to rest, we sat down immediately; none of us had the strength to chat.

It had been planned to open the hospital at Nyurebin at the western foot of the mountain range. But as 2nd Lt Mananji, who came back from Rangoon, reported that the city was in confusion, and Army Headquarters was being evacuated, the Hospital Director decided that we should cross the Pegu Mountains and the Sittang plain and move to the Shan plain. The Burmese nurses who accompanied us were discharged and sent back to their homes in Bassein escorted by Medic Sergeant Ito, who was their trainer. We wished them a safe journey back home. (As Sergeant Ito did not return to our group nor to Japan, we do not know what happened to them.) I gave my Japanese cotton kimono to one of the girls as a souvenir.

After staying there for three days, we started the march. One day our leader told us that we would cross the enemy line, the Rangoon–Mandalay road. We advanced silently and found a good chance to cross the road. At about 6 a.m. (probably 18 May) we arrived at a village called Wedaung for a long rest. We were allocated a bamboo house. It was the first time after 21 days' march that we could rest under a roof. We felt fairly relaxed and those on cooking turn prepared meals while others washed our dirt-stained clothing.

As we were just going to eat, I saw a medic hurriedly putting on shoes: an alarming situation. Then bullets flew into the house. Someone cried, 'Nurses, escape towards the mountain!' So we ran away scattered, as we were advised not to form a group. I ran as fast as I could into the tall grass.

I came to a dry road that ox-carts used. As I stood there still dazed, Chief Nurse suddenly came out from the grass. She did not wear glasses and seemed to be in low spirits. She just said, 'Ah, Hideko.' As we looked back at the village, smoke curled up high. Chief Nurse and I started to plod on. She did not talk; she only said that she wanted to meet the leader.

After walking for ten minutes we met Tadako. When Chief Nurse saw Tadako, she held her tightly and wept for a while. As I watched them, I recollected that Chief Nurse did not weep when she met me. I had to realise that I was not trusted by her.

After some time we met Kiyomi who was not wearing shoes. She had had no time to put on shoes when we were attacked at the village. Then we came to a river, which seemed not too wide. But I could not swim, so I would be unable to reach the mountain we were heading for. Suddenly a Burmese lady came out of the bush and told us by sign language: 'Lots of Americans. Now is dangerous. We will send you by boat when it gets dark.'

The sky became dark and heavy rain fell. The Burmese lady led us to a small hut and told us to wait. (As we knew later, eight of our nurses were hiding in the bush nearby, and heard Japanese spoken from somewhere but it was dangerous to shout loudly. So I did not meet them for a long time.) Ten minutes later the Burmese lady came and told us, 'Many women who wear the same clothes as you are weeping on the other side of the river. Come with me. We will send you by boat.' At the river an old man operated a small boat skilfully with a long pole and ferried us. On the other bank six of our nurses were weeping. They were weeping because Sadako and Fusako had been swept away by the current when they swam across the river.

After watching the river for five or ten minutes, Chief Nurse said, 'We may be found by the enemy if we keep standing here.' We started to walk. Then I opened a packet that the lady gave me. It was raw sugar and boiled rice wrapped in a tree leaf. I divided them among ten nurses. Though the amount was tiny I felt her kindness keenly, and regretted that I did not thank her.

We went through a marsh for a while and came to a dry road. Seven of us did not have shoes and our feet were bleeding, cut by sharp grass leaves. As we walked into the tall grass the sun came out. Seeing that Chief Nurse sat down, everybody quietly lay down on the grass and fell into a deep sleep.

Next morning we woke up when the bright sun was shining on us. We followed four Japanese soldiers who happened to pass by. Those without shoes wrapped their soles with banana leaves but they were worn out in a short time. We walked quietly; nobody dared to speak. It started to rain, and when the sun set we lay down on the ground and slept.

Next morning it was not raining. We walked following the soldiers.

I felt something strange, and looked around. I heard 'click,

click' from below and then 'click, click' from the opposite direction. When I looked ahead, I could see men with rifles. Suddenly four or five young Burmese came out from the bush. We ten ran into a bush, where a senior private was. We sat around him and asked, 'Please kill us with your grenade.' 'Quick, quick!' Then I saw a young Burmese close by pointing his rifle towards us. The private looked at his grenade and said, 'Ten cannot die with one grenade.'

Chief Nurse sat down on the grass and loosened her belt saying, 'I will kill myself here. You over there!' As everybody looked at her, the private said, 'We could kill ourselves in the final five minutes.' He started to run. Everybody jumped up and left the place; eight of us slipped beneath a fallen trunk of a rotten tree, except Kiyomi and one other.

There horrible worms were slithering around, and as Sumie muttered, 'I don't like these worms', a stray bullet hit Chief Nurse. I untied my belt, wrapped it around my neck and tried vainly to strangle myself, and then tried to bite my tongue with my teeth. Then I heard Japanese spoken, 'Girls, girls! Don't do the foolish thing.' Instantly I stood up and started to run. Chief Nurse said to me, 'Hideko, don't be captured!' She then gasped, 'Long live the Emperor!' and fell dead.

When I came to myself, I was taken, staggering in semi-consciousness to a small hut. I sat there in a daze. I thought without any anxiety that I would be killed. I was concerned that my hair was in a terrible mess. After a while Chiyoko arrived, painfully supported on the shoulders of the Burmese; she was shot through the right arm and right thigh. Then Sumiko was carried in as she was unable to move, being wounded in six places.

That evening I was told, 'Your friends will be buried.' I went and made sure five bodies of nurses were carefully buried in a deep hole with ritual services. I was given a finger of each of them, cremated and wrapped in paper. Chief Nurse and four nurses were killed in action and were buried on 21 May 1945. I did not know what had happened to Kiyomi and Tadako.

We slept in the bamboo hut; I lay in the middle to take care of the two wounded. Next morning the Burmese and a British officer (or maybe an NCO) came and asked our names and unit. We did not give them correct answers. The officer slept in a nearby hut using a mosquito net.

Next morning the officer came with the Burmese, who introduced himself as Mofran, and abruptly asked, 'Do the Japanese believe in ghosts?' I peeped at Chiyoko and answered, 'Yes, we do.' Then the Burmese told us: 'A young girl was killed in the next village last night.' We thought that might be Tadako. I was sorry not to have gone to identify the dead body.

The officer gave us some gauze and cotton, so I made a make-shift bandage using cut-pieces of pantaloons, but as there was no medicine to treat them their situation did not improve; pus was oozing out and the body temperature was high. Sumiko seemed to be suffering severe pain due to her complicated fracture, but I had no way of setting the bones.

When two weeks had passed, Mofran came and told us that we would be sent by light plane as it was painful for the injured to be carried on an ox-cart. People were building a landing strip. After staying in the hut for about three weeks we three boarded a light plane and flew to Rangoon airport, from where we were taken by a truck to a hospital. It was the hospital which had been used by Japanese as an Isolation Branch, where I had once come as escort to contagious patients. At the hospital Chiyoko had a bullet removed from her thigh, and Sumiko's broken bones were fixed. A Nisei interpreter came and showed us the familiar signatures of the six nurses of our team with whom we had lost contact after the attack at Wedaung village. We were happy to know that they were safe at the British hospital in Pegu.

Two days later we boarded a hospital ship and disembarked at Calcutta, where I was also hospitalised due to malarial high fever and diarrhoea. Ten days later we were transferred by train to Delhi Military Hospital. Sumiko was still in bad way while Chiyoko and I recovered fairly well.

In November we were transferred by train to the camp for Japanese located in central India. The camp was in the midst of a big desert and was surrounded by barbed wire fences. There we were so happy to meet Etsuko and Harue of our team. They told us : 'We two together with four nurses were captured by Burmese guerrillas in the evening after the attack at Wedaung, and were taken to the British Hospital at Pegu, where we worked as nurses for captured Japanese soldiers. Then we two were ordered to escort Japanese chronic patients in a hospital ship. At Calcutta we were separated from the soldiers and, to our surprise, were put in the British police prison; we felt uneasy. After two days in the prison, we rode by train for seven days and arrived here and were accommodated in a separated quarter.' They told us that more than two thousand Japanese civilians who were taken from Singapore, Rangoon and the southern area were in the camp with a few Germans and Italians.

After some time, we volunteered to work at the hospital in camp, and lived in the hospital building. A German doctor, Indian nurses and British nurses worked there and three Japanese ladies were in the kitchen. Soon after I moved to the hospital I attended a birth. When I touched the soft skin of the baby, I felt that now I was in a different world after having nursed only the soldiers.

We received a letter from the Victory Group of Japanese in the camp who believed that Japan had won the war and it was enemy propaganda that she was defeated. And another – the Defeated Group – wrote to us that Japan had surrendered unconditionally. Through lack of information we could not judge which was correct. One day the Victory Group attacked the Defeated Group with bamboo sticks and the situation in the camp became chaotic. In order to quell this riot, soldiers were brought into the camp and fired rifles recklessly; twenty-four men of the Victory Group were killed. Unfortunately many innocent women and children were shot by their bullets and were brought to the hospital for treatment, which made us very busy. We bandaged their wounds expertly and by this were recognised as experienced Red Cross nurses and were told that we would be paid 16 rupees a month, which according to the interpreter was good pay. But for some unknown reason we never received the money.

In May 1946, we left the camp and then awaited the next boat at Singapore, when a British captain visited us and told us in fluent Japanese, 'Two of your comrades, Fusako and Sumie, drank poison and died at Rangoon Hospital. Though doctors pumped out their stomach, regretfully they did not recover. There were suicide notes written by the two, which I left with my friend in Rangoon assuming that you would still be in Burma. As I found your names in the list of people going back to Japan, I came here to meet you.'

We wept on hearing the bad news and thanked the captain for visiting us. I still cannot understand why they committed suicide. I knew Fusako had a strong character and had promised, 'I shall return to my parents come what may.'

We embarked on a ship and arrived at the port of Otake in our lovely homeland on 2 July 1946, to which we once thought we would never return.

61 · Japanese Nurses at a British Hospital

Nurse Fusako Ikeda, 490 Relief Squad (Wakayama)
Japan Red Cross

Rangoon, Paungde, Pegu

While we were resting in a hut at Wedaung village on 18 May 1945, after walking over the Pegu Mountains, we were suddenly attacked by men with rifles. Hearing the sound of shooting I ran out of the hut without carrying anything; I could only put on shirt and pantaloons. I felt the bullets came flying one by one close to my ears, which fortunately did not hit me. (Later I realised that even a bullet flying far away sounds like a close shot.) It was my first experience of being under fire. I ran for my life without fear. Enemy planes flew over us, and we dispersed and ran into tall grass, by the direction of Chief Nurse.

In the grassy field six of us were able to meet again and walked towards the east, and came to a big river which I thought to be the River Sittang. We tried to cross so that we could reach the mountain where Japanese soldiers would be, but the river was too deep to wade, so we turned back. When we were contemplating what to do, two Burmese came and ferried us to the other bank in two canoes.

We were taken to a big house, probably of the village elder, and his family loaned us their clothes and dried our shirts and pantaloons, gave us a warm supper, invited us to stay and prepared beds for us. As we had slept outdoors for the past twenty days, thin cushions and mattresses on a bamboo floor were very comfortable for us; so we slept very well. Had we been soldiers we might have suspected that it could be dangerous, but we just accepted their kindness with thanks.

Early next morning when we tried to leave, the master of the house brought out a rifle and aimed it at us. There was nothing we women could do. By then we realised that we had been captured by the enemy from last night. Too late! Several Burmese men in lungi with rifles came and took us outside and ordered us to line up, pointing their rifles at us. I vacantly accepted the situation as an inevitable consequence and did not ask for mercy. As I stood still the leader of the Burmese happened to notice the Red Cross badge I wore on my dirty shirt and ordered his men to put down their rifles saying, 'Nurse, nurse.' Thus we were not shot but became dishonourable Prisoners of War. They made us walk barefoot a long way to a bridge. After crossing the River Sittang, they took us to a small town by car and gave us lunch. Then, as we were loaded on a British lorry, our eyes were covered by blindfolds, which surprised us; we held one another's hands.

We got off the lorry and were led into a small house and were each handed fine blankets such as we had never seen in the Japanese army. After a while a British man in civilian clothes came and introduced himself as an interpreter and asked our names one by one in fluent Japanese. Then a British officer (who we were told was the commander) asked the name of our commander, numbers of patients and the place we worked, but we insisted that we did not know. However, we were surprised to be told that 'You are nurses of the Wakayama team of the Japanese Red Cross.' The reason that the commander knew our identity was from our relief squad notebook which was in our luggage left at Wedaung village. And he said repeatedly: 'You Japanese are barbarians. If you had been walking holding up the Red Cross flag, you would not have had such terrible experiences.' Lastly he asked us what kind of work we would like to do. As we answered that 'We wish to work as Red Cross nurses,' he told us that we should work at a hospital.

We recollected that our leader used to say, 'We would not be attacked by the enemy if we walked in line holding the Red Cross flag.' But when we were attacked, he took a rifle to cover our escape rather than urge us to show the flag. Probably because it was so sudden, he could not tell who were attacking us: Gurkhas, Burmese National Army, guerrillas or local bandits who were known to kill Japanese and rob them of their belongings; guerrillas and bandits were not likely to recognise the flag.

Next day we were taken to the British Army Hospital in Pegu. As we plodded with dirty swollen legs, without shoes and dressed in worn-out stained clothes, many British patients looked down on us from all the windows. I had never felt so ashamed and miserable in my life. We were led into a room and an interpreter introduced us to an Indian soldier who was to take care of us. We were surprised that the soldier brought in a bucket of water and started to wash our legs. We had a hard time explaining to him in sign language that we would wash by ourselves. Many large-size sports shoes were offered by the patients 'to the brave Japanese ladies'. The soldier brought a big plate piled up with rice and curry with six spoons, which tasted delicious. We finished it quickly and then the next course was brought in.

A British nurse with the rank of captain led us to a tent where we were to live and told us we were allowed three days' rest. She gave us British uniforms and cloth recovered from parachutes. We adjusted the uniforms to our size and made our underwear from the parachute cloth.

After the rest we were assigned to attend our patients, captured Japanese soldiers. Looking at them I felt keenly how miserable these Japanese prisoners of war were. They did not chat. They never mentioned their names. They wore tattered uniforms and were sad and ashamed at being captured. They thought that they would never return home. Influenced by them, we felt that it would be impossible for us to go back to Japan, as we must also remain prisoners of war, having worked for the army. However, the British director of the hospital gently told us, 'You are not prisoners of war. We protect you under the Red Cross Convention.' Under his guidance hospital staff and interpreters treated us kindly so we could gradually relax and work comfortably.

In mid-June Etsuko and Harue were ordered to go to Rangoon to escort chronic patients. As their departure was so sudden I could not say goodbye to them, and we felt worried about our future.

In late June, Kiyomi came to our hospital from Toungoo; it was so unexpected that we cried, holding each other. Kiyomi told us her story: 'After we were attacked at Wedaung, I met Chief Nurse in the evening and made for the mountain. Two days later we ten were surrounded by armed Burmese; I ran away on my own following a Japanese soldier into a bush. While we were wandering in the jungle we met guerrillas twice and barely escaped. As we became very hungry and exhausted, having eaten only a few unripe bananas in ten days, I risked going into a house and begged for food. Fortunately the family was kind and gave us rice and napi, and they checked our belongings. Our grenades, the last weapon of the soldier, were taken away. We were moved on foot for five days to a prisoners' camp at Toungoo, where I was separated from the soldier and shown six names of our nurses. I was recognised as a Red Cross nurse and worked on preparing bandage materials at a field hospital. After a few days an officer asked me to work in the hospital but I insisted that I would like to join my comrades, and was sent here on the following day.'

Among the imprisoned patients there was a soldier who was in 118 Base Hospital at Paungde, who told us that Hospital Director Medical Major Matsumura and many men fought bravely at Wedaung and were killed. We mourned their death and were still concerned about other nurses.

A few days later we were told that two nurses would be sent to a military hospital in Rangoon, so we tossed up in Japanese style and selected Yoshiko and Sadami. When the two left we told them that we were sure to meet again and we would survive any hardship.

Now three of us, Ayako, Kiyomi and I stayed in Pegu. From that time more and more Japanese military patients were sent to the hospital and we were kept too busy; often we had to work continuously for two days without sleeping.

At that time Mr Emden, the Indian soldier who took care of us, seemed depressed and said, 'I am very sad today. My dear friend died, so I can't eat or sing songs.' So we tried to console him. A few days later another Indian told us that Yoshiko and Sadami who went to Rangoon had committed suicide. We just exclaimed, 'Why! How come?' And we could only guess that something terrible must have happened to them. We mourned for them with deep sympathy to their heart-breaking suffering. I remember that Yoshiko said to me, 'I will go home to my mother whatever hardship I have to endure.'

We now realised that Mr Emden had a kind considerate heart and did not want to make us unhappy by telling us the truth.

Around that time, members of the International Red Cross Committee visited our dormitory tent, and announced: 'If you want to go back to Japan, we Red Cross are willing to send you to Japan by plane.'

'As we want to go on helping the wounded Japanese soldiers, we now wish to stay here.'

'We do not strongly advise you to go home, so take good care of your health. Have you any problems?'

'No. Everybody we meet here is kind to us. We thank them.'

'We are happy to hear it.'

They left.

One day the Indian soldiers were bursting with joy, saying that the war was ended and they could go home soon. So we thought Japan must have been defeated.

Then we were transferred to a hospital established in the camp for Japanese Surrendered Personnel at Payagyi. The chief of the hospital was Medical Major Bando of the 1st Field Hospital of the Japanese 53 Division. Doctors and medics were very kind and sympathetic, and the work there was not hard as in the British hospital; we had easy days. Still we were worried what had happened to Chief Nurse and other comrades; we talked about them every day and could not be happy.

When we had worked at the JSP hospital for nearly a year, we were notified that we would be repatriated. We wanted to stay in Burma until the last group so that we might get any information about the nurses in our team. But our request was not granted.

We boarded the hospital ship, *Arimasan-maru,* and went to Singapore, where we worked at a hospital for a month while the ship was repaired.

We landed at Saseho in Kyushu on 13 October 1946; the return to our homeland!

When I got home I was told that my funeral had been held in July 1946. Yoshiko, who committed suicide, was mistakenly reported to Japan as me. My parents were overjoyed to see me back home, having been convinced they would never see me again.

The following nurses of 490 Relief Squad were killed:

One died of fatigue and sickness on 11 May 1945

Two killed at Wedaung village on 18 May

Two drowned in the River Sittang on 18 May

Five killed near Chorau village on 20 May

One missing, from Chorau village on 20 May

Two committed suicide in Rangoon in July

Only eight nurses (including two badly wounded) out of twenty-one were able to return home.

Also two men of the squad (leader and assistant) were killed at Wedaung on 18 May.

Fifteen Red Cross Relief Squads (total 315 nurses) went to Burma and most nurses in other squads returned home except for a few who were killed in air-raids or died of sickness.

62 · The Hukawng Valley and Meiktila

Lieutenant Shuichiro Yoshino, 11th Epidemic Prevention and Water Supply Unit, 18 Division

Taunggyi, Hukawng Valley, Meiktila

In November 1943 our unit went to the Hukwang Valley, in the north of Burma, with 18 Division who were fighting with the Chinese–American forces under General Stilwell, whose aim was to march into northern Burma from Ledo in Assam. The Hukawng Valley was known for its severe climatic conditions and as a breeding ground for cholera and malaria, where the control of epidemics was of prime importance. I worked hard to detect disease and to supply clean water to the fighting soldiers. When the supplies were cut off by the long-range penetration groups commanded by General Orde Wingate, we Japanese had to retreat gradually. And food became scarce, so that we had to live on local yams and bamboo sprouts from the fields. This made me weak and I had to spend two months at a field hospital. Hearing that the unit was to retreat to the railhead, I left the hospital without the doctor's permission and rejoined my colleagues just before the final withdrawal, leading a group of patients with ox-carts and eight horses to the base camp. During the difficult retreat one soldier was killed in an air attack and all the horses were lost. After returning to the base with the patients I was exhausted and was sent to the rest camp in Maymyo for a month.

On 10 March 1945 I went to the headquarters of the 56 Infantry Regiment to make arrangements to supply water. As the regiment was advancing towards Meiktila I and three others moved with its headquarters. As the sun rose, we arrived at a village with a pagoda surrounded by palm trees, where we fortunately found a shallow shelter with cover. It was on a road nine kilometres north-east of Meiktila. Anti-tank guns were on our right and the headquarters were behind us.

As the sun rose higher, British aircraft started to fly over us, and the sound of tank guns gradually came nearer. Japanese anti-tank guns opened fire on the tanks. British tanks surrounded the village and continued shelling. A shell from a tank gun hit a palm tree and broken branches fell on us. We suffered no damage, thanks to the cover.

The noise of our rifles and light machine guns was mixed with artillery fire and the shouts of the regimental commander. Sand, dust and the smoke of exploded shells: I could see only the trunks of the palm trees with their branches blown off, and the white tip of the pagoda.

I was fatigued and sleepy from the previous night, and felt no hunger. After a long day, with the noise of the tanks and the commander's shouted orders, the sun began to set and the shelling stopped. Then the tanks advanced towards us, making a loud noise, followed by troops firing Thompson submachine guns. We were fearful that the tanks would run over us, but fortunately they turned round just in front of us and retreated. We came out from our shelter and looked around at each other. We were happy to be alive.

I could see five tanks burning with black smoke, all hit by our anti-tank guns, but most of our guns had been destroyed in the fighting. I was sorry that we had no means of treating the wounded anti-tank crews.

During the night the regiment retreated two kilometres. We started to supply drinking water to the regiment, first by drums carried on lorries. As the soldiers who came to get water attracted British shelling, we visited the front-line trenches carrying water bags on our shoulders. The soldiers in the trenches held out their canteens and gratefully received the water with a 'thank you'.

After several days the Japanese decided to abandon Meiktila, and in our retreat our only remaining filter car, and all the lorries, were burnt in air attacks. We walked to Sittang struggling through the muddy road along the river.

The war ended on 15 August 1945, and we were then disarmed, labelled 'Japanese Surrendered Personnel' (JSP) and put in a concentration camp. One day a brigade commander of 'The Black Cats' (17 Indian Division) came to our camp. We assembled and listened to him. He said: 'You have not become prisoners as you have been defeated in war. Don't hang your heads; you stopped fighting by order of the Emperor. I know from my experience of fighting with you that you Japanese have great ability. I believe that you are sure to make Japan a first-rate country after you have returned to your home country. Be confident and behave yourselves so that you can get home without trouble.'

What a splendid speech by a high-ranking officer of the victors! We were really moved. At that time we did not know when we would get home and what the situation was in Japan under the occupation of the Allied Forces, so we were in a depressed mood. The speech was a great encouragement to us. We called 17 Indian

Division 'The Black Cats' because of its divisional emblem. It was the most familiar British division for us as it fought in Burma from early 1942 to the end of the war against the Japanese 33 (White Tiger) Division.

We left Rangoon on 13 June 1946 by the US ship *Whitehead* and landed in Japan on 10 July. My parents were so happy to see me.

Notes

PART 1

The Japanese army advanced into Burma with two divisions (33 and 55) until the capture of Rangoon. Both divisions were about two-thirds of full strength. 33 Division comprised 214 Infantry Regiment, 215 Infantry Regiment, 3rd Battalion 33 Mountain Gun Regiment, 1st Company 33 Engineer Regiment and other units. 55 Division comprised 112 Infantry Regiment, 143 Infantry Regiment, 55 Mountain Gun Regiment (12 guns only), 55 Cavalry Regiment and other units. On 8 December 1941, when Japan declared war, the 143 Regiment force landed in south Thailand. 112 Regiment was in north Indo-China, and 214 and 215 Regiments were in China. They moved to the mid-west of Thailand and marched over the rugged mountain range which divided Thailand and Burma.

55 Division occupied Moulmein on 30 January, 1942, and the 33 Division took Pa-an on the River Salween on 3 February. After the battles of Kuzeik (12 February), Bilin(17–20 February) and Sittang (22–23 February), the British–Indian forces retreated westward. On 3 March Japanese troops crossed the River Sittang and 33 Division advanced through the forests and occupied Rangoon on 8 March. 55 Division met with strong resistance from British tanks and occupied Pegu on 7 March, after they had retreated towards Upper Burma.

The British–Indian forces who fought with the Japanese Army as related in each of the stories are as follows, according to the *Official History of the Indian Armed Forces in the Second World War: The Retreat from Burma 1941-42*, unless otherwise specified.

Two British battalions were originally in Burma in December 1941: the 1st Battalion Gloucestershire Regiment and the 2nd Battalion King's Own Yorkshire Light Infantry.

Tavoy: The 3rd and 6th Battalions Burma Rifles

Kuzeik: The 7th Battalion 10th Baluchi Regiment. The casualties suffered by the 7/10 Baluchi were 15 officers and some 400 men whereas 17 Japanese men were killed.

Bilin: The 2nd Battalion King's Own Yorkshire Light Infantry, the 1st Battalion 7th Gurkha Rifles and the 1st Battalion 4th P.W.O. Gurkha Rifles and the 4th Mountain Gun Battery.

Wanetchaung: 'Later that night (7 March) there arrived at Wanetchaung the last train to leave Rangoon. This train was wrecked by hostile action at a bridge near Wanetchaung station. The troops, Military Police and civilian personnel in the train were attacked by the Japanese and hostile Burmans. They drove off the attackers, killing twenty of them, and during the morning of 8 March joined the main body of the retreating troops.'

North of Pegu (around Payagyi): The 7th Armoured Brigade. Pegu: The place where the Japanese 8th Company fought is not specified. It was probably north-west of Pegu.'(In the evening of 5 March) Headquarters and two companies (B and D) of the 1st Battalion West Yorkshire Regiment covered the north-western area of Pegu. B Company was posted north of and astride the junction of the main railway lines with the Moulmein branch line.'

At Kuzeik, the 2nd Battalion 215 Regiment carried out a silent night attack with bayonets against 7/10 Baluchi, who had not expected this type of attack. Meanwhile the 1st Battalion 215 Regiment blocked the retreat route from Kuzeik capturing about 237 Indian soldiers, and also repulsed the advance of the British reinforcements.

The Sittang Bridge: Brigadier N. Hugh Jones commanded the attack around the bridgehead but details of the units involved are not mentioned except the following: 'A company of the 1st Battalion 4th P.W.O. Gurkha Rifles and a detachment of the 1st Battalion 3rd Q.A.O. Gurkha Rifles endeavoured to dislodge the Japanese Light Machine Gun but failed owing to intense darkness and thick jungle.'

The Sittang Bridge was demolished prematurely while about two brigades were still on the eastern side of the river. Those men had not been able to cross the bridge as it was within shooting range of the Japanese machine guns from Point 135 which the Japanese had occupied in the morning of 22 February. Many men swam or rafted across the river, while 173 men surrendered to 215 Regiment. As most of their lorries and weapons were lost, this was the turning point in the Burma Campaign in 1942.

On the morning of 7 March, the 3rd Battalion 214 Regiment with two mountain guns blocked the Prome road between Taukkyan and Hmawbi. The Rangoon garrison, with General Sir Harold Alexander, fought hard to break through the roadblock until early the next morning, when the Japanese broke their lines of communication. 215 Regiment and the 3rd Company 214 Regiment went straight to Rangoon bypassing this engagement, as the capture of the harbour was vital for the Japanese to get supplies and troops. The steep muddy road over the Burma–Thailand border could not be used in the rainy season (June to October).

PART 2

The Japanese Army advanced into Burma with two under-strength divisions. 33 Division took Rangoon on 8 March 1942, then started to advance north along the River Irrawaddy while 55 Division occupied Pegu and moved toward Mandalay. Two more divisions came to Burma through Rangoon harbour: 56 Division from Japan on 24 March; and 18 Division from Singapore on 7 April. Meanwhile a Chinese army of 50,000 strong entered Burma, and its 200 Division resisted the Japanese advance at Toungoo, a key city on the Mandalay road. After Toungoo was captured the Japanese 55 Division and 18 Division advanced north, fighting mostly with the Chinese, while 56 Division went north-east to Shan State and the River Salween. The Japanese 33 Division advancing on the Prome road was reinforced by its third regiment, 213, and was supported by 105mm field guns, 150mm howitzers and 40 motor boats. The British took offensive action to defend Prome but lost 10 tanks, 200 vehicles and many weapons at Schwedaung on 30 March. A concentrated Japanese airforce attacked British bases at Magwe and Akyab on 21–24 March. Many planes having been destroyed, the British airforce retreated to India.

While the Japanese 215 Regiment failed in the attack on Kokkogwa, 214 Regiment went secretly to Yenangyaung and captured the city on 19 April. The British 48 Brigade resisted the advance of 18 and 55 Divisions at Kyaukse and covered the withdrawal of British and Chinese forces to the north. The Japanese occupied Mandalay, the second largest city in Burma, on 1 May.

33 Division captured Monywa on 2 May, and its two battalions advanced on the Chindwin River and seized the British embarkation site at Schwegyin on 10 May. The British had to leave on foot, abandoning 60 tanks and many vehicles.

The British Army in Burma marched through rough mountains and reached Imphal in India just in time before the drenching monsoon started. Thus the Japanese occupied all Burma by the end of May 1942.

British–Indian forces who fought with the Japanese in each of these stories are as follows:

Shwedaung: 7th Hussars, 7th Armoured Brigade, 1st Glosters, 1st Cameronians, West Yorks, Duke of Wellington's Regiment and 414 Battery RHA.
Kokkogwa and Thadodan: 48 Brigade and 2 Royal Tanks
Yenangyaung: 1 Burma Division (1 Brigade and 13 Brigade) and 7 Armoured Brigade (less 7th Hussars)
Kyaukse: 48 Brigade (1st/4th, 2nd/5th, 1st/7th and 1st/3rd Gurkha battalions) 7th Hussars, 414 Field Battery RHA and 95 Anti-Tank Battery RA.
Monywa: 1 Burma Division, 63 Brigade, 48 Brigade and 7th Hussars.
Shwegyin: 48 Brigade, 1 Jats, 7th Hussars and 3 Indian Battery.

PART 3

After the British Army and Chinese Army had retreated from Burma, Japanese 15 Army commanded by Lt. General Shojiro Iida occupied all Burma by four divisions, whose headquarters were located at Taunggyi (18 Division), Yenangyaung (33 Division), Mandalay (55 Division) and Hsemwi (56 Division).

On 10 August 1942 Gandhi, Nehru and many Indian leaders were arrested by the British and violence spread in India. At that time Southern Army ordered 15 Army to start preparations for an attack into India. The idea was that 18 Division should advance on Tinsukia through Hukawng Valley and 33 Division was to move into Imphal and on to Dimapur. However, both divisional commanders, Reny Mutaguchi and Shozo Sakurai, opposed the plan and the operation was stopped.

Late in 1942 it was decided to move 55 Division to Arakan where a British offensive was anticipated. Then 18 Division moved to north-west Burma and defended the Hukawng Valley.

Brigadier Orde Wingate with 3,000 men (Chindits) crossed the Chindwin on 14 February 1943 and went eastwards into Burma, supplied by air, and put the Mandalay–Myitkyina railway out of action for four weeks. The Chindits returned to India in May and lost about 1,000 men.

PART 4

One company of Japanese infantry occupied Akyab in Arakan on 4 May 1942 followed by a fighter squadron. The Japanese were reinforced by two battalions of 213 Regiment in October 1942.

14 Indian Division occupied Maungdaw and Buthidaung on 17 December and advanced toward Akyab, but the Japanese resisted at Donbaik and Rathedaung.

55 Japanese Division arrived piecemeal in February 1943, and its 112 Regiment moved across the Mayu Range and occupied Indin by 6 April, forcing 6 and 47 Brigade to retreat. The Japanese reoccupied Maungdaw and Buthidaung by 14 May. After the rainy season was over, the main force of 55 Division, under the command of Major General Tokutaro Sakurai, went through the British lines north-east of Buthidaung unopposed and captured Taung Bazar on the morning of 4 February 1944, and then attacked 7 Indian Division from the rear and surrounded it at Sinzweya Basin, where it formed a strongly defended Admin Box. The Sakurai Column could not penetrate through the defence and had to retreat on 26 February. 'For the first time a British force had met, held and decisively defeated a major Japanese attack.' (Slim) It was a turning point in the Burma Campaign. Despite the defeat, the Japanese kept the Maungdaw–Buthidaung line against the attack of 26, 36 and 25 Indian Divisions until the rainy season. The advance of 81 West African Division in the Kaladan Valley was opposed by Koba Column in Kyauktaw area on 1 March. 22 Koba Column consisted of 111 Regiment (about half-strength), 2nd Battalion of 143 Regiment, 55 Cavalry Regiment, a temporary battalion composed of 1,200 replacement men and two 105mm cannons. The Japanese kept Akyab until 28 December 1944, and retreated eastward.

British forces who fought with Japanese in each of these stories:

Donbaik: 47, 55 and 6 Brigade (14 Indian Division)
Point 105 (north of Rathedaung): a detachment of 55 Brigade
Indin: 6 Brigade
Sinzweya: 7 Indian Division
Ngakyedauk Pass: A mixed squadron from the 25th Dragoons commanded by Major James Allanson.

PART 5

General Mutaguchi, Commander of Japanese 15 Army, saw that the mountains and forests of north-west Burma were not the barrier, as proved by Wingate's raid in 1943, and believed that the best method to defend Burma was to capture the British base at Imphal. Having captured Imphal, he proposed to press on into Assam and to start an uprising that would force the British out of India, with the aid of the Indian National Army commanded by Subhas Chandra Bhose, a past President of the Congress Party.

In March 1944, the Japanese advanced towards Imphal – 33 Division from the south and 15 Division from the east. Meanwhile 31 Division went from the east to Kohima.

Japanese 33 Division advance on the Tiddim Road was confronted by 17 Indian Division. These two divisions had clashed before in 1942 during the British retreat from Burma. The Japanese first encircled 17 Division but failed to destroy it. Then the Japanese prepared a final all-out thrust for Imphal, reinforced by tanks and heavy artillery, but British IV Corps struck first. After ferocious fighting over a wide area, the Japanese were defeated.

Japanese 15 Division, with only four infantry battalions, marched across the mountains north-east of Imphal, and cut the main road between Kohima and Imphal north of Kanglatongbi. They remained astride the road until they were forced off it in early July.

Japanese 31 Division marched from the Chindwin across the mountains. After its 58 Infantry Regiment took Ukhrul, General Miyazaki decided to attack Sangshak, which resulted in the fatal delay of one week, allowing the British to strengthen their defences. 31 Division took all but a few hill patches in Kohima while suffering high casualties, and blocked IV Corps' reinforcement and supplies from the railhead at Dimapur, completing the isolation of Imphal, except for the large-scale air transport.

Mutaguchi planned that his men were to be fed first with meat on the hoof, then with rations and arms captured from the British. But the cattle died, and the British destroyed almost all the dumps before they retreated. As the supply across the rugged mountains was ineffective, General Sato, Commander of 31 Division, finally decided on 1 June 1944 to retreat from Kohima without permission from Mutaguchi.

Starving and diseased remnants of the three Japanese divisions and the Indian National Army staggered through the mud back into Burma. It was the biggest defeat the Japanese Army had sustained. In the four months, Japanese casualties were over 60,000 men – an increase caused by Mutaguchi's insistence on continuing the attack, thus delaying retreat. British casualties were 17,000 – a severe loss for the British.

PART 6

After the defeat at Imphal, the Japanese planned to halt the advance of the British XIV Army on the banks of the Irrawaddy. Japanese 15 Army (15, 31 and 33 Divisions) was to secure Madaya, Sagaing and Pakokku area though it was under strength and lacked mobility. 33 Army (18 and 56 Divisions) was to hold a line from Lashio to north-east of Mandalay, and 28 Army (54 and 55 Divisions) would hold Yenangyaung, Bassein and Rangoon.

British 20 Division started to cross the Irrawaddy on 12 February 1945 and in three weeks of fighting established its beachhead, where two battalions of Japanese 33 Division lost 953 men out of 1,200. The 17 Division crossed the Irrawaddy on 17 February and broke out of the bridgehead four days later, spearheaded by 255 Armoured Brigade, and captured Meiktila by surprise. Japanese 18 and 49 Divisions counter-attacked to recapture the area, but after bitter fighting decided to retreat on 28 March.

British 19 Division, supported by 2 and 20 Divisions, took Mandalay on 19 March. Then the Japanese 15 and 33 Armies retreated via east of the Sittang River to Tenasserim and Thailand.

From Pegu Yomas 38,000 men of the Japanese 28 Army broke out eastwards on 20 July 1945, but were attacked by the waiting 17 Division, and only 15,000 men were able to cross the Sittang.

On 15 August the Emperor of Japan announced the war was over, and all Japanese troops were gradually accommodated in JSP (Japanese Surrendered Personnel) camps. They worked on the restoration of Burma, and were sent back to Japan by July 1947.

Out of 305,501 Japanese officers and other ranks who fought in Burma, 185,149 men were killed or died of sickness and only 39 per cent (118,352 men) were able to return to their homes.

The Authors

DR KAZUO TAMAYAMA was born in Japan in 1919 and graduated at Hokkaido University in 1941. He later took a Master's Degree at Carnegie Mellon University in the USA and a PhD at Hokkaido University.

From 1941 to 1947 he worked for the Hokkaido Synthetic Oil Company on a project to produce oil from coal. For a period after the Second World War he was a civil servant. Following this he was employed by an American pharmaceutical company and subsequently became President for eight years of a British company, a Beecham subsidiary.

It was during this last appointment that he began his study of the military operations in Burma. On retirement he became Secretary of the Japan-British Society and organised the visit to Japan of British Burma Campaign veterans for the purpose of reconciliation between the peoples of Britain and Japan. He also organised and presented a series of lectures by Burma survivors.

A member of the Japan War History Society, he has published a translation of Harry Seaman's *The Battle of Sangshak* and co-authored *Burma 1942: The Japanese Invasion,* published in 1999.

In 1998 Kazuo Tamayama was appointed an Honorary Member of the Order of the British Empire.

JOHN NUNNELEY was born in Sydney, Australia in 1922 and was educated in England. He spent most of the Second World War as an officer in a colonial infantry regiment, the King's African Rifles, in East and North-east Africa, Ceylon (Sri Lanka), India and Burma. In 1944 he was wounded while fighting the Japanese 214 Infantry Regiment of 33 Division, The White Tigers, in the British advance down the Kabaw Valley in the drive to recapture Burma. As leader of numerous successful reconnaissance and fighting patrols he was Mentioned in Despatches for distinguished service.

In 1990 John Nunneley joined the newly created Burma Campaign Fellowship Group (BCFG) whose aim is to promote reconciliation between former enemies and renewed friendship between Britain and Japan. He was elected Chairman of BCFG in 1996. In 1999 the Japanese Government awarded BCFG 'The Foreign Minister's Commendation' in recognition of the group's major contribution to the cause of reconciliation.

John Nunneley edited *Tales from the Burma Campaign 1942–1945*, a collection of sixty personal accounts by BCFG members (1998). He is author of *Tales from The King's African Rifles: A Last Flourish of Empire* (1998).

In 1986 he was awarded France's La Medaille de la Ville de Paris.